ILLUSTRIOUS AMERICANS:
CLARA BARTON

This volume is one of a series of books in depth, each on a man or woman who has contributed such outstanding service to mankind that his fellow Americans are proud to acclaim him. Miss Barton is such a person. In the painting below she is on a relief mission during the Spanish-American War (see page 119).

ILLUSTRIOUS AMERICANS:

By Marshall W. Fishwick
and the Editors of Silver Burdett

Editor in Charge: Sam Welles

Designer: Frank Crump

*Miss Barton is here studied in three significant ways:
a candid new biography, a full pictorial documentation,
and a long, revealing selection of her own writings.*

BIOGRAPHY

PICTURE PORTFOLIO

HER OWN WORDS

SILVER BURDETT COMPANY
The Educational Publishing Subsidiary of Time Inc.
Morristown, New Jersey
Park Ridge, Ill. • Palo Alto • Dallas • Atlanta

Library of Congress catalog card number: 66-20553
© 1966 Silver Burdett Company
All Rights Reserved
Printed in the United States of America
Philippines Copyright 1966 by Silver Burdett Company

CLARA BARTON

BIOGRAPHY

This biography was written by Marshall W. Fishwick, Project Director of the Wemyss Foundation in Wilmington and Adjunct Professor of American Studies at the University of Delaware. Dr. Fishwick took his Ph.D. at Yale and taught 12 years at Washington and Lee. He has published seven books. The editors, in turn, have prepared the boxed comments on Miss Barton, all the illustrations, and the chronology covering her life and era. She is pictured at left in a large detail from a stained-glass window at the Winchester, Massachusetts, Unitarian Church—also shown on pp. 2, 13.

PICTURE PORTFOLIO

In this 32-page color document the editors survey Miss Barton's stirring career, from the shy, teenaged teacher to the indomitable nonagenarian whose heritage has lastingly benefited not merely her own land but the whole world. Each of the illustrations depicted above is a detail drawn from some part of the portfolio.

respect of every one of them,

are before you,

my request appear unreasonable, an

ll submit, patiently, ~~though~~ sorrow

y better things. I beg to subsc

with the Highest Respect

Your d.

Clare

HER OWN WORDS

The editors have here selected more than 50,000 words Miss Barton wrote, with a commentary putting each excerpt in the context of her life, thought, actions, and times. The letter at left, one of the many specimens of her handwriting included, is described on page 153.

CHRONOLOGY

1821–1854

Childhood and Teaching

1821 Born on Christmas Day near North Oxford in Massachusetts.
1825 Her sister Dorothy teaches Clara to read soon after her third birthday, and the little girl quickly begins to spell out three-syllable words.
1832-34 Nurses her seriously injured brother, David.
1836 L. N. Fowler predicts she will never exert herself on her own behalf—only for others.
1851 Her mother dies.
1854 Has first nervous collapse.

1839 Starts 11 years of teaching school in Massachusetts.
1850 Enrolls at Clinton Liberal Institute in upstate New York.
1852 Establishes a free public school at Bordentown, New Jersey.
1853. Despite her great success in Bordentown, a male principal is made her superior.
1854 Becomes a government clerk at Patent Office in Washington.

1855–1871

Wars at Home and Abroad

1857 Suffers from malaria.
1862 Returns home to care for her dying father.
1863 Illness forces her brief withdrawal from Civil War activity.
1868 Loses her voice during a lecture tour.
1869 Sails to Europe after doctor orders her to take "three years of absolute rest."
1870 First encounters the Red Cross when some of its early leaders call on her as she is convalescing in Geneva.

1857 Leaves Patent Office, a victim of political "spoils system."
1860 Recalled to her government post in Washington.
1861-65 Does heroic work in Civil War, much of it under fire.
1865-69 Locates missing soldiers, marks graves at Andersonville, lectures on war, and makes eloquent speeches supporting the cause of woman's rights.
1870-71 Forgets her own ailments while doing notable relief work during Franco-Prussian War.

1872–1895

Establishing the Red Cross

1872-73 So ill in Europe she cannot sail home for a year.
1873-76 Settles in Washington and then has a complete collapse.
1876-85 Gradually recovers her health during long but intermittent stays at Dansville, New York.
1886 Sells home in Dansville and returns permanently to Washington.
1891 Roughs it on a long Western camping trip just before celebrating her seventieth birthday.

1876-81 Struggles to organize Red Cross in America.
1881-95 Leads Red Cross relief after fires, floods, hurricanes, famines, earthquakes, yellow fever, cyclones, and other calamities.
1884 Only woman among 400 delegates from 30 countries at the international Red Cross conference that adopts her pioneering type of peacetime relief for worldwide use.

1896–1912

The Final Phase

1897 Builds home, "Red Cross," in Maryland just outside Washington and makes it her headquarters for the last 15 years of her life.
1899-1907 Publishes series of books on her life and work.
1910 Takes up tree grafting and typewriting, and travels alone to Chicago for speeches.
1911 Makes her will.
1912 Dies at home, April 12, of double pneumonia and is buried near her birthplace in Massachusetts.

1896 Works in Turkey after the Armenian massacres there.
1898-99 Aids both civilians and soldiers in Cuba before, during, and after the Spanish-American War.
1900 Leads Galveston relief work.
1902 Heads American delegation to Red Cross conference in Russia.
1904 Resigns from Red Cross.
1905-12 Founds and heads National First Aid Association; is pleased when the Red Cross again adopts first aid, which it had dropped after she resigned.

POLITICAL–MILITARY EVENTS IN AMERICA	CULTURAL–ECONOMIC EVENTS IN AMERICA	WORLD EVENTS
1821 Spain cedes Florida to U.S. **1823** Monroe Doctrine stated. **1829-37** Andrew Jackson President. **1835-36** Texas gains independence. **1837** Michigan statehood. **1843-44** Frémont in California. **1845** Texas annexed. **1846-48** War with Mexico. **1850** California statehood. **1850** Compromise of 1850. **1854** Republican party organized.	**1825** Erie canal opens. **1831** Discovery of chloroform. **1833** First coeducational college, Oberlin, is founded. **1835** Colt patents revolver. **1837** Severe depression begins. **1843** Dorothea Dix challenges existing treatment of the insane. **1845-47** Thoreau lives at Walden. **1846** Elias Howe invents sewing machine. **1851** Melville's *Moby Dick*. **1852** Otis invents elevator.	**1823** Spanish monarchy restored. **1825** First steam locomotive passenger service, in England. **1836** Charles Dickens' *Pickwick Papers*. **1837-1901** Queen Victoria reigns. **1839** Britain seizes Hong Kong. **1845** Potato blight in Ireland leads to terrible famine. **1848** *Communist Manifesto* issued. **1853-56** Crimean War; Florence Nightingale provides remarkable, pioneering nursing services.
1855-56 Bitter fighting in Kansas. **1857** Dred Scott decision. **1858** Lincoln-Douglas debates. **1859** John Brown's raid. **1861-65** Civil War. **1863** Emancipation Proclamation. **1865** Lincoln assassinated. **1866** Ku-Klux Klan organized. **1867** Alaska bought from Russia. **1869** Wyoming becomes first state to let women vote.	**1855** First American kindergarten, at Watertown, Wisconsin. **1855** Whitman's *Leaves of Grass*. **1859** A Northerner, Daniel Emmett, writes "Dixie." **1862** First federal income tax. **1863** Door-to-door mail delivery. **1865** First oil pipeline. **1869** First transcontinental railroad completed. **1871** Great Chicago fire.	**1855** Mexico ousts Santa Anna. **1859** Darwin's *Origin of Species*. **1861** Russia frees its serfs. **1861** Kingdom of Italy organizd. **1863-64** First steps taken to form International Red Cross. **1865** Mendel's laws of heredity. **1867** Canada becomes a dominion. **1869** Suez Canal opens. **1871** German Empire and Third French Republic are both proclaimed after Franco-Prussian War.
1873 A new record of 459,803 immigrants in one year. **1876** Custer's "last stand." **1880** Census records 50,155,000 inhabitants. **1883** Civil Service reform. **1890** Sherman Antitrust Act. **1892** First national use of secret ballot.	**1873** Severe financial panic triggers a long depression. **1876** Mark Twain's *Tom Sawyer*. **1876** Bell patents the telephone. **1878** First American bicycle. **1881** Tuskegee Institute founded. **1883** Brooklyn Bridge completed. **1886** American Federation of Labor organized. **1889** Mayo Clinic founded. **1893** Ford builds his first auto. **1895** Supreme Court declares income tax unconstitutional.	**1873-74** First Spanish Republic established. **1876-1909** Abdul Hamid II reigns over Ottoman Empire. **1877** Tolstoi's *Anna Karenina*. **1879** Ibsen's *A Doll's House*. **1882** Britain occupies Egypt. **1886** Gold rush in South Africa. **1889** Japan adopts a constitution. **1891** Pope Leo XIII's *Rerum Novarum*. **1895** Röntgen discovers X rays.
1896 Supreme Court establishes "separate but equal" doctrine that holds until 1954. **1898** Hawaii annexed. **1898** Spain cedes Puerto Rico, Guam, and the Philippines after the Spanish-American War. **1901-09** Theodore Roosevelt President. **1906** Pure Food and Drug Act. **1907** Oklahoma statehood. **1912** Wilson elected President.	**1896** Rural free delivery starts. **1897-98** Klondike gold rush. **1899** Spinal anesthesia first used. **1899** Hall of Fame founded. **1901** Oil discovered in Texas. **1903** Wright brothers make first airplane flights. **1904-14** Panama Canal constructed. **1909** National Association for the Advancement of Colored People organized. **1911** Edith Wharton's *Ethan Frome*.	**1896** Olympic Games revived. **1898** The Curies discover radium. **1899-1902** Boer War. **1900** Boxer Rebellion in China. **1901** First successful radio transmission across an ocean. **1903** Shaw's *Man and Superman*. **1905** Russian workers revolt unsuccessfully. **1907** Hague Peace Conference. **1910** Freud's *Psychoanalysis*. **1911-20** Mexican revolution. **1912** China becomes a republic.

ACKNOWLEDGMENTS

Henry Moscow wrote the text accompanying the Picture Portfolio in this book. The text research for the volume was done by Denise Farrell and the picture research by Patricia Smalley. Wayne Young was responsible for the layouts, while Elaine Brown did the copy editing and Louella Still Culligan prepared the index.

Considerable help was received from both the American Red Cross and The Friends of Clara Barton.

Excerpts from the following books have been used with permission: From *Clara Barton, Daughter of Destiny*, by Blanche C. Williams. Copyright 1941 by Blanche C. Williams. Published by J. B. Lippincott Company. From pp. 5-6, 19, 149 of *Angel of the Battlefield*, by Ishbel Ross. Copyright 1956 by Ishbel Ross. Reprinted by permission of Harper & Row, Publishers, and Brandt & Brandt. From *Under the Red Cross Flag at Home and Abroad*, by Mabel T. Boardman. Copyright 1915 by the American Red Cross.

PICTURE CREDITS

CLARISSA HARLOWE BARTON—who later shortened her first name to Clara—was a born fighter. It was in her blood, her era, her destiny. She was pert and petite, but that was not what distinguished her. A certain toughness of body and soul, and a dedication to others before herself, highlighted the life she lived and the legend she created.

Nineteenth-century America was a man's world. That's what four quart-size teen-age lads must have thought when they saw a pint-size girl—just over five feet tall, and not yet eighteen—walk up the dewy grass road to District School Number 9 in rural Massachusetts. It was May 10, 1839; Clara Barton was about to launch one of America's memorable careers and to show that a woman's place was in the world.

"On entering, I found my little school of 40 pupils all seated," Clara recalled later. "I was too timid to address them, but holding my Bible, I said they might take their Testaments and turn to the Sermon on the Mount. All who could read, read a verse each, I reading with them in turn."

The verses, and the discussion that followed, launched the first day well. Night found them, Clara recalled, "social, friendly, and classed for a school." But this apparent "Era of Good Feeling" was only a lull before the storm. A day or two later the four large boys—who had driven a previous teacher from the school—began acting very roughly in the playground, and waited to see what the new girl-teacher would do about it. She promptly showed she could play their sports as well as they could. She matched muscle and skill, as well as wit, with her biggest students. She was a girl, but she was also the boss. Her skirts whirled as, with perfect timing, she jumped to catch a ball thrown wide or high. It is even said she could swing a keg of sweet cider to her shoulder as handily as any young man could.

"When they found that I was as agile and as strong as themselves," she later wrote, "that my throw was as sure and as straight as theirs, and that if they won a game it was because I permitted it, their respect knew no bounds."

Four bullies in a little New England schoolhouse had learned a lesson that thousands of men would learn in the decades ahead. Clara Barton was no pushover.

She was proudly Yankee at a time when New England was alive with ideas and enterprise. The year she began to teach, a great quintet of Massachusetts writers were in their early prime. John Greenleaf Whittier and Henry Wadsworth Longfellow were thirty-two, Nathaniel Hawthorne was thirty-five, Ralph Waldo Emerson was thirty-six. Oliver Wendell Holmes had just turned thirty—so had a lank Westerner named Abraham Lincoln, and an eloquent poet then living in Virginia, Edgar Allan Poe.

At twenty-two, Henry Thoreau was too young to have been heard from yet. James Russell Lowell, Walt Whitman, and Herman Melville were only two years older than Clara herself. Another sensitive and brilliant New England girl had not yet given any indication that she would become one of America's finest poets; after all, Emily Dickinson was only nine.

A rural childhood

All of them were, like the Bartons, close to a rural life where men in homespun clothing and coarse leather shoes plowed and hoed and hoped. Churches were simple and severe buildings; the God worshipped in them was a strong, full-blown, sinewy Jehovah. This was a world full of hunting shirts, corn shucks, barnyards, wheat-growing hillsides, maple syrup, sorghum, and crackling wood fires defying the sharp cold of icy winter nights. Men knew from personal experience what Emerson meant when he described "The Snow-Storm":

"The sled and traveller stopped, the courier's feet
Delayed, all friends shut out, the housemates sit
Around the radiant fireplace, enclosed
In a tumultuous privacy of storm."

An excellent portrait of Clara, painted from life, is this oil done by Cornelia Fassett in Washington about 1877.

There were potatoes to peel, cows to milk, catechisms to learn. There was wading and plowing in springtime, berrying and swimming in summer, nutting and harvesting in autumn, sleighing and snowballing in winter. Yet for all the activity, it could be exceedingly lonely country. Often whippoorwills made the only sound, except for water gushing over a limestone ledge. A child could play all day with no other company but her own hands.

Into such country Clara Barton was born near North Oxford, Massachusetts, on Christmas Day in 1821. Stephen Barton, her father, had been a noncommissioned officer under "Mad Anthony" Wayne in the Indian campaigns along the western frontier in the 1790's and bore the honorary title of "Captain." He had seen American blood spilled in the nation's defense. Clara was very much the baby of the family, being 10 years younger than her sister Sally, 13 younger than brother David, 15 younger than brother Stephen, and 17 younger than sister Dorothy.

The age gap helped to make her shy and withdrawn, though she never lacked for attention and affection. Her father's pet, she stretched out with him before the fireplace and played "Battle" with grains of corn. The red grains fought it out with the yellow ones—and whichever grains were the Americans generally won. Military tactics and strategy fascinated her all her life. Duty and courage were words Clara learned before she could walk. She never forgot them.

Her parents

Although Clara's father was a prospering farmer and fairly prominent in his community at the time of her birth—he had served not only

From the time she was six years old Clara wrote verses, which seldom attained a very high poetic standard. Also, from girlhood onward she enjoyed reading the outstanding Massachusetts authors of her time. These included (from left) Ralph Waldo Emerson, Henry Wadsworth Longfellow, Oliver Wendell Holmes, Nathaniel Hawthorne, and John Greenleaf Whittier. Holmes was always one of her favorite prose writers, thanks especially to his collection of essays entitled "The Autocrat of the Breakfast-Table."

as a town selectman but also as a Massachusetts state legislator—her birthplace was quite unpretentious. A plain frame structure, it had eaves that slanted up from the first floor to provide a partial second story.

Almost every stick of furniture in the house (including Clara's crib) was homemade. A center hall divided the ground floor of the house through the middle; Clara was born in the rear room on the left side of the first floor. The flagstones in front of the main door bore the marks of her father's hand tools and were flanked by lilac bushes and a grassy yard where Clara was permitted to play alone after she had learned to walk.

The military spirit that Clara's father possessed was accompanied by a gentle disposition, a broadly philanthropic outlook, and a confirmed urge toward hard work. She was always especially close to him, and throughout her childhood she spent more time with him than with her mother. He seems to have been more responsible than anyone else in forming her character; until the time of his death, when she was past forty, Clara greatly valued his counsel.

Clara's mother, Sarah Stone Barton, bore her first four children before she was twenty-eight. An experienced, middle-aged matron by the time Clara arrived, she was already well set in her own practical household ways. She had a hot temper, which her daughter inherited but usually kept in check through use of the benign poise that she had evidently inherited from her father.

However, Clara also derived from her mother her decisiveness, common sense, warm heart, and strong will—and she seldom found need to keep any of these qualities in check during her adult years. Mrs. Barton, firm in her techniques of family management, did teach her daughter many housekeeping methods she valued all her life. And of her mother, Clara said: "Her efforts have been as lasting and as much honored by me as any."

There was little of the soft and sentimental in her upbringing. Her mother forbade dolls and toys—but there were cats in the haymow, chickens in the henhouse, calves in the barnyard, and pedigreed colts in the pasture. She rode well when she was only five. Button, a sprightly white-haired dog, grew up with Clara. He followed her everywhere, and slept by her bed at night.

The elder Bartons had helped establish the Oxford meeting house—one of the first Universalist churches in existence. Universalism had a more liberal theology than the Puritan doctrine of the Barton ancestors, but the family maintained all the fundamentals of conscience in the older ethic. Every Sunday, despite rain, wind, or snow, the Bartons drove five miles to church. Decades later, Clara wrote: "A fire in a church would have been sacrilege in those days, and I can just remember being taken home one bitter

cold Sunday with frozen feet. I had not dared complain and fell in the pew when they set me down."

The results of such rearing were permanent. Clara commented, after she had spent a number of years as a teacher: "Show me a child well disciplined, perfectly governed at home, and I will show you a child that never breaks the rule of school. A silken thread will bind that child."

Her inner dynamo

The Bartons were a family of schoolteachers —Sally, Stephen, and Dorothy all taught while Clara was a child. "I had no playmates, but in effect six fathers and mothers," Clara recalled later. "All took charge of me, all educated me, each according to personal taste. My two sisters were scholars and artistic, and strove in that direction. My brothers were strong, ruddy, daring young men, full of life and business."

Dorothy taught Clara to read when she was three; Sally taught her geography; and Stephen, arithmetic. Thus, when she started at Colonel Richard Stone's one-room neighborhood school at four, she did not have to begin spelling with the one-syllable words on the first page. "I spell in 'Artichoke,'" she told the teacher—that being the first word in the three-syllable column of her speller. The act was typical—she wanted to be ahead of, not simply with, others around her. Inside her was a kind of dynamo that ran incessantly, urging her to excel.

THE "QUAKER POET, SO DEAR TO US ALL"

Miss Barton had a special fondness for the writings of Whittier; she called him "the loved Quaker poet, so dear to us all." Among her favorite lines from Whittier were these in which he expressed his faith in God:

"I know not where His Islands lift
  Their fronded palms in air;
I only know I cannot drift
  Beyond His love and care."

She herself was reared a Universalist, always kept a keen interest in religion, and believed in immortality. However, she never became a formal member of any church.

In 1829, when Clara was nearly eight, her parents sent her to boarding school at Oxford, near the city of Worcester in Massachusetts. Timid and unhappy, she wore only one dress and ate little at meals. Undone by bashfulness and loneliness, she turned pale and thin, but improved once she was back home with her family again.

Meanwhile her parents had moved from the hilltop farm where Clara was born to one with broad fields in the valley below that same hill. Now they occupied an old Colonial-era house that needed a lot of fresh painting and papering. Nearly 80 years later, Clara recalled: "Painting included more then than in these later days of prepared material. The painter brought his massive white marble slab, ground his own paints, mixed his colors, boiled his oil, calcined his plaster, made his putty and did scores of things that a painter of today would . . . never think of doing."

She begged to learn all these processes, and spent joyous weeks getting callouses on her hands as she did so. She also "was taught to trim paper neatly, to match and help hang it, to make the most approved paste, and even varnished the kitchen chairs to the entire satisfaction of my mother, which was triumph enough for one little girl." In adult life Clara often helped paint and plaster her own homes.

One episode at the new farm was equally lasting (but more tragic) in its effects upon Clara. To the anguish of her parents, the farm's hired men let her see an ox slaughtered "with a terrible blow. The ox fell; I fell too; and the next I knew I was in the house on a bed, and all the family about me, with the traditional camphor bottle, bathing my head to my great discomfort. As I regained consciousness, they asked me what made me fall? I said 'some one struck me.' 'Oh, no,' they said. . . . Happy ignorance! I had not then learned the mystery of nerves. . . . But, singularly, I lost all desire for meat."

After she had witnessed this ox-slaughtering, Miss Barton was a sparing eater of meat during the rest of her life. Nevertheless, when the mood for eating meat was on her, she would cheerfully tackle a beefsteak at breakfast or broiled bacon as part of her meal at teatime.

In 1831 her father gave her a Morgan horse named Billy, and her mother added a silver-trimmed saddle. Clara loved to ride over the green hills, and to feel the bright air sting her face and bite her ears. Moving fast excited her. Almost 80 years later, writing of her childhood, she commented: "To this day my seat on a saddle or on the back of a horse is as secure and tireless as in a rocking chair, and far more pleasurable."

In this period, while Andrew Jackson was President, country people came together to raise barns, bringing with them their families, axes, saws, and their ready muscles. Such neighborly acts made it possible to do big jobs in short order. You helped so that you would, in turn, be helped. That is how America was built. So, in the year 1832, neighbors came to raise a

barn for Captain Barton. The Captain's son David fell from the ridgepole when a plank broke, and was seriously injured.

"From the first days and nights of illness, I remained near his side," Clara recalled later. "I could not be taken away from him, except by compulsion, and he was unhappy until my return. I learned to take all directions for his medicines from the physician, and to administer them. . . . I was the accepted and acknowledged nurse of a man almost too ill to recover." She wrote that in two years, "I only left his bedside for one half day." David did finally recover—and Clara Barton had meanwhile found, before she even reached thirteen, the role in life for which she was entirely suited.

But it was schoolteaching, not nursing, that first attracted the dark-haired, sharp-featured Clara. At Lucian Burleigh's school near her father's farm she studied ancient history, as-

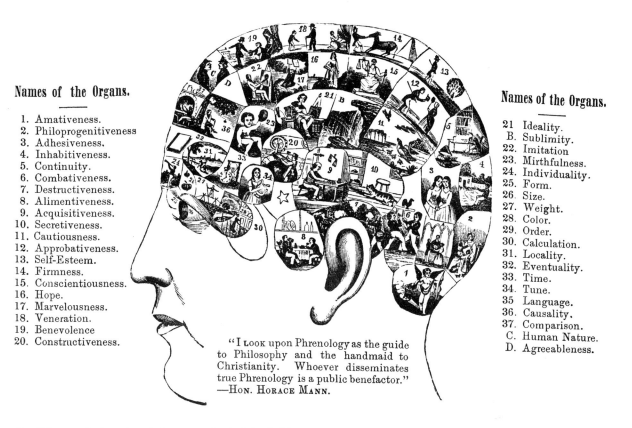

Names of the Organs.

1. Amativeness.
2. Philoprogenitiveness
3. Adhesiveness.
4. Inhabitiveness.
5. Continuity.
6. Combativeness.
7. Destructiveness.
8. Alimentiveness.
9. Acquisitiveness.
10. Secretiveness.
11. Cautiousness.
12. Approbativeness.
13. Self-Esteem.
14. Firmness.
15. Conscientiousness.
16. Hope.
17. Marvelousness.
18. Veneration.
19. Benevolence
20. Constructiveness.

Names of the Organs.

21 Ideality.
B. Sublimity.
22. Imitation
23. Mirthfulness.
24. Individuality.
25. Form.
26. Size.
27. Weight.
28. Color.
29. Order.
30. Calculation.
31. Locality.
32. Eventuality.
33. Time.
34. Tune.
35 Language.
36. Causality.
37. Comparison.
C. Human Nature.
D. Agreeableness.

"I LOOK upon Phrenology as the guide to Philosophy and the handmaid to Christianity. Whoever disseminates true Phrenology is a public benefactor." —HON. HORACE MANN.

Practitioners of phrenology felt a person's skull to decide which of the organs shown in this old chart dominated that person's character. Horace Mann, a notable educator of the day, was a leading supporter of phrenology.

This certifies that the **School Committee** *of the Town of Millbury have examined M*__s *C. H. Barton* *and satisfied themselves that* her *literary attainments and moral charac-ter are such as to qualify* her *to teach the* Winter ____ *School in* Grace Hill District ____ *the present year.*

J. F. Bronson ____ *Sec'y Sch. Committee.*

Millbury, Dec 8 ____ *184*9

tronomy, and languages. She was home sick with the mumps when a famous English lec-turer, L. N. Fowler, visited her family. He was interested in the subject then called phrenology, which bore some resemblance to what we today call psychology.

Seeing that Clara was restless and questing, Fowler examined her, and reported to her par-ents. Clara overheard him say: "She will never assert herself for herself . . . but for others she will be perfectly fearless. Throw responsibility upon her. She has all the qualities of a teacher. As soon as her age will permit, give her a school to teach."

Firm, warm teaching

All those who heard Fowler's suggestion took him seriously. Completing her course work, Clara applied to the local committee of three examiners (a clergyman, a lawyer, and a justice of the peace) for a certificate to teach school. On May 5, 1839, they "approbated her" for the ensuing term. She was soon in her first class-room, described at the start of this chapter.

Almost to that moment, her family had still looked upon her as a mere child. Realizing this, Clara had asked them with all her dignity, "But what am I to do with only two little old waifish dresses?" Her family conceded that the question was pertinent, and aided her efforts "to look larger and older" by acquiring new frocks that fell below the tops of her shoes. These dresses were not simply longer than the two fit only for a waif, but were also more adult in their cut and style. One was an elegant, tight-fitting green dress beautifully trimmed with velvet.

The first term of teaching was such a success that, when it ended, the students "sobbed their way down the hill after the last goodbye." The authorities came to District School Number 9 to congratulate Clara for the discipline she had maintained. She felt she had learned as much as she had taught—and what she learned as a teen-age teacher was the rocklike foundation on which her life of service to others was built.

Managing rural schoolhouses, with students of all ages in one room, was trying, tiresome work. The girl-teacher mastered it impressively. She spared neither smile nor rod when neces-sary, encouraging the shy and shaming the bullies. By molding the young, Clara knew she would shape the community. Even when former students came back years after graduation, she called them "my children." Teaching—like courage and conscience—seemed to be in her very blood.

Though it brought her professional pleasure, her attitude toward teaching blocked off the possibility of marriage. She considered her work "more fruitful of good than matrimony," but was haunted by romantic longings and indecision. Slight and attractive, she had thick brown hair parted in the middle and clustered over her ears in ringlets; high cheekbones and classic features; slim waist and hands; and dark dancing eyes.

Several men courted her—one actually sent $10,000 after he "struck it rich" in the California gold fields. (She tried to return the money but he insisted on her keeping it—so she invested the sum and it helped to support her in later life.) But Clara Barton never married. Loneliness and quiet despair were frequent companions, as diary entries, like this one made in 1852, show: "I contribute to the happiness of not a single object and often to the unhappiness of many and always my own, for I am never happy. . . . How long I can endure such a life I do not know."

After teaching in various schools not far from her parents' farm for about 10 years, and with her thirtieth birthday approaching, Clara decided she must not only get more education, but also move farther away from the home nest, if she were to find happiness and fulfillment. So in 1850 she resigned her teaching position and enrolled in the "Liberal Institute" for female teachers at Clinton, New York. Brothers Stephen and David drove her to the station on a crisp winter morning in the "jingling cutter" used when snow was on the roads. As she waved goodbye, Clara realized that a chapter in her life had ended. The New England years were past—Clara Barton was entering a wider world.

Following women pioneers

"I broke away from my long shackles," Clara later said of this major decision, which she took at a time when there were almost no colleges for girls. The pioneering leaders for both civil rights and higher education for women "had not

---

MISS BARTON AND MARRIAGE

At least occasionally, she seems to have thought of matrimony—but apparently matters never got so far as a formal engagement, much less marriage itself. Her nephew Stephen E. Barton, who was close to her for more than 50 years and was named her executor, wrote:

"My aunt said to me at one time that I must not think she had never known any experience of love. She said that she had had her romances and love affairs like other girls; but that in her young womanhood, though she thought of different men as possible lovers, no one of them measured up to her ideal of a husband. She said to me that she could think of herself with satisfaction as a wife and mother, but that on the whole she felt that she had been more useful to the world by being free from matrimonial ties."

Another intimate of her young womanhood put it somewhat differently:

"Clara Barton had many admirers, and they were all men whom she admired and some whom she almost loved. More men were interested in her than she was ever interested in; some of them certainly interested her, yet not profoundly. I do not think she ever had a love affair that stirred the depths of her being. The truth is, Clara Barton was herself so much stronger a character than any of the men who made love to her that I do not think she was ever seriously tempted to marry any of them."

---

labored and succeeded as they have now. Every girl should bless these pioneer women in her daily prayers. I got all the institute could give me . . . and I was free to take my course in the world and seek its work."

Clara "had not expected so charming a teacher" as the head of the institute, Miss Louise Barker, to whom she subsequently paid warm and affectionate tribute as possessing "an unlooked-for activity, a cordiality, and an irresistible charm of manner . . . a winning, indescribable grace which I have met in only a few persons in a whole lifetime." Since Clara still looked much younger than her years and since no biographical particulars or outline of past work was required, she never told anybody at the institute that she had taught, let alone that she had already spent more than a third of her life teaching. "There was no reason why I should volunteer my history, or step in among that crowd of eager pupils as a 'schoolmarm' expected to know everything. The easiest way for me was to keep silent, as I did."

Clara's thirst for knowledge was enormous. She took all the courses that the institute offered, and even spent her holidays at the school. Mary Norton and Abby Barker, fellow students, and Samuel Ramsey, divinity student at nearby Hamilton College, became her close friends. There were lively talks, long walks in the country, dreams of the future.

Then, after a full and stimulating year at Clinton, came stunning news from brother Stephen: "Our excellent mother is no more." Crushed by the letter, Clara went to her room "without a word." Because of the slow communications of the period, Stephen's letter reached her too late for her to get home for the funeral, but she did return later to console her father. Again despair gripped her. "I am," she wrote, "badly organized to live in the world, or among society."

Outer gaiety; inner gloom

From about 1850 until her death in 1912, there is a startling contrast between Clara's dealings with other people (even those nearest to her) and her private diaries. As her biographer Ishbel Ross has observed: "The melancholy thread of her inner life is traceable through 60 years of diary entries, in juxtaposition to the bright and purposeful picture of her daily activities as revealed in her letters, her accomplishments, the comments of her friends, and the newspaper accounts of her successful career. By this time she was already committed to the constant note-taking which was to illumine every facet of her life, reflecting her thoughts, motivations and actions with the accuracy of a mirror."

Yet, because of her bright exterior, her immediate family and friends—even when they were with her daily—seldom caught a glimpse of her interior gloom. Thus, at this very period of inner despair, Clara was gaily saying that social rivalry in her circle consisted of loading a table down with as many sorts of cake as possible: "The prestige of one family that set 14 varieties before its guests was eclipsed by neighbors who increased the number to 17."

Challenge in New Jersey

Having completed her studies at the institute, Clara went to Bordentown, New Jersey, planning to spend a few weeks with Mary Norton, who lived in a nearby town. But idle visiting or sitting was not for the hypersensitive Yankee lady. In Bordentown she saw many children roaming the streets. Talking to several of these obviously idle urchins, she found out there were no free public schools in operation. Clara Barton was never one to accept a situation when she thought she could improve it. The laws of New Jersey said free schools were to be conducted. Why were there none in Bordentown?

Peter Suydam, local postmaster and chairman of the school board, shrugged his shoulders at her indignant protests. Many of the street loafers, said Suydam, "were more fit for the penitentiary than school—a woman could do nothing with them." "Free schools for paupers" —for that is what the townspeople called them— were unpopular and impractical. Worthwhile people paid for private schooling.

Such talk got Clara's dander up. She promised to teach without pay if she were furnished with a school building. The board reluctantly granted her a teacher's certificate on July 1, 1852, and refitted a shabby old schoolhouse for her use. In a few months, they suspected, she would be ready to quit and go home.

The first day six pupils came. A year later there were 600. The astounded citizens of Bordentown had watched one tiny visitor do what they had been unable to do—open and operate a successful free school. Swamped with pupils, Miss Barton sent to North Oxford for Frances (Fannie) Childs to come and teach with her; Jenny Suydam became a student assistant, as overflow classes were moved to a hall above a tailor's shop.

In Bordentown, as in all her previous schools, Clara won not just lasting affection and respect but solid effort from her pupils. Until the end of her life, men and women kept writing to tell Clara how much her inspired teaching had always meant to them. Meanwhile, after school hours, she enjoyed long strolls around the Bordentown area, with "the silver flow of the Delaware below its rocky bluffs," its handsome old brick houses, and its historical associations with signers of the Declaration of Independence and other founding fathers.

All her life Clara was fascinated by the career of Napoleon. So not least of Bordentown's charms in her eyes was that, for some 20 years, Napoleon's brother Joseph (the former king of Spain) had lived there in exile. Much of the handsome estate Joseph Bonaparte had laid out in Bordentown had changed little since his day. Clara considered the estate's "miles of shrubs and flowers, its walks, its rests, the ripple of brooks, and the unceasing song of birds—the repose of nature—a home fit for a king."

In 1853 a new $4,000 building was approved, and the job of principal established. But it was not offered to Clara; women seldom headed up sizable operations in the 1850's, even if they themselves had personally developed them, as Clara most assuredly had developed the Bordentown school. A young man was placed over her. Stung by the board's ingratitude and the way the new man treated her, with pettiness and jealousy, she decided to resign. Her brother Stephen urged her not to quit, but to "continue the straightforward, just, independent system you have commenced, and I think that all will be right."

Then nature intervened. Worn down by long hours, constant strain, and frustration, Clara lost her voice completely. The woman who had brought the sound of happy school children to Bordentown was too hoarse to talk when she submitted her resignation. No one knew it, but when she walked out of the schoolroom that day, her teaching career was over forever.

A "pest in petticoats"

On a raw February day in 1854 Clara started out for Washington, D.C., with her friend Fan-

FREQUENT LAUGHTER IN BORDENTOWN

Fannie Childs, who later married Clara's nephew Bernard Barton Vassall, was her assistant teacher at Bordentown—and thus recalled it:

"Clara and I boarded and roomed together. The editor of the Bordentown *Gazette* roomed at the same place. He frequently commented on the fact that when Clara and I were in our room together, we were always talking and laughing. It was a constant wonder to him. He could not understand how we found so much to laugh at.

"Clara was so sensitive, she felt it keenly when any pupil had to be punished, or any parent was disappointed, but she did not indulge very long in mourning or self-reproach, she knew she had done her best and she laughed and made the best of it. Clara had an unfailing sense of humor. She said to me once that of all the qualities she possessed, that for which she felt most thankful was her sense of humor. She said it helped her over many hard places.

"Clara had quick wit, and was very ready with repartee and apt reply. I remember an evening . . . at the home of the Episcopalian minister, who was one of the School Committee. The discussion turned to phrenology. Clara had great faith in it. The minister did not believe in it at all. They had quite an argument about it. He told Clara of a man who had suffered an injury to the brain that had resulted in the removal of a considerable part of it. He argued that if there was anything in phrenology, that man would have been deprived of a certain group of mental capabilities, but that he got on very well with only a part of a brain. Clara replied quickly, 'Then there's hope for me.' So the discussion ended in a hearty laugh."

Clara's first Bordentown school is now a memorial to her.

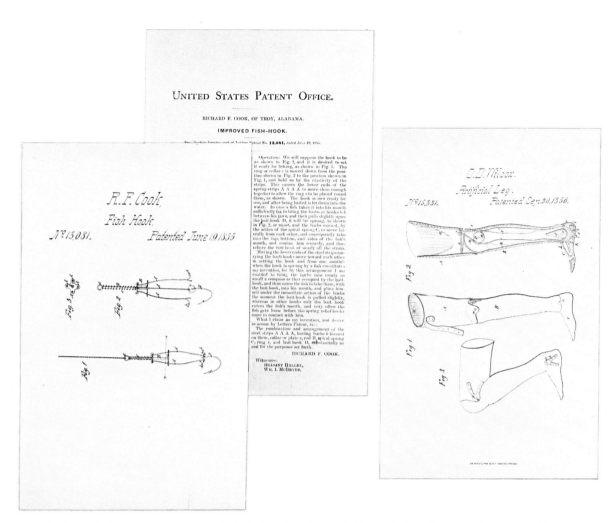

Two patents granted while Clara Barton was in that office. She helped to blaze a trail for female clerks in Federal jobs.

nie Childs. There she hoped to recuperate in the milder climate, and perhaps find another job. With the coming of spring sunshine, she felt "healthy, wealthy, and spunky," as she wrote home.

Most of the capital's streets were unpaved. Many government buildings had not been finished when Clara Barton walked about as a sightseer. The Washington Monument was halted below the halfway mark, with its top encased in wooden scaffolding. The Capitol had two unroofed wings, and a small dome that would shortly have to be replaced. There were mud puddles and ruts everywhere, as Clara made her way to and from her lodging at 1013 T Street. With her health restored, she was

ready to work again. Perhaps her Massachusetts congressman, Colonel Alexander De Witt, could help her find a government job.

He could and did. At De Witt's suggestion, Judge Charles Mason hired Clara Barton as a copy clerk in the Patent Office—reportedly, the first woman to copy secret papers in a United States government department. Earning 10 cents for every 100 words copied, she was able to make between $70 and $80 a month. "My arm is tired, and my poor thumb is all calloused holding my pen," she wrote. But she progressed so well that Mason soon made her his confidential clerk and raised her salary to $1,400 a year. For a woman in the 1850's (and, in fact, for a great many men of the time), this was considered a splendid salary, seldom achieved.

One reason for her rapid rise, Clara explained long afterward, was that (unlike most human beings) she could keep a secret—and "the secrecy of its papers had not been carefully guarded" in the Patent Office. Serious leaks had occurred. Some clerks were selling off various patent secrets for their own profit and to the grave injury of the patent owners. Thus, Judge Mason considered Clara "a very valuable ally in his reforming work in the Patent Office."

The men with whom she worked resented her presence and success. She was a "pest in petticoats," at whom they whistled, blew smoke, or spit tobacco juice. "I'm terrified," she wrote to David, "but I'll never let them know it." If those who taunted her expected Clara Barton to give up or run, they were to be disappointed. She might look small as a lapdog, but she held on like a bulldog.

This is how a typical day in her life went. She arose at four o'clock in the morning, read her Bible, prayed, and dressed. She straightened out her room, studied French, and fixed herself breakfast. By then it was time to walk a mile to work, where she was always seated by nine o'clock. Her only time off was during a brief lunch break. After the day was done she frequently took work home by special permission and continued until she fell asleep, often close to midnight.

Fortunately her sister Sally (married now to Bernard Vassall), who lived in Washington, provided regular company. There was also the drama of, and excitement at, being in the nation's capital where great issues were being debated and decided. Talk of slavery and secession was everywhere. Clara was not an Abolitionist, though strongly opposed to slavery. Believing that sudden emancipation of the Negroes would only worsen matters, she favored a more gradual solution.

When she could, she slipped down to the Capitol and listened to the congressional debates. In May 1856, for example, she was in the Senate chamber when Charles Sumner delivered his speech on "The Crime Against Kansas."

Two days later the irate Preston Brooks, a congressman from South Carolina, caned Sumner into unconsciousness on the Senate floor. The young copy clerk knew, as did many others, that the Union was in grave danger. In a sense the war had already begun. "It began not at Sumter," she said later, "but at Sumner."

"I am to blame..."

Meanwhile Clara had her own problems. She was a staunch supporter of the new Republican party, formed in 1854 and ready to challenge the Democrats in the 1856 national election. The Republicans chose John C. Frémont to run against James Buchanan. When the Democrats won, it was easy to predict what might happen to government employees who had deserted the party. "A day of general decapitation is looked for in all offices," Clara wrote in her diary. She was right.

Colonel De Witt had not been reelected to Congress, and Judge Mason resigned from the Patent Office. In 1857 Miss Barton's resignation was requested. Soon she was on her way home to Oxford, where her eighty-three-year-old father was infirm. Clara's eyes and throat gave her trouble. At thirty-six her career seemed ruined by overwork, antifeminism, and the political spoils system. The next few months were one of the most difficult periods she ever experienced.

She considered teaching again, and was actually offered a job in Rome, New York. "I have outgrown that, or that me," she wrote. "I dread the routine of such a life. I am to blame, I know, for nobody teaches so easily or has so little trouble with it." Instead, Clara took painting lessons and thought of teaching art somewhere in the South. She also considered writing to Sam Houston, a frontier hero she greatly admired, and asking him for a position in Texas.

The whole picture was changed when a letter came from Washington, asking Clara to return to the Patent Office. She had been badly missed; it seemed more important to have a highly efficient clerk straighten out the patent records than to debate her politics.

Captain Barton urged his daughter to return. Her friends, her life, and her destiny lay in Washington—which would be her headquarters for more than half a century. So back to the capital she went, where some congressmen now wore daggers and pistols, while others shuddered at news of John Brown's bloody raid on Harpers Ferry, Virginia. In December 1859, Brown was hanged for treason. But his soul was marching on, and hundreds of thousands would be marching before the issues he so dramatically raised were settled.

The little lady on the train bound from Massachusetts to Washington was riding through an all but severed Union; her destination was the focal point at which the ability of an Illinois politician named Abraham Lincoln would soon be tested. No nation, he insisted, can endure half free and half slave. With this central conviction, he sought and won the Republican candidacy in the 1860 election. Three other major candidates ran for the office; with the Democrats split among themselves, Lincoln with a minority of the popular vote polled a great majority of the electoral votes.

"If Lincoln Is Elected," a notice in the Charleston *Courier* had warned the nation in early November, "South Carolina Will Lead Boldly for a Southern Confederacy." On December 20, 1860, South Carolina did secede and solemnly proclaim: "The Union is dissolved." Delegates of the state came to Washington to

During Brooks's assault, other Southerners smile or hold back Sumner's friends. It took Sumner years to recover.

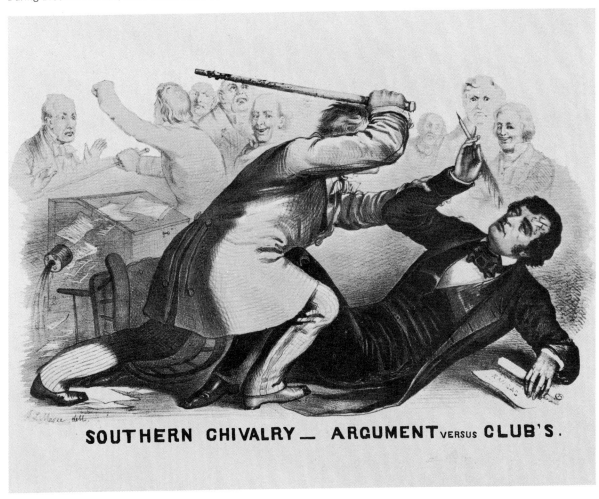

SOUTHERN CHIVALRY _ ARGUMENT VERSUS CLUB'S.

claim possession of all United States property within its boundaries, including Fort Sumter in Charleston harbor.

President James Buchanan (who remained President until March, even though his successor had already been elected) answered by sending reinforcements to Fort Sumter. They never got there. The supply ship was fired on and turned back at the harbor's mouth.

Six other Southern states followed South Carolina in secession. Their delegates met, formed the Confederate States of America, and elected Jefferson Davis of Mississippi their first president. He was inaugurated on February 18, 1861. Suddenly the nation that, since the days of George Washington, had been headed by only one president at a time had two at once.

"I'll help soldiers"

In this atmosphere, fifty-two-year-old Abraham Lincoln came to Washington to begin his term of office. On March 4, 1861, he was inaugurated on the Capitol steps, beneath a half-completed dome. Chief Justice Roger Taney administered the oath of office to the gangling Lincoln, who then said: "We are not enemies, but friends. We must not be enemies. Though passion may have strained, it must not break our bonds of affection." Lincoln was shrewdly leaving the onus of attack on the Confederacy.

Few in the audience knew that underneath the platform on which he spoke were 50 armed men. One of the persons listening was Clara Barton. "We have a *live Republican* president," she wrote to her friend Annie Childs the following day. "The inaugural address was first delivered in a loud, fine voice. . . . Only a very few of the United States troops were brought to the Capitol at all, but were in readiness at their quarters and other parts of the city; they were probably not brought out, lest it look like menace."

Far to the south the troops of South Carolina were in readiness, too; General Pierre G. T. Beauregard was completing his plans for an overwhelming attack on Fort Sumter. The day of coolness and compromise had passed.

BROWN DRESSES THAT TURNED TO GREEN

In her youth, and occasionally in later life, Clara was a painter; she enjoyed mixing colors on a palette. Throughout her life, she had a preference for bright colors—her favorites were green and red. Her elder sister Sally said, "When Clara goes to town to buy a brown dress, I know she will get it, for Clara always does what she says, but one way or another, that dress always changes to green, before she can get home."

She loved to set off a green dress with touches of red, especially since she considered that the red rose was the Barton family symbol. (Red apples were her first choice in fruit.) Her biographer Ishbel Ross noted: "Long before she heard of the Red Cross it was her custom to add a dash of scarlet to her costume. 'It is my color,' she would explain, swinging a scarlet scarf around her neck, often with a green dress . . . .

"Sometimes it was nothing more than a red ribbon at her throat or her waist. At other times it was a hood or uister. She donned a scarlet scarf as she sailed for Cuba and the Spanish-American War. She sported a scarlet-lined cloak while she stood on a New York dock, watching grain being loaded for shipment to Russia for the famine victims of 1892. In her late eighties she was observed milking her Jersey cow, dressed in a black gown with checked apron, a brown Quaker bonnet, and a red shawl gleaming with the jewels of two of her foreign decorations."

Cut off from supplies and relief, Major Robert Anderson and his Federal garrison of only 75 men had no chance of holding Fort Sumter. They would and did hold out as long as they could—but in due time the "Stars and Stripes" would be hauled down, and the new Confederate flag, the "Stars and Bars," would take its place. Meanwhile President Lincoln appointed his cabinet and prepared for action. On April 14, 1861, Fort Sumter fell. The next morning President Lincoln issued a call for 75,000 men to put down the rebellion.

Clara Barton read the news in her small apartment on T Street. "This conflict is one thing I've been waiting for," she wrote that tragic spring. "I'm well and strong and young—young enough to go to the front. If I can't be a soldier, I'll help soldiers."

She was only eight months short of forty—an

age at which many women consider the major events and struggles of their lives past. Clara Barton had worked and struggled much in her first four decades, in jobs that were "not for ladies." And the saying that "life begins at forty" might have been coined to describe her.

Those whom she had taught or worked with, loved and respected (or, in some few instances, scorned) her. In the nation at large, she had no wide reputation. But now, with the advent of the Civil War, all that was to change. The diminutive but tireless Yankee schoolteacher was destined to become the Angel of the Battlefield—one of the best-known and most deeply admired women in the whole great sweep of American history.

The start of the Civil War was pictured in this fashion by what was then America's leading illustrated newspaper. During the bombardment of Fort Sumter (center) from Fort Moultrie (left) and Cummings Point (right), crinolined women and frock-coated men gathered on Charleston's roofs to observe the event. Most of them were overjoyed at the smoke-laden scene of such victorious destruction. But one witness reported "prayers from the women and imprecations from the men." Later in the war, during the 1863 siege of Charleston by Union forces, Clara worked close to Sumter on the far side. At that time she was on Morris Island, nursing white and Negro troops wounded in the bloody assaults on Charleston's outer defenses.

HARPER'S WEEKLY.
JOURNAL OF CIVILIZATION.

VOL. V.—No. 227.]   NEW YORK, SATURDAY, MAY 4, 1861.   [SINGLE COPIES SIX CENTS.
[$2 50 PER YEAR IN ADVANCE.

Entered according to Act of Congress, in the Year 1861, by Harper & Brothers, in the Clerk's Office of the District Court for the Southern District of New York.

THE HOUSE-TOPS IN CHARLESTON DURING THE BOMBARDMENT OF SUMTER.

Chapter 2
HEROINE AT WORK, IN CIVIL WAR AND AFTER

APRIL 1861 saw the American Union fall apart. It also saw Clara Barton sitting in the presiding officer's chair of the United States Senate, reading a newspaper to Yankee recruits who had been rushed south to put the Union back together.

In that month of confusion and chaos, no one knew what to expect. Virginia, which had provided the United States with four of its first five presidents, seceded. This brought the Confederacy right to the banks of the Potomac, and, with strong secessionist sentiment in Maryland, lightly garrisoned Washington was in immediate danger. A pro-Confederate mob in Baltimore cut rail and telegraph connections; for several days no reinforcements reached the capital.

General Winfield Scott, seventy-five-year-old chief of the Union armies, who had been three when the Constitution was adopted, thought the city "in danger of being attacked on all sides in a day or two."

"It does seem to me, General," Lincoln remarked to Scott, "that if I were Beauregard I would take Washington."

Little wonder that the 6th Massachusetts Regiment, en route to Washington, was attacked by a mob on April 19 while changing trains in Baltimore. Four soldiers were killed, and dozens wounded; the remaining troops hurried on to Washington and safety. Among those waiting to greet them at the station was Clara Barton. One promptly called out her name—he was a lad from the farm next to her brother David's. The men were from Worcester, near her hometown; some of them had been her pupils.

Hearing that the regiment was to be billeted in the Senate chamber of the Capitol, Clara followed after "her boys." And when she saw they had lost all their baggage and clothes in Baltimore, she swung into action. From her own rooms she brought linens, tearing up sheets to make handkerchiefs. With her money, and her sister's, she bought baskets of food, and had five Negro porters carry them to the Capitol. Next the soldiers begged her to read aloud the one available copy of their hometown paper, the Worcester *Spy*.

Suddenly she had been whisked to the front of the chamber and placed in the big chair reserved for the Vice President. The men were quiet as she read "hometown" accounts of the attack on them in Baltimore. They clamored for a second reading, and applauded as she finished.

Clara Barton had performed the first of what would be a memorable sequence of selfless acts for human beings suddenly set adrift in a time of trouble and pain.

Towels, soap, needles, thread, stationery, reading material—how many things the soldiers needed! Quickly Clara sent a notice to the Worcester paper: she would receive and distribute any food, supplies, or money sent to her. She did not represent the government, state, or army—only herself, and the heartfelt needs that would not let her sleep at night.

The citizens of Worcester, and dozens of other towns who saw the message, responded. Soon women were knitting and sewing, canning and packing, so that loved ones would not go wanting. Clara's own small quarters were crammed full to the ceiling, with no place for incoming boxes. Like the "sorcerer's apprentice," she had found the magic way to get supplies—but not how to regulate or stop them.

The key to her work

At this point Clara Barton drew upon the quality that was the key to her whole character and program—the ability to organize. Think straight, plan carefully, act boldly: a six-word summary of her life. A warehouse was rented for the excess material. Systems for acknowledgment, storage, and distribution were worked out. A substitute was found for her in the Patent Office—she was not going to dismiss her job the way officials had dismissed her from it four years earlier. Like others whose lives were pledged to preserving the Union, Clara understood that in the days ahead it was plan or perish.

The Federal army, which was so critically needed now, was still pathetically inadequate for the Herculean task ahead. The withdrawal of Southerners reduced the regular army to a meager 13,000 men. Congress quickly raised the authorized strength to 42,000 but that figure was not reached in 1861. In effect the Union army, created by the act of July 22, 1861, was a volunteer force; the method of recruiting was clumsy, inefficient, and marred by politics.

Not until March 3, 1863, was a draft law enacted. Even after that, draftees could hire a substitute or be exempted by paying $300. Pay was low—$11 a month for a private, later increased to $16. This inexperienced citizens' army had to learn its lesson in the mud and blood of battle.

The first bitter lesson came on July 21, 1861, when overconfident Union generals pushed

This wartime panorama includes the White House at far left, the unfinished Washington Monument, and the Capitol.

southward to meet the Confederate forces at Bull Run, Virginia. Washington officials and ladies followed in carriages, to see the victory. What they saw was a Yankee rout: 500 killed, 1,000 wounded, 1,500 missing.

If military arrangements for Bull Run had been inadequate, medical preparations were scandalous. Almost no provision had been made to take decent care of the wounded—they were returned, untended, to the Potomac River docks, to wait in the sun or rain until they could be taken into improvised hospital tents. Clara Barton cared for all she could in her rooms then. She repeatedly went down to the docks to see the pathetic sight and render whatever service she was able.

That day, and for many days following, she kept asking three questions: (1) Why couldn't the wounded be tended at or near the battle? (2) Why couldn't a better system of nursing and care be devised? (3) Why should men who fought like heroes be left to die untended and unwanted by people they were defending?

Of course medical techniques and supplies in 1861 were vastly inferior to those of a century later. Few of the drugs used today were known, and there was inadequate anesthesia. Camp life fostered infection and epidemics, which were hard to check. Battle conditions made it almost impossible to provide help or treatment quickly.

Many gallant doctors and aides did all they could, as Clara Barton well knew. But she also knew and saw "elegantly dressed ladies who ride over and sit in their carriages to witness 'splendid services,' and . . . learn very little of what lies there under canvas." The United States Sanitary Commission (similar to the later Red Cross, though on a smaller and less permanent scale) was overwhelmed by the emergency. The whole system needed revising; that human touch for which there is no substitute must be added. Women, Clara was convinced, could best supply it. Why could not *she* serve as a nurse, on the battlefront?

To the mid-nineteenth-century mind, the idea was ridiculous, even though England's Florence Nightingale had done this during the Crimean War in the 1850's. A woman's place was in the home—to send women out on the firing line was a shocking idea. New ideas always meet some opposition: her ideas ran into stone walls.

Still Clara asked, requested, insisted. Going home in November of 1861 to be with her dying father, she raised the questions in Massachusetts. With Colonel De Witt, she visited Governor John A. Andrew. The governor's letter endorsing Clara's proposal brought a tart reply from a key official: "I do not think at the present time Miss Barton had better undertake to go to Burnside's Division to act as a nurse." But she *was* going, and finally found a man who would help her—Major D. H. Rucker, Assistant Quartermaster General.

There was a good deal more red tape to cut, but Clara snipped away. Finally, in July of 1862, William A. Hammond, the army's Sur-

geon General, wrote this historic directive: "Miss C. H. Barton has permission to go on the sick transports in any direction—for the purpose of distributing comforts for the sick and wounded and nursing them—always subject to the direction of the surgeon in charge."

To the front

On August 3, 1862, Clara Barton climbed into a supply wagon pulled by a team of mules, and headed for the battlefront. Small but vigorous, she wore a dark skirt (free from all crinoline and stiffening), plaid jacket, and kerchief. She had done all she could back in Washington. Her job henceforth was to seek the place where she could do the maximum good.

While Clara moved south, jouncing along beside the driver of her mule wagon, General "Stonewall" Jackson was rushing north with his Confederate army. On August 9 he met and defeated the Yankees at Cedar Mountain, near Culpeper, Virginia. "Concluded to go to Culpeper," Clara wrote in her journal for August 11. "Packed goods. . . . And so began my work."

It was midnight when her four-mule team

APPEARING AS THE SHELLS WERE BURSTING

Surgeon Dunn, who was from Conneautville, Pennsylvania, asserted subsequently that he was the first to call Clara the "Angel of the Battlefield." He was certainly the first frontline doctor she helped; here and later she showed her amazing talent (or her luck) for appearing at just the right time with just the right supplies that were required. "I first met Miss Barton," wrote Surgeon Dunn, "at the battle of Cedar Mountain, where she appeared . . . with everything needed . . . and while the shells were bursting in every direction took her course to the hospital on our right, where she found everything wanting again."

Concerning the battle of Chantilly, soon afterward, Surgeon Dunn wrote: "Soon the wounded began to come in. Here we had nothing but our instruments. . . . When the cars whistled up to the station, the first person on the platform was Miss Barton, again to supply us with bandages, brandy, wine, prepared soup, jellies, meal, and every article that could be thought of. She stayed there till the last wounded soldier was placed on the cars, then bade us goodbye and left."

---

pulled up in front of the hospital tent of Brigade Surgeon James L. Dunn. "We were entirely out of dressings of every kind," he wrote in his report. "After doing all she could on the field, she returned to Culpeper, where she stayed dealing out shirts to the naked wounded, and preparing soup, and seeing it prepared in all the hospitals. . . . I thought that night if heaven ever sent out a holy angel, she must be one, her assistance was so timely." The title "Angel of the Battlefield," coined that first day she spent at the front, stuck with Clara until the last day of her life. Her diary shows that, in keeping with her selfless devotion, she nursed not only the Union but the Confederate wounded while she was at Culpeper.

Back in Washington, she stepped up the campaign to get supplies from citizens throughout the North. "Your wine brought strength to the fainting," she wrote to the women of Hightstown, New Jersey. "Your clothes stanched the blood of the dying." She must not only use supplies, but also secure new ones, in ever larger amounts.

Soon afterward the second battle of Bull Run was fought—another disaster for the North. Climbing into a freight car loaded with supplies, Clara rushed to Fairfax, Virginia, where the casualties had been dumped onto open bales of hay and straw. Death was everywhere: dead men, dead dreams, dead predictions. Young voices were no longer "shouting the battle cry of freedom." They were groaning and asking for food or a drink of water. Clara Barton, who had taken three women volunteers with her, described the scene: "We were a little band of almost empty-handed workers literally by ourselves in the wild woods of Virginia, with 3,000 suffering men crowded upon the few acres within our reach."

All night they worked, Clara making her inventory by candlelight. The next morning, units of the Confederate cavalry were seen through the trees. Would the casualties and their nurses all be overrun before the little Union train puffed to the siding and picked up the wounded? After hours of delay, it finally arrived. The last

This newspaper illustration of the first battle of Bull Run helped civilians see the need for nursing at the front itself.

human wrecks were put on flatcars; the painful journey back to safety began. Had not the Angel hovered over them, many who made that journey would have died.

The second battle of Bull Run merged into the battle of Chantilly. The whole drama was played over again. This time Union General Philip Kearny was killed and his men were demoralized. "All day they came," Clara wrote, "tired, hungry, ragged, defeated, retreating they knew not whither."

The Union's low morale

Through all this dark period of the war, Pope, Burnside, and Hooker all tried in vain to organize a Union fighting machine to stop the Confederates. Greed, confusion, anguish, and profiteering cut deeply into morale on the home front. All this did not lessen Clara Barton's

determination to do her work well—instead, her determination increased.

Thus, when a message came on September 13, 1862, saying she was needed at Harpers Ferry, she swung once more into action. Major Rucker gave her a wagon. No other women were allowed to make the rough and dangerous 80-mile trip, but the Reverend Cornelius M. Welles (one of her reliable co-workers, though never an official associate) and three other men accompanied Miss Barton. Soon they were in the debris of war—dazed prisoners, dead animals, grown men reduced to sobbing boys. Then the wagon of mercy caught up with an army wagon train 10 miles long.

The usual order of march was in effect—first ammunition, then food and clothing, and finally hospital supplies. If she remained in line, Clara could not hope to arrive in time for the worst of

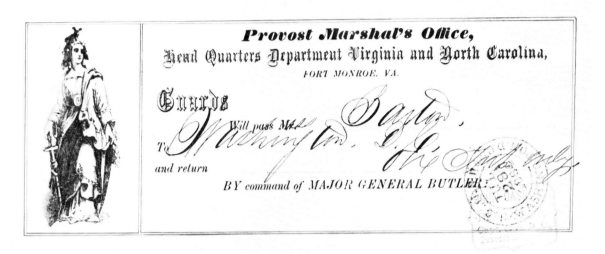

Wherever she went, in any military zone throughout the war, Clara had to have a pass similar to this one.

the fighting. So at one o'clock the following morning she aroused her small crew, had them harness the mules, and hurried to outflank the army wagons ahead.

Harpers Ferry had already fallen to Jackson, but she had no trouble finding the Army of the Potomac drawn up for what was to be the bloodiest battle of the whole Civil War—Antietam. By pushing forward during the night, Clara Barton was on the battlefield soon after the first gun fired. She did not leave until the last wounded soldier had been treated.

The battle was a military turning point. Having crossed the Potomac into Maryland, Lee was moving deep into Union territory. Concentrating at Frederick, he sent Jackson to take Harpers Ferry and Longstreet to hold South Mountain. Lee himself stood at Sharpsburg, on the Antietam Creek. Although the Confederates beat off McClellan's attacks, they could not advance. On September 19, Lee withdrew across the Potomac, leaving 9,000 Confederate casualties. The Union forces had suffered 12,000 casualties.

Of this vast number, many on both sides were treated by Clara Barton and the 30 helpers she managed to round up in the emergency. One medical station had been reduced to using corn leaves for bandages, when she arrived with sup-

plies. A doctor was trying to operate with light from the two-inch stub of a candle, when she brought him lanterns. While the ground outside the barn she occupied was being fought over, Clara calmly mixed gruel from water and meal, baked slabs of hardtack, and meted out precious medical supplies that made the difference between life and death. The volunteer nurse did not waver and she did not sleep.

By the time the regular army supplies arrived on the third day, Clara was utterly exhausted, burning with fever. Her assistants wrapped her in an old quilt and put her on the wagon floor. Then she was jogged back to Washington. At home she looked in the mirror and found that her face was "the color of gunpowder, a deep blue." It was more than a week before she had strength to rise again and return to work. Then she paid an early call on Major Rucker—to tell him how much better she might have done at Antietam had she been given more wagons!

Winter warfare

By now Clara Barton's name was on everyone's lips. When Abraham Lincoln reviewed the Union troops in October, 1862, she was asked to attend. The 21st Massachusetts Regiment gave her an honorary title—"Daughter of the Regiment." Nothing they could have given could have brought her so much pleasure and joy.

Yet there was no time to bask in the glory of new titles or fame. Soon she was off again, moving south with six wagons, an ambulance, and eight drivers—the increased allotment that Major Rucker had solemnly promised her. The weather was bitter cold, and would get colder. Clara insisted on maximum effort from herself and those under her. When the drivers tried to stop in midafternoon, she ordered them forward, then regained their loyalty by fixing a piping hot meal when they stopped. Soon the little party caught up with General Burnside's troops at Berlin—and with another endless army wagon train, trudging toward another bloody encounter.

By November, Clara's exposure to burns, bruises, and frost led to an intensely painful bone inflammation in her hand. She decided to return to Washington to have it treated and to get more supplies. But she had scarcely got home before a telegram from her colleague Cornelius Welles arrived: "Hundreds of wounded men but few to work. Come." Back she went into numbing cold that would freeze

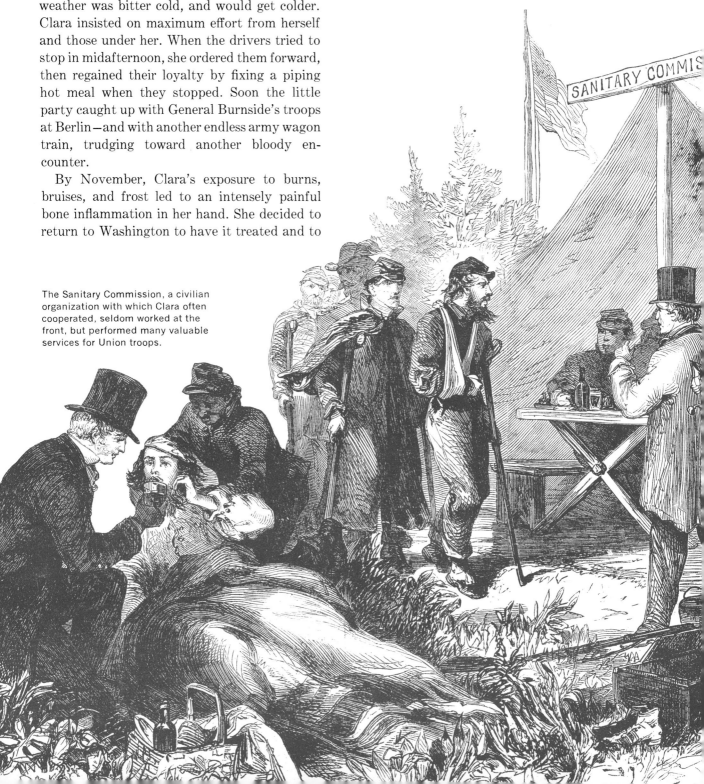

The Sanitary Commission, a civilian organization with which Clara often cooperated, seldom worked at the front, but performed many valuable services for Union troops.

wounded limbs and frostbite aching fingers. She was assigned the Lacy House, an old colonial mansion at Falmouth, a stone's throw from the Rappahannock River, for her operations. The battle of Fredericksburg was about to begin.

General Lee, regrouping after Antietam, had established an army of 78,000 men on the Fredericksburg side of the Rappahannock. General Burnside was across the river at Falmouth, with 120,000 men. In biting December weather Union engineers set out to build a pontoon bridge across, despite heavy fire from sharpshooters and well-entrenched forces on the other side. Finally the bridge was in place.

Six Union assaults were made, all of them repulsed. At the height of the fighting Clara got a "crumpled, bloody slip of paper" from the embattled Union surgeon Clarence Cutter on the other shore: "Come to me. Your place is here." Off she went on one of the most hazardous missions of her life. Soon she was rocking across the swaying bridge, the water hissing with shot on both sides. An officer rushed forward to help her. One shell exploded so close that it blew away part of their clothing.

"The next instant," Clara wrote, "a solid shot thundered over our heads, a steed bounded in the air, and with his gallant rider, rolled in the dirt, not 30 feet in the rear. Leaving the kind-hearted officer, I passed on alone to the hospital. In less than a half-hour he was brought to me— dead."

The whole night and the next day, Clara worked feverishly with Dr. Cutter, until the Northern forces were compelled to retreat across the river in terrible confusion. Red blood covered the white snow. One batch of wounded Confederate prisoners, whose bloody clothing was frozen tight to the ground, had to be chopped free with axes. Back in the Lacy House, Clara tried to keep all of the fires roaring, to wrap hot bricks in rags for the shivering bodies salvaged from the battle, to find warm words for numbed warriors. Some of those brought in wore blue, others gray. To Miss Barton, there were no enemies when the wounded and dying were brought in. Her mercy did not acknowledge sides or stop at political boundaries.

Eventually 1,200 men had been crammed into the 12 rooms of the old Virginia mansion. Wounded men filled the floors, porticoes, corridors, and stair landings. Some actually had to be put on the shelves of a large cupboard. "Think of trying to lie still and die quietly, lest you fall out of a bed six feet high!" Clara wrote sadly. And again: "When I rose from the side of the couch where I had knelt for hours . . . I wrung the blood from the bottom of my clothing before I could step."

On a raw, dreary day the gallant humanitarian, numb with cold, pain, and grief, returned to Washington. As she wrote her friend Annie Childs, she was "shoeless, gloveless, ragged, and blood-stained," full of "desolation and pity and sympathy and weariness, all blended." People stared at Clara in the streets. They had no way

MRS. JANE C. HOGE.   MRS. MARY A. BICKERDYKE. "MOTHER BICKERDYKE"

MISS MARY J. SAFFORD.   MRS. CORDELIA A. P. HARVEY.

Four famous nurses of Union soldiers are grouped above.

of telling what sights those dark eyes had seen, what kind deeds those small hands had performed. But many soldiers knew—and would never forget.

To another front

As her strength returned, and bright spring blossoms appeared on the boughs, Clara Barton asked to be sent to Hilton Head, an island off the South Carolina coast in an area where fierce battles would soon be fought. Her brother David was quartermaster there. Her brother Stephen, who had moved South before the war to establish a sawmill and other plants, was not far away. Now that the Army of the Potomac was well provisioned, she wanted to see what she could do in another theater of operation.

On April 7, 1863, she arrived at Hilton Head on the transport *Arago*, along with an ambulance, horses, and drivers to assist with her work. Miss Barton's fame had preceded her; cheers and salutes greeted the tiny nurse whenever she made an appearance. Once she was about to cross a small stream when a Union captain approached with his men. "Now boys, there stands Clara Barton," he said. "I want every one of you to kneel on your right knees and let her walk across the stream on your left knees." Thus Clara crossed, without getting her shoes wet. No wonder she called herself the best-protected woman in the United States.

Soon after she arrived, there was a lull in the siege of Charleston. Clara often had a chance to ride horseback with the army officers; once she galloped five miles in 20 minutes just after dawn and then went on to pick enough blackberries to make a shortcake for breakfast. She also taught some Negro boys how to read, and worked hard at cheering up various homesick young soldiers. Even so, she had an uneasy feeling that she was not doing enough; unless a sharp battle soon took place, she thought that she should return to what she termed "my own army" (because she had worked so much with it) in Virginia.

Clara wrote in her diary: "God's will, not mine be done. I am content. How I wish I could always keep in full view the fact and feeling that

---

CLARA'S CALMNESS UNDER FIRE

A surgeon from Wisconsin who saw Clara's work at Antietam later described her utter calmness under fire:

"With sleeves rolled up to the elbows (I'm not certain whether sporting an apron or not), with dress skirt turned up and that portion which should normally constitute the bottom, pinned around her waist, a lady of pleasing countenance stood beside a huge iron kettle hung or placed otherwise over a roaring fire, using a ladle to stir something like a barrel-full of soup, which, by the frequent tasting, she appeared to be seasoning, to make it palatable to the hundreds of wounded heroes."

God orders all things precisely as they should be; all is best as it is." But she did not confine herself to religious reflections; she also sent her quartermaster brother a requisition for a flat-iron with a note: "My clothes are as well washed as at home, and I have a house to iron in if I had the iron. I could be as clean and sleek as a kitten. Don't you want a smooth sister enough to send her a flatiron?" And all too soon, a resumption of active hostilities was putting a cruel tax on her strength.

For eight months Clara labored in the area, face sunburned and raw, eyes sore from the blowing sand. The glaring sun was like a demon; the only escape was a small floorless tent pitched in shifting sand. Fort Sumter was smashed, Fort Gregg and Fort Wagner were regained, but proud Charleston would still not surrender. The siege failed. Because of illness, Clara returned to the North. She had seen only her brother David; later in the war her brother Stephen did reach her in Virginia—but he died soon after.

By the spring of 1864 she was well again, gathering supplies for her next battle assignment. Early in May she was sent to the Wilderness campaign. In the thick woods and tangled undergrowth across from the Rapidan River, General Lee knew, the Union's two-to-one superiority in numbers and artillery would be somewhat neutralized. In his earlier skillful maneuvering in the Wilderness area (even though he lost his great supporting general, "Stonewall" Jackson, at Chancellorsville in 1863), Lee had won a major Confederate victory by daring flank movements. Now in 1864 the Wilderness was again a death trap for the Union troops; it turned into an inferno when the brush caught fire and burned many of the wounded to death.

When Clara Barton reached Belle Plain, where the injured from the battles had been brought, the sight was dismaying. Torrential rains had made transportation all but impossible. Hundreds of wagons, including those carrying the wounded, were mired hubdeep in the mud. Thus the "poor mutilated starving sufferers of the Wilderness," as Clara called them, had to go unfed and untended. Doing what she could, Clara saw that no one on the scene could bring about much improvement. This was so bad a muddle that only direct action in Washington could save it.

Rescue in the Wilderness

Using all the pressure she could muster, Clara rounded up four fast horses to dash to the Federal dock, and then took the first steam tug to Washington. There she stormed into the office of Senator Henry C. Wilson, Chairman of the Senate Military Committee. He was so moved by what she reported that he went directly to the War Department at ten o'clock that night.

Early the next morning the Quartermaster General and his staff started out to the scene of the Wilderness debacle. While they oversaw matters there, Clara rounded up carloads of supplies and returned in three days. The deadlock was broken. The wounded were rescued from their horrible plight. One of the most tragic chapters of the Civil War was ended.

Clara Barton's reputation and influence reached a new peak. Late in June of 1864 she was appointed Superintendent of the Department of Nurses for the Army of the James, serving under General Benjamin F. Butler. The general—whose vanity ranked high among his various shortcomings—did appreciate her. He

MISS DIX, MISS BARTON

Neither in the Civil War nor later was Clara Barton a trained nurse. Relatively little of her lifetime of service took place in hospitals. The outstanding *nurse* of the Civil War was Dorothea Dix, one of the truly remarkable women in American history. The careers of Miss Dix and Miss Barton had many similarities and contrasts—vividly summed up by Dr. William E. Barton, a leading Congregational clergyman and Clara's distant cousin. She named him her literary executor; he wrote the definitive biography of her.

"It must be remembered that Miss Barton's service was . . . voluntary. . . . The system of army nurses was under the direct supervision of Dorothea Lynde Dix, a woman from her own county. . . . It is one of the fine manifestations of good sense on the part of Clara Barton that she never at any time attempted what might have seemed an interference with Miss Dix, but found for herself a field of service, and developed it according to a method of her own. . . .

"Dorothea Lynde Dix was born April 4, 1802, and died July 17, 1887. . . . Until the publication of her biography by Francis Tiffany in 1890, it was commonly supposed that she was born in Worcester County, Massachusetts, where she spent her childhood. But her birth occurred in Maine. Unlike Clara Barton she had no happy home memories. Her father was an unstable, visionary man. . . . She began teaching, as Clara Barton did, when she was fifteen years of age. And like Clara Barton she became a pioneer in certain forms of educational work. Dorothea Dix opened a school 'for charitable and religious uses' . . . and in time she inherited property . . . so that she was able to devote herself to a life of philanthropy. . . .

"In her work for the insane she was especially effective. . . . Like Clara Barton she found an especially fruitful field of service in New Jersey; the Trenton Asylum was in a very real sense her creation. . . . By 1861 her reputation was well established. She . . . had gained the well-merited confidence of the medical profession . . . and was spending a few days at the Trenton Asylum, when the 6th Massachusetts was fired upon in Baltimore. . . . Like Clara Barton she hastened immediately to the place of service. On the very next day she wrote to a friend: 'I have reported myself and some nurses for free service at the War Department, and to the

Surgeon-General [wherever nursing is needed].'

"Her offer was accepted with great heartiness and with ill-considered promptness. She was appointed 'Superintendent of Female Nurses.' She was authorized 'to select and assign female nurses to general or permanent military hospitals; they not to be employed without her sanction and approval except in case of urgent need.'

"Whether the United States contained any woman better qualified to undertake such a task as this than Dorothea Dix may be questioned. Certainly none could have been found with more of experience or with a higher consecration. . . . Her biographer very justly says: 'The literal meaning, however, of such a commission as had thus been

Miss Dorothea Lynde Dix

hastily bestowed on Miss Dix—applying as it did to the woman nurses of the military hospitals of the whole United States not in actual rebellion . . . involved a sheer, practical impossibility. It implied, not a single-handed woman, nearly sixty and shattered in health, but immense organized departments at 20 different centers.'

"The War Department acted upon what must have appeared a wise impulse in turning this whole matter of woman nurses over to the authority of a woman known in all the states—as Miss Dix was known. . . . But she had never learned to delegate responsibility to her subordinates. It had been well for Clara Barton if she had known better how to set others to work, but she knew better than Dorothea

Dix and was 20 years younger. Indeed, Clara Barton was younger at eighty than Dorothea Dix was at sixty, but she herself suffered somewhat from this same limitation. Dorothea Dix could not be everywhere, and with her system she needed to be everywhere, just as Clara Barton under her system had to be at the very front in direct management of her own line of activities.

"But Dorothea Dix, besides needing to be simultaneously on 20 battlefields, had to be where she could examine and sift out and prepare for service the chosen from among a great many thousand women applying for the privilege of nursing wounded soldiers, and ranging all the way from sentimental schoolgirls to sickly and decrepit grandmothers. Again, Mr. Tiffany says: 'Under the Atlas weight of care and responsibilities so suddenly thrust on Miss Dix, the very qualifications which had so preeminently fitted her for the sphere in which she had wrought such miracles of success began to tell against her. . . . She had for years been a lonely and single-handed worker, planning her own projects, keeping her own counsel, and pressing on, unhampered by the need of consulting others, toward her self-chosen goal. The lone worker could not change her nature. She tried to do everything herself. . . . Ready to live on a crust, and to sacrifice herself without stint, her whole soul was on fire at the spectacle of incompetence and callow indifference she was doomed daily to witness. She became overwrought and lost the requisite self-control. . . . Inevitably she became involved in sharp altercations with prominent medical officials and with regimental surgeons.'

"It is necessary to recall this in order to understand Clara Barton's attitude toward the established military hospitals. . . . She had no intention whatever of becoming a cog in that great and unmanageable machine. Clara Barton held Dorothea Dix in the very highest regard. In all her diaries and letters . . . there is no word concerning Dorothea Dix that is not appreciative. In 1910 the New York *World* wired her a request [for] eight names of women whom she would nominate for a Woman's Hall of Fame. . . . She . . . named [Miss] Dix. . . . Few women understood so well as Clara Barton what Dorothea Dix had to contend with. . . . In some respects the two women were too much alike in their temperament for either one to have worked well under the other. For that matter, neither one of them greatly enjoyed working under anybody.'"

General B. F. Butler sits by his tent for a photograph.

quickly became one of her enthusiastic admirers and supporters. "Honor any request that Miss Barton makes without question," he told a staff officer. "She out-ranks me."

After months, even years, of struggle, Clara was given an organization and backing that enabled her to do well the job at hand. Her headquarters were in a former plantation near Petersburg, where the main action of the struggle shifted. Seeing that he could not force his way through Lee's lines in the dense thickets of the Wilderness, Grant had decided to take the longer but more open southern route, through Petersburg.

On June 12, 1864, he started his army to the James River, crossing by pontoons at Wyanoke Neck. Lee's army dug in near Petersburg. A long and bloody siege began. The Confederates held out all summer, repulsed the enemy at Hatcher's Run on October 27, and stabilized the lines for the winter. Clara Barton, meanwhile, had become an executive, supervising nurses, stewards, orderlies, and clerks, while overseeing a "family" that contained more than 1,500 people.

By now it seemed certain that the North was going to win—but who could say when Lee, the Gray Fox, would give up? Sherman marched across Georgia, burning all in his path, and captured Charleston in February, 1865. Union generals Thomas and Sheridan were moving ahead steadily. Grant kept hammering away. The common soldier on both sides, who bore the brunt of every attack and danger, must still face loneliness, doubt, and death as he sang:
"We're tenting tonight on the old camp ground,
   Give us a song to cheer
   Our weary hearts, a song of home
   And friends we love so dear . . ."

Lincoln had words to cheer them in his Second Inaugural Address, of March 4, 1865: "Let us strive on to finish the work we are in; to bind up the nation's wounds . . . to do all which may achieve and cherish a just, and a lasting peace among ourselves and with all nations."

The Union army did strive, and finally the bloody brutal work was finished. The barrel-chested General Ulysses S. Grant led the way. He knew what had to be done to defeat the Confederacy, and he did it. The weight of his extra men, extra materials, and indomitable will was slowly but surely felt.

Suffering beyond calculation

Of the estimated 600,000 Southern troops in the field in 1863, over half of those still alive by the winter of 1865 had left the ranks. Desperately short of men—he could put only 1,100 to the mile outside Petersburg—General Lee finally broke under the pressure and abandoned Petersburg and Richmond. The doomed Confederate capital faced the worst day of its history as the Sabbath sun rose on April 2. Looting and burning followed the official order to burn all supplies that might be useful to the North. Flaming balls of tar turned the waterfront into a bonfire. Powder magazines and arsenals exploded with whooshing booms. Crying, raging, snarling mobs took over.

At dawn on April 3, the 4th Massachusetts Cavalry—from Clara Barton's home state—entered the beleaguered city. The next day President Lincoln boarded the S.S. *Malvern* and made his way to captured Richmond, via a river littered with dead horses, abandoned barges, and broken ordnance. When the ship ran aground, Admiral Porter shifted Lincoln to a 12-oared barge that carried him to the edge of Richmond.

"Glory, hallelujah!" a Negro yelled as he landed. He and several others fell on their knees as the President approached.

"Don't kneel to me," Lincoln said. "You must kneel to God only and thank Him for your freedom." Meanwhile Lee retreated westward as Grant wrote home to his wife: "The suffering which must exist in the South next year will be beyond calculation." Although he had less than 28,000 troops in the field, Lee was not yet defeated. If he could link up with General Joseph Johnston, or get safely to the mountains, he might hold out. While his men munched dried corn and their horses gnawed tree bark, the "Johnny Rebs" sang:

"The race is not to them that's got
The longest legs to run,
Nor the battle to that people
That shoots the biggest gun."

But the Confederates did not get far. The story was written along the roads, littered like a beach with driftwood from fastebbing tides: discarded equipment, abandoned wagons and ambulances, starving stragglers, shell-shocked

"FANNING MY FEVERED FACE"

Colonel John J. Elwell, who was wounded in the assault on Fort Wagner, paid this tribute to Clara:

"I was shot with an Enfield cartridge within 150 yards of the fort and so disabled that I could not go forward. I was in an awful predicament, perfectly exposed to canister from Wagner and shell from Gregg and Sumter in front, and the enfilade from James Island. I tried to dig a trench in the sand with my saber, into which I might crawl, but the dry sand would fall back in place about as fast as I could scrape it out with my narrow implement. . . .

"Two boys of the 62nd Ohio found me and carried me to . . . an extempore hospital. After resting awhile I was . . . started for the lower end of the island one and a half miles off, where better hospital arrangements had been prepared. . . . My soul longed for sleep, which I got in this wise: an army blanket was doubled and laid on the soft side of a plank with an overcoat for a pillow, on which I laid my worn-out body.

"And such a sleep! I dreamed that . . . my dear wife was trying to soothe my pain. . . . My sleepy emotions awoke me and a dear, blessed woman was bathing my temples and fanning my fevered face. Clara Barton was there, an angel of mercy doing all in mortal power to assuage the miseries of the unfortunate soldiers."

gunners. "I've fought my men to a frazzle and I can do nothing unless Longstreet supports me," Colonel Charles Venable told Lee. Longstreet

Members of the Union army's hospital corps do an ambulance drill as they prepare for the harsh reality of battle.

A Currier & Ives print depicts Booth assassinating Lincoln as Major Henry Rathbone vainly tries to intervene.

had nothing to support him with. On April 9—Palm Sunday—Lee surrendered the Army of Northern Virginia to Grant at Appomattox, Virginia. The war was virtually over.

"Charity for all"

Clara Barton was in Washington when the news came—one of the most joyful days in her life. Now she and all the others could put behind them the fear of a severed Union and a destroyed capital. No one could ever remove the memories and the nightmares endured: of men blackened by powder, homes gutted by fire, the bleak croak of vultures, fields grown over with weeds and brambles, bodies washed out from shallow graves, the sightless eyes of cold faces staring at the sky. But all this was past, thank God. Now under President Lincoln the wounds would be healed. With "malice toward none; with charity for all," America would reunite.

A week later the Washington of hysterical joy was sunk into gloom. On April 14 the Lincolns attended the Ford Theater to see a play. That night American history was changed by a lead ball, about half an inch in diameter, which crashed into Lincoln's head and lodged a few inches behind his right eye. The assassin, John Wilkes Booth, escaped from the theater and

Abraham Lincoln died the next morning. The noble Captain had fallen. At the moment of greatest triumph, death had prevailed.

One of the last letters Lincoln wrote—on March 11—read: "To the Friends of Missing Persons: Miss Clara Barton has kindly offered to search for the missing prisoners of war. Please address her at Annapolis, giving her the name, regiment, and company of any missing prisoner. (signed) A. Lincoln."

Cherishing the letter, and the assignment Lincoln had given her, Miss Barton carried out this work with the same vigor and courage she had shown at the battlefront. She went to Andersonville, a notorious Confederate prison camp where thousands of Union soldiers had perished, and set up a national cemetery. Anxious to tell about her war experiences, and needing employment to meet heavy expenses, she decided to lecture around the country. The tour began in October 1866. A handbill was prepared advertising the lectures.

The "Heroine" who walked to the platform (and it was always an ordeal—"all speech-making terrifies me," she often said) was only five feet three inches tall. Slender and straight, simply dressed with her black hair combed severely back, she spoke in a clear deep-toned

LECTURE!

MISS CLARA BARTON,

OF WASHINGTON,

THE HEROINE OF ANDERSONVILLE,

The Soldier's Friend, who gave her time and fortune during the war to the Union cause, and who is now engaged in searching for the missing soldiers of the Union army, will address the people of

LAMBERTVILLE, in

HOLCOMBE HALL,

THIS EVENING,

APRIL 7TH, AT 7½ O'CLOCK.

SUBJECT:

SCENES ON THE BATTLE-FIELD.

ADMISSION,   25 CENTS.

voice, from a manuscript small enough to fit in her purse. She knew her material so well that she did not look at the pages often, and felt her material so strongly that she immediately gripped her audience. The speaker tried to be accurate, but she made no effort at impartiality. She did not attempt to conceal her feeling about the haughty slaveholders who had tried to wreck the precious Union. She did not lecture in the states of the vanquished Confederacy.

Well-received in New England and along the eastern seaboard north of Washington, she moved on to Illinois, Iowa, Nebraska, and Kansas. Hers was a backbreaking schedule, in country where transportation was still primitive and hardships were many. The psychological and physical strain made itself felt on that part of Clara Barton's physique which always went first—her vocal cords. Attempting to give a talk in the winter of 1868 at Portland, Maine, she opened her mouth and no sound came forth. There was nothing to do but walk off the stage. Her lecturing career was halted.

Back in Washington, she was put to bed for a rest. With the money earned from lectures (about $15,000) and with that repaid to her by Congress (in connection with her searching for missing persons), she was able to move from her modest rooms to a house on Pennsylvania Avenue close by Capitol Hill. Five days after her forty-seventh birthday on Christmas Day, 1868, Clara Barton moved into the shabby but comfortable old house.

Her diary records: "December 30, 1868, Wednesday. Moved . . . in the midst of a fearful snowstorm and a good deal of confusion. . . . Took my first supper in my own whole house." In advance, she had agreed to pay the movers $6, but their work so pleased her that she gave them $10. Considering Clara's very thrifty ways, this showed deep satisfaction indeed!

For Clara tried never to waste a dime. As William E. Barton has observed, she was "economical to a very marked degree. . . . A list of her actual economies . . . would produce on many minds the impression that she was stingy. This would be wide of the truth. . . . She was parsimonious but not penurious."

On December 31, aided by her two Negro servants and some friendly neighbors, she settled snugly into her new home. The day was tempestuous and she was weary, yet glad indeed to be safely ensconced in a dwelling all her own.

Looking out her window, she could see the Capitol. There, seven years earlier, she had read the Worcester *Spy* to young men from her district of Massachusetts, in the days before the fighting began. What years they had been, from 1861 to 1868! In her mind's eye a thousand visions must have appeared as the names of battles and sieges passed like troops marching into action: Cedar Mountain, second Bull Run, Chantilly, South Mountain, Antietam, Falmouth, Fredericksburg, Morris Island, Charleston, Wagner, the Wilderness, Fredericksburg again, Petersburg, the Mine, Deep Bottom, Richmond.

Almost everything had changed. An obscure clerk in the Patent Office had become a famous heroine, known and admired throughout the land. The once timid Clara Barton had boldly endured every hardship and danger, and proved that women could do work for which they had never been considered before. These were, by all odds, her most critical as well as dangerous years—the platform on which a distinguished and unique career could be built. The Mistress of the School Room had become by 1868 the Angel of the Battlefield. But a great many of her hardest battles were yet to come.

Chapter 3
ANGEL IN ACTION
ON FOREIGN BATTLEFIELDS

THOUGH fought on native soil, the American Civil War was, in a real sense, part of a world upheaval. In the mid-nineteenth century, European nationalism reached flood tide and broke down the old dikes, while in the United States nationalism was overcoming sectionalism and the appeal to states' rights. Nation-states—centralized and closely knit units whose political authority rested upon and represented the will of the people—sprang into being.

In 1850 two major powers, Britain and France, dominated the scene. A cluster of smaller nations—including Denmark, Sweden, Switzerland, and the Netherlands—had proud heritages but little power. Much of Europe was a checkerboard of principalities, dukedoms, and free cities. Central Europe, heartland of the defunct Holy Roman Empire, was a political patchwork, half Catholic and half Protestant. The United States was a loose confederation of quarreling states, half slave and half free.

Yet by 1871 new countries, like Germany and Italy, loomed large in Europe, while the wobbly American Republic was firmly and permanently united under a triumphant federal government. Much of today's history stems from that critical generation, now a century past, when Europe moved toward the crest of its power and controlled most of the globe.

To that restless and expansive continent a bone-tired Clara Barton set out in 1869. "Your throat is exhausted," a doctor told her after she

The ancient Tower of London was one of the places that most fascinated Clara on her first trip to Europe.

left the stage, unable to finish a lecture, in the winter of 1868. "Rest is the only cure. You ought to go to Europe. Get away from everything and everybody, and let your system build up again." The doctor prescribed "three years of absolute rest."

Physically and emotionally tied to her memories of an America of fast-filling cemeteries and a martyred President, Miss Barton found this decision a "hard sentence." "Still," wrote the lady who had spent months with soldiers and military commands, "the order was obeyed and I went."

In August of 1869 she sailed for Europe and opened a whole new chapter of her life. Lecture fees, and a congressional grant of $15,000 for personal expenditures while doing her missing-persons work on behalf of the government, provided a comfortable cushion for the future. After years of endless labor and anxiety the Angel of the Battlefield was ready for a change.

So the pert little lady with well-combed dark-brown hair, broad chin, and eagle-bright eyes disembarked in Scotland to enjoy the lakes and hills of that rugged land which was not unlike parts of her native New England. Then she moved south to London. Always an eager sight-seer, Clara was thrilled by London Bridge, the Tower, the Thames, Guildhall, and other spots that make London a seedbed of history. But the English climate was not good for her throat, and she had to move on.

Doctors said that Geneva, Switzerland, was ideal for throat ailments. By chance, she knew a family there named the Golays, having written letters for their soldier-son who had fought in the American Civil War. She crossed the English Channel (finding the water too choppy for her liking), stayed a while in Paris (which was beautiful, but a bit lavish for her Yankee blood), and went by train to Geneva.

The Geneva Convention

Curled around a crystal-clear lake, within sight of Mont Blanc and other Alpine peaks, Geneva was, she reported, "a spectacular spot for the American visitor." Clara had no way of knowing that, next to Washington, Geneva would prove to be the most important city in her life. She only knew she liked the people's looks and the sense of history there.

She described in her diary sights that especially struck her: the Romanesque cathedral of St. Peter, the Renaissance town hall, and the house of Jean Jacques Rousseau. The spirit of John Calvin, who lived there physically in the sixteenth century—and in Massachusetts spiritually for a dozen generations—still hovered over the old town. Clara had known that spirit since childhood, and was at home with it. The Golays also made her feel thoroughly at home. They took Clara in like one of their own family, and showed her the local sights.

Genevans spoke often of the international convention held in their city five years earlier. The resulting treaty dealt with the treatment and care of wounded and sick in armed forces on land; the wounded, sick, and shipwrecked members of military vessels at sea; the treatment of prisoners of war; the protection of civilians under wartime conditions; and the protection of hospitals and military transports. These were much the concerns that had been occupying Clara Barton at the moment the provisions of the Geneva Convention were being debated and adopted in 1864—she had been too busy with her own affairs to take note of international declarations.

But Clara's heroic activities had not escaped the world's eye. As she was soon to discover, she was known and admired throughout Europe. One day a group of gentlemen, led by Dr. Louis Appia, called on her. The Swiss visitors com-

---

AN INVALID ON HER WAY TO IMMORTALITY

Martin Gumpert, an authority on the Red Cross, would later write: "She traveled for her shattered health to Europe, never suspecting that there in the meantime a work had begun that would henceforth fill her whole life, and to which . . . through the founding of the American Red Cross, she was to render immortal services."

plimented her for what she had done, and asked her why her country had failed to ratify the Geneva Convention. To what does America object, Dr. Appia asked, and sought advice on how these objections might be overcome.

"What could I say?" wrote Clara later, in some embarrassment. "What could each or any of you have said? . . . I could only answer these gentlemen that I feared the matter was not sufficiently understood, being in a foreign language."

Thanks to Dr. Appia, Clara soon learned not only about the Geneva Convention but also of Henri Dunant's *Un Souvenir de Solferino*. It was a fascinating story. Henri Dunant, a Swiss humanitarian, found himself in northern Italy in 1859, when Italian and French soldiers clashed with the Austrians. One of the many sharp, bloody encounters during the rise of a unified Italy, the battle of Solferino left 40,000 dead, maimed, and wounded.

Receiving no special protection, the medical corps on both sides had to risk enemy action and retaliation; when the course of battle changed, the wounded were pushed aside, overrun, or abandoned. Dunant watched the battle from a nearby hilltop. Horrified by the needless suffering and pain, the visitor organized a local mercy group, and spent generously of his own money for relief measures. He even went to the French emperor, Napoleon III, and persuaded him to release captured Austrian doctors to tend the wounded.

Like Florence Nightingale, the gallant British nurse who had done so much for the wounded in the Crimea a few years earlier, Dunant saved many lives by personal concern. What of *later* battles, where there would be no Dunant, no provisions for aid? This thought caused him to publish in 1862 one of the century's pivotal pamphlets: *Un Souvenir de Solferino* (A Memory of Solferino). He told of his own adventures in clear and moving prose, ending with this question: "Would it not be possible to found and organize in all civilized countries permanent societies of volunteers who in time of war would give help to the wounded without regard for their nationality?"

The Franco-Prussian War

The plea, which for humanity's sake might well have been made generations earlier, came

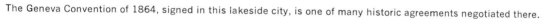

The Geneva Convention of 1864, signed in this lakeside city, is one of many historic agreements negotiated there.

just in time for men to act before the Franco-Prussian War. Dunant's countrymen, proud of their mountain homeland and its long record of avoiding foreign wars, read his book and sought an answer to his question. The action taken at Geneva in 1863 and 1864 was the first step in establishing an effective agency of mercy for men all over the world.

In 1863, representatives of 16 nations conferred on how to effect "the relief of the wounded in armies in the field." A second meeting, in August of 1864, produced an international pact, designed "to render neutral and immune from injury in war the sick and wounded and all who cared for them." Reversing the Swiss flag (white cross on red background), the new relief organization took as its emblem the red cross on a white background. Clara Barton saw this

Red Cross flying for the first time in Geneva. It would envelop her life until she died.

Puzzled at why America had not joined, Clara investigated. She found that two Americans had been unofficial observers at the 1864 meetings: George C. Fogg, the United States Minister to Switzerland, and Charles S. Bowles, European agent for the United States Sanitary Commission. They had no power to act; and, though two formal petitions were presented later in Washington, neither was accepted.

Fearful of the ancient quarrels and plots of the Old World, and aware of George Washington's admonition to avoid all permanent alliances with other countries, the battered American Republic had not wanted to assume obligations under any European treaty. Now fate had brought Clara Barton, most famous of

This painting of the 1864 Geneva meeting shows its president, General William Dufour, receiving a report from Charles Bowles, an

Civil War relief workers, to the very city where the International Red Cross had taken root.

While she was enjoying the calm Swiss scene and thinking about what her Swiss visitors had told her, ominous war clouds were gathering in the east. Otto von Bismarck, Prussia's stern prime minister, promised to unite Germany with blood and iron—and that was just what he set about to do. The North German Confederation (Norddeutscher Bund) encompassed the 22 states north of the river Main, and was bent on further expansion. Napoleon III, elected Emperor of France in 1852, was trying desperately but vainly to thwart Bismarck's plans.

In the spring of 1866, while Clara Barton was helping to locate missing Union soldiers, Prussia sprang into action. Led by General von Moltke, and armed with a new rifle called the "needle

gun," which fired six times as fast as the Austrian rifle, the Prussians crushed resistance in Saxony, Hanover, and Hesse-Cassel.

The battle of Sadowa, fought on July 3, 1866, brought complete victory to the invaders. In five weeks and three days the Prussians had routed all enemies to the south and humbled the Austrian army. The resulting peace treaty excluded Austria from all participation in German politics, and gave Prussia nearly 25,000 square miles of territory and 5,000,000 new subjects.

The stage was set for a conflict between Prussia and France. Clara did not need to have the American consul in Bern, whom she visited in 1870, tell her this. Writing home to her brother David, Clara described the forboding and suspense. "All France and Prussia with both Northern and Southern Germany are armed and marching to the Rhine," she wrote. "Little Switzerland, bright as a diamond in her rough mountain setting, proclaims a neutrality which she means." Of France she added: "Nothing can be 'too foolish,' and no pretext too slight, where personal interest, royal dignity, ambition, or pride are injured or threatened. . . . Her populace, wild with enthusiasm, shouts, '*Vive la guerre!*'" In July 1870, the ambitious and overconfident Napoleon III declared war on the kingdom of Prussia.

France, its minister of war declared, was ready "down to the last button on the last gaiter of the last soldier." Paris streets resounded to the cry of "On to Berlin!" Many thought French troops would celebrate the *Fête Napoleon* (August 15) in Bismarck's capital. But the Prussians, much better trained and equipped, dashed such extravagant hopes. Though she came to Europe to forget cannon shots and soldiers' yells, Clara Barton would soon be on the field of action. Being Clara Barton, she could not stand idly by when others needed her.

Back into action

One European noblewoman perceptive enough to grasp this was the Grand Duchess of Baden, daughter of King Wilhelm of Prussia.

unofficial American observer at the conference.

In this contemporary print, a helmeted German sentry waves Miss Barton into the conquered city of Strasbourg just after its fall. She conducted notable relief work there.

This intelligent aristocrat, modest yet assured, who had helped organize the Geneva Convention of 1864, visited Clara at the villa where she was then living in Bern. Her coach was manned by servants in the gold and scarlet liveries of the royal house of Baden; Clara could not help being stirred by the Duchess' plea for her aid in the impending conflict. She hailed Clara in the name of humanity, and praised her achievements in the Civil War.

Clara explained that she was in Europe merely to recover from her illness, but admitted that her health was improving.

And when she learned that a group from Bern was going to Basel to arrange for relief supplies, she cast doubts aside. Under the auspices of the Red Cross, but as an independent American citizen, Clara Barton threw herself into the cauldron that was the Franco-Prussian War.

The Red Cross warehouses at Basel, built on a bluff overlooking the Rhine River, were well stocked with medical supplies. Clara had had no such stores to draw from in America; no trained nurses and clerks with Red Cross armbands to assist.

She met a tall, blue-eyed Swiss girl named Antoinette Margot, who soon became her close friend and assistant. Together the two started for Mulhausen in a private carriage, as the railroad had been destroyed. The road was filled with refugees in every sort of vehicle and on foot—oxen, sheep, cows, families, peasants' carts, gilded coaches, all fleeing to get out of the Prussians' path.

"Turn back. You will be killed!" some of the refugees shouted at the couple headed toward the battlefront. But when they heard that these two were nurses, they added, "God bless you."

At Mulhausen Clara found no suffering to relieve. So she proceeded to Strasbourg, and, after 24 hours of struggle, reached the walls of that garrisoned city. The United States consul and vice consul, both American Civil War veterans, knew of Clara Barton. They arranged to get her and Miss Margot seats on a bus going to a depot for the wounded at Karlsruhe.

They began their journey in a heavy rain, with the United States flag on the front of the bus. En route, Clara took the red ribbon she wore on her throat, made it into a cross, and sewed it on her sleeve. By that simple yet deeply significant act, she became the first American to wear in an official capacity the insignia of the International Red Cross.

As Clara was moving, so was the well-drilled Prussian army. All the fighting took place on French soil; a long list of French disasters began to be written on the pages of history: Wörth, Colombey, Mars-la-Tour, Gravelotte. Clara was not interested in political and military questions—only in the men who bled and died for them.

"Six or seven miles from Strasbourg," Clara later recalled, "we came into a German camp. Troops without number. . . . We were ordered back. Somebody must do something, and I asked for the 'Colonel commanding.' He came . . . struck an attitude, and stood before me. . . .

" 'You speak English, I presume, Colonel?'

" 'A little, madame,' evidently a trifle flattered by the presumption. I explained our desires.

"He replied with dignified courtesy . . . 'We are an army entire, madame, and proceed to the bombardment of Strasbourg. You are free to return but not to advance, save on one condition.'

" 'What may that be, Colonel?'

" 'Capture, madame! You can pass our lines, but you will be a prisoner from that moment.'

" 'Do you mean by this, Colonel, that we shall be thrown into confinement and held there?'

" 'Oh, no, madame,' he answered, returning my incredulous smile. 'Oh, no, you will be prisoners of war, free within our lines, but not [under any circumstances will you be free] to pass out of them till the close of the war.'

" 'The wounded will be within your lines?'

" 'We hope so, madame, as we intend to lose no fields.'

" 'And your lines extend from Belgium to Switzerland?'

" 'Certainly.'

" 'That is space enough for me, Colonel. Let me in.'

" 'You accept the conditions, then?'

" 'Fully, Colonel.'

"The bayonets were withdrawn, our horses moved on, and for the first time in my life, I was a prisoner."

Having passed through the German lines, she and her companion reached Karlsruhe, where the Grand Duchess Louise greeted them warmly. Soon they were all at work, tending the wounded, consoling the dying, moving back and forth from the nearby battlefields. It was Fredericksburg, Richmond, and Antietam all over

For more than 40 years, from the time of the Franco-Prussian War, Clara's closest friend among European royalty was the Grand Duchess Louise of Baden, depicted here with the Grand Duke on the day they were married in the Berlin palace of her parents.

51

again, but with far better medical facilities and equipment. Now nearly fifty, Clara showed the same incredible endurance and fortitude that had made her legendary in America.

One day in late September, seated with her friend the Grand Duchess, she saw a courier come with the news that Strasbourg had fallen to the Germans. Knowing that she would be desperately needed there, Clara set out immediately for the conquered and shattered city. She found what she expected—more than 20,000 people without food, clothing, or shelter, with many others wandering about not knowing where to turn or what to do. This was the grim face of war: bloody, tear-stained, haggard, hopeless.

A way to self-respect

Of course they must be fed and clothed; but that was only part of the problem. They must be brought back to normal, given work and hope. Clara told Antoinette that they did not require charity so much as a new faith in themselves and in life—and that this was the real job confronting the two of them in Strasbourg.

Using her own private money and drawing from her own boundless inner faith, Clara decided to set up a workroom for women. Instead of giving out clothes, she would let the needy make them. Hiring a few local women, buying material and clothes patterns for them, she located the first operation in the yard of a ruined house. Soon the women were turning out dresses, skirts, and trousers—so many, in fact, that Clara secured an empty warehouse from which to distribute them.

The needles darted and the scissors snipped. Soon some 300 women were at work, and the "Barton Brigade" was turning out some 1,500 finished garments a week. Additional items were pouring in from Clara's friends back in Worcester and Boston. Suits and dresses were important, but the women's main product was self-respect. They were not begging, but earning their chance to survive. Watching the successful operation, Clara began to visualize a pattern of rehabilitation that she would employ time and again during the years ahead.

One formidable visitor to her Strasbourg workroom was the "Iron Chancellor" Otto von Bismarck, who for a generation was the most feared single statesman in Europe. Clara (who was never really afraid of anyone) found him "a little stiff"—but, with her usual generosity of spirit, noted, "He is gentle and good at heart, I think." Bismarck strongly endorsed the relief work she was doing, just as Abraham Lincoln had endorsed her plans for locating missing soldiers. Not the least of all Clara Barton's varied achievements was the solid respect she won from these two men, who were both assuredly among the nineteenth century's most remarkable—and hard-to-fool—leaders.

Letters to American friends expressed Clara's inner satisfaction with her seamstresses: "It was such a comfort to see them week by week grow better clothed, themselves and the children, till by and by a woman and a baby came to look only like a big and little bundle of the same clothing she carried in her basket." Seeing how the work was thriving by late in 1870, she decided to go back to her post in Paris early in 1871. Christmas Eve found Strasbourg as "cold as Greenland" as she packed.

A knock came at her door, and outside her house was "a Christmas tree in full blaze all for myself"—set up by grateful townspeople. It shone with a myriad of lights like stars, and was surrounded by flowers and gifts. "In the delicate shadows, falling like tracery upon the snow which spread beneath its branches, I sat down," Clara wrote to Fannie Childs Vassall. "I could not truly say that my hand did not sometimes brush across my eyes."

Paris was grim and gaunt. Darkness had fallen over the City of Light. Even the animals in the zoo had been eaten by the starving populace before the city surrendered in January. Once more the Prussian war machine was unbeatable. Clara, who had entered the city on foot before transportation was restored after the siege ended, gave tirelessly of her effort and money to the needs of the Parisians.

In 1872, worn out by constant work and suffering from eyestrain, she finally joined American friends and rested in a little cottage on the Isle of Wight—one of the few true holidays of her whole life. In London, where she went next, Clara became so ill that her niece Mamie (David's youngest daughter) came over from Massachusetts to help nurse her back to health. Not until the autumn of 1873 was Clara strong enough to undertake the sea voyage home.

The four-year period that ended while she was bobbing about on the north Atlantic was pivotal. In the earlier American war, patriotism had been her motivating force; but in Europe, far from home, humanitarianism had been the spur. She had labored from 1870 to 1873 not to preserve her own nation or any other political union, but to bring comfort and aid to the wounded and distressed. Though wearing and challenging, these years had broadened her scope, knowledge, and confidence immensely.

The pattern through which she could channel such efforts existed in the relatively new Red Cross. In Geneva, she was the right person at the right spot at the right time. By moving quickly and decisively when war struck, she won admiration of both sides, as well as warm support from the European-centered Red Cross. Her rehabilitation work showed that she had both audacity and astuteness. No wonder she ended up with some of the most splendid awards that royalty could bestow (the Jewel of the Red Cross of Serbia, the Iron Cross of Merit from the newly proclaimed German Emperor, and the Gold Cross of Remembrance from the Grand Duke of Baden, for example).

Instead of being the closing years of her active field campaigns, the 1869–1873 period was a time of renewal. Unlike many American visitors to Europe in those years, she was not discouraged by the nationalistic struggles of the Old World.

Coming as a convalescent to a continent of foreign cultures and languages, she became a leading actor in, rather than a mere observer of, the tempestuous Franco-Prussian War. She came, she saw, and, again as an Angel of the Battlefield, she conquered. Showered with praise, gratitude, and honors, she returned to the United States to undertake the major campaign of her life: the long, often discouraging effort to plant the banner of the International Red Cross firmly and permanently on American soil and in the American conscience.

Chapter 4
SINGLE-HANDED STRUGGLE FOR THE RED CROSS

DRAMATIC changes took place in the United States during Clara Barton's absence in Europe. The heroism of the 1860's gave way to the materialism (sometimes cynicism) of the 1870's. Hopeful trees were stripped of life; the Civil War shook down their leaves and blasted their promise. Harassing storms and rains of Reconstruction destroyed the sense of summer. A sadder, more disillusioned America tried to knit together a blood-soaked Union that had been wounded to the core.

Dead men's pictures stared down from the walls; the all-black garments known as widow's weeds were everywhere. Ghosts stalked memorial services and legislative halls. The dead would not stay buried, as orators recalled their sacrifice and politicians waved the "bloody shirt." The newly rich were reluctant to turn from money-making to nation-making. Swift and reckless exploitation gripped the land. Lessons of pain and humility were soon forgotten as scandals, profits, and production mounted. The ambitious and capable worked alongside the greedy and lawless to create what was— despite its manifold shortcomings—the greatest technological revolution yet known to history.

To this bustling scene Miss Barton returned in October 1873, in her own words "worn out, sleepless, wretched, and despairing." Her old home in Washington, on Pennsylvania Avenue and Capitol Hill, was so noisy that her physician ordered her to move to a quieter spot at 14th and F streets. As she was settling here in May 1874, word came that her sister Sally was dying in Massachusetts. Rising from her bed, Clara rushed home, only to arrive a few hours after Sally died.

"It was too much," Clara noted. "Body and soul were stricken." Then followed the worst years of her life. She was subject to colds, severe headaches, a weak back, digestive trouble, and periodic attacks of the camp diarrhea from which she, like many soldiers, continued to suffer years after the war. Her voice and her eyes failed; doctors spoke of complete nervous prostration.

"I could not tell you the suffering, physical and mental . . . and I would not if I could," Clara wrote in retrospect. "Only a small portion of the time could I stand alone; averaged less than two hours' sleep in 24 for almost a year; could not write my name for over four months, and could not have a letter read to me or see my friends or scarcely my attendants."

For a period she had to be waited on almost hand and foot by Minnie Kupfer, one of her aides in the Franco-Prussian War, who had followed Clara to America and had now perforce become her housekeeper, her nurse, and (on doctor's orders) her guardian against even the

Presidential aspirant John Sherman used the "bloody shirt" appeal to Civil War veterans to help his campaign along.

"I'll astonish the nation,
    An' all creation
By my great Presidential Aspiration!
I'll sail over Blaine like a soarin' eagle,
And swoop over Hawley higher 'n a sea-gull,
I'll dance on old Evarts, I'll stand on Depew,
I'll fly clean over the hull low crew—
    Thet's what I'll dew!
I'll light on the libbe'ty-pole, an' crow,
An' I'll say to the gawpin' fools below;
  'This ain't no sort of a Flyin' Merman,
  Nor Flyin' Dutchman, nor Flyin' German—
    It's ol' John Sherman,
  Lightin' out hot fer the nomination,
  The liveliest candidate in creation!'"
            *
Slowly, ruefully, some fine day,
We may not hear—or, again, we may—
    It's likely enough—
An aged voice of misery say,
"Wal, I like flyin' well enough,
B'gosh—but the' ain't such a thunderin' sight
O' fun in 't when ye come to light!"

slightest sort of strain. Months later, when Clara was once more able to scribble a few lines at a time, she wrote her niece Mamie: "They let me see no one at present—I am weak—Night before last I had a chill which lasted 10 hours without once letting up. I was cold and wet as a fish every minute of the time."

Could this be the same heroine who endured almost every physical and mental strain on the battlefields of America and Europe? Could the woman who had endured so much now abide no single or trivial unpleasant episode or word?

Certainly she had an abnormally sensitive temperament, with psychic as well as physical problems. Confronted with the need for direct decision and action, she could withstand everything. Once the tension was gone, and she had no cause to which to attach herself, she became a different person. When the pressure went down, Clara Barton collapsed. The best example of it is her long, painful transition back to useful service in America in the 1870's.

"Utter prostration"

"You will understand from *theory*, and I pray the great and good God that you may *never* know from *experience*, what helplessness and suffering may follow in the strain of utter prostration of the nervous system," Miss Barton wrote in 1877 to her devoted European friend, the Grand Duchess Louise of Baden. She complained of a "hot sore spot on the spine . . . leading up to the base of the brain, bursting into flame at every over-taxation."

But in 1876, when matters were at their blackest, a young woman friend urged Clara to enter the sanitarium at Dansville, New York, famous for its climate and curative waters. Remembering the town happily from visiting it during lecture tour days Clara went—and spent much of the next 10 years of her life there.

First she was enrolled in the sanitarium—called "Our Home on the Hillside." Her outlook improved so steadily that she bought a private house and began the long journey back to wholeness and strength. "I have done everything to surround myself with healthful and strength-giving influences," she wrote. "The climate is delicious and I almost live in the open air. Sleep, which in all years has been only a visitor, has come back to abide with me more constantly. My flesh is also returning and I am regaining some power of endurance."

News of politics and current affairs was kept from her, lest she be emotionally upset. She had quiet walks in the morning, piano concerts and stereopticon slides at night, soothing sermons on Sunday. There was even time to catch up on her diary, compose poetry, and write to friends.

Some of her most winning letters, written in these quiet years, tell of a favorite black-and-white cat named Tommy who ate raw beefsteak for breakfast, drank milk from a saucer, and spent most of the day sleeping. "Toward dusk he generally helps himself to a fresh meat lunch with the fur on, from the cellar or barn or field and about seven he comes in for his tea, and it is real tea, with a little sugar, and a good deal of milk and a small plate of crackers. . . . He wants to sit in my lap and have me feed him his soaked cracker from my fingers and then be told he is a good pussy for about 15 minutes." Warmth and affection began to shine through her life again.

Other letters from Dansville reveal clearly some of the attitudes that Clara Barton developed as a child and kept throughout her life. She never accepted cities and urban life. Like Thomas Jefferson, whom her father taught her to admire, Clara found cities "sores on the body politic."

To a visiting German professor, who came to America while she was recuperating, she wrote: "I am sorry that you must perforce see our country . . . through the slum, and mire, and haze of a lens like New York City. Out on our millions of acres of hills, valleys, and plains is a better, purer, nobler population, the force of whose earnestness and honesty will save our Nation long ages after the pollution of its cities would have turned it into a Sodom and Gomorrah. . . . Tweed and his 'ring' didn't go to the farmers sweating in their hay-fields. . . . They went to the politicians, and burrowed in the cities and made their nests like the bats and owls, under the eaves of churches and in halls and steeples."

She added: "We are not so near destruction as it would seem from *your* standpoint, and because a few poor, vain, foolish women, with little money and less brains and shriveled hearts, have betaken themselves to the boarding-houses

This photograph of Manhattan's Lower East Side in the 1880's depicts the urban slums that Clara hated.

THE FRUITS OF A DECADE IN DANSVILLE

Blanche Colton Williams, one of her most perceptive biographers, wrote of what her years at Dansville signified to her:

"Clara Barton grew old only in the last year or so of her ninety-odd years; but to one who has read 40 of her diaries and a 'Journal' or so in addition, besides hundreds of documents and letters, the 10 years in Dansville, New York, marks a transition of sorts. If her career be indicated up to the age of fifty-five by a steadily rising line, however jagged or saw-teethed with advances and depressions, the decade in Dansville may be figured by a horizontal, also marked by little peaks and pits—at the end of which the line descends? Never.

"It rises again, not to cease its triumphant long ascent to the final plateau—a very short line. . . . At the age of sixty or so, when most women and most men consider the emoluments of rest, she was only at the beginning of a quarter-century that, for magnitude of achievement and spectacular importance, surpasses all preceding years."

of New York City, and are living false, empty, silly, idle lives for *show*, it does not make it that this is the character of life of *all* women in America. . . . Get another standpoint, and a wider outlook . . . than New York City . . . before you judge . . . this great country."

Spearhead in the struggle

Certainly Clara Barton, recuperating in rural New York, did not intend that *her* life be empty, silly, or idle. She sought and found a cause. The instrument that brought it about was a letter she wrote on May 17, 1877, to Dr. Louis Appia in Geneva, asking if she might try to establish the International Red Cross in America; the direct inducement was his reply, urging her to spearhead and direct the fight.

At Dansville, also, she found a devoted helper—Julian B. Hubbell. Ambitious and intelligent, this Iowa farm boy was born in 1847 and came East for his education. A chemistry teacher in the Dansville school when Clara met him there in 1876, he became a close friend, confidant, and aide.

But her greatest confidant was the Lord. Through this dark period, Clara sought and

found strength in religion. "God has stood very near," she wrote, "my trust in Him has never faltered, and my faith has never wavered nor changed." The mirror showed a drawn face, but in Clara's heart there was no retreat.

Her plans for the new relief organization were boldly conceived. She envisioned a national headquarters, with smaller offices in every state and local chapters in every city and town. The organization should not only be prepared for wartime service, but for disasters and emergencies of any type: fire, flood, epidemic, tornado, drought, catastrophe. American generosity must be harnessed and directed toward human needs whenever they arose.

Always a realist, Dr. Appia commended the large plan but counseled Miss Barton to start with three objectives: (1) to win public opinion to her side; (2) to gain the President's active support; (3) to secure the adoption of the Geneva treaty by the United States Senate.

Dr. Appia had conferred with President Gustave Moynier of the International Committee of the Red Cross, who also wrote Clara, enclosing a letter to President Rutherford B. Hayes that he urged Clara to deliver in person.

A campaign—an order! The letters electrified the long-time invalid. In October 1877, Clara packed her bag and headed for Washington, D.C.—the 400-mile trip was her longest since 1873. Old times, old fires were alive again. Undaunted by the President's absence from Washington, she called on other officials and congressmen, pleading her cause.

Her years as an invalid had not dimmed Clara's expertise at every kind of legitimate lobbying maneuver that could be practiced in the nation's capital. In her view, the Red Cross had never been accepted by the Federal government because the groundwork had never been effectively laid so that all the key officials who must pass on the matter in both the administrative and the legislative branches had a chance to understand what it was all about before they rendered their verdict.

With her customary flair for military tactics and terminology, she resolved "to guard the outposts" by doing everything she could to "create an interest and secure cooperation whenever the matter should come up for discussion or decision." She wanted to give a full advance briefing about the Red Cross to as many people as she could before she even approached President Hayes.

She wrote and published a pamphlet called *What the Red Cross Is*, arguing vigorously for "the neutrality of all sanitary supplies, ambulances, surgeons, nurses, attendants, and sick or wounded men, and their safe-conduct, when they bear the sign of the organization, viz., the Red Cross."

Finally she saw President Hayes early in 1878. Courteous but evasive, he passed her request on to Secretary of State W. M. Evarts, who promptly passed it on to his assistant secretary, Frederick Seward. The official skepticism was couched in such questions as:

"Don't you think we've had enough war for a while?"

"Can't Americans look after themselves?"

"But isn't this a strange task for a *woman* to undertake?"

"Isn't this the work of churches, not reformers?"

Such opposition would have stopped most people—but not Clara Barton. When she realized the Hayes administration would not actively support the Red Cross, she continued to publicize the movement—and bided her time. In the last months of Hayes's term she campaigned for the 1880 Republican candidate, James A. Garfield, and then headed back to Washington. She intended to fight on, and to win.

The election of Garfield was a lucky break. A Civil War veteran, he knew and admired her earlier work; his own youthful privations in Ohio had instilled the humanitarian viewpoint in him. He endorsed Miss Barton's plans enthusiastically, and commended them to his Secretary of State, James G. Blaine. Blaine and two other cabinet members, William Windom and Robert T. Lincoln, added valuable support. Her spirits soaring, Clara held a meeting and

organized the "Association of the American Red Cross" on May 21, 1881.

In other lands, monarchs and chiefs of state served as the president of their nation's Red Cross, so Clara had asked President Garfield to assume this office in the United States. He declined, insisting that Clara herself take the post—and she was duly elected president. At the May 21 meeting, which was held in the parlor of Clara's own apartment at 1326 I Street in Washington, Walter Phillips, then general manager of the Associated Press, acted as secretary. A constitution drafted by Judge William

Dr. Julian Hubbell, Clara's chief aide in the Red Cross, had the flowing side-whiskers known as "Dundrearies."

59

Lawrence of Ohio—who became first vice-president of the fledgling organization—was adopted; it emphasized that the American Red Cross would place great importance on peacetime relief activities.

The historic scene in Clara's parlor was subsequently described by Mrs. Peter V. DeGraw, one of those present: "The chairs were pushed back against the wall in a square. At the end of the room stood Miss Barton. She spoke of the horrors of war and of the need for an impartial society to treat the wounds of the injured, friend and foe."

Of course, the organization had not yet won the Senate's approval of formal United States ratification of the Geneva Convention, nor linked itself with the Red Cross in Europe. However, with President Garfield's support, all this was practically assured.

Another assassination

But Garfield's days were numbered. On July 2, 1881, he went to Washington's Baltimore and Potomac Railroad Station to board the presidential train. A short, hollow-faced man named Charles J. Guiteau stepped from the crowd. Two shots rang out. Garfield fell to the ground. For 80 days the President hovered between life and death, and life in Washington was in a state of suspense.

Clara Barton, however, during the weeks of waiting before Garfield's death, busied herself setting up the first local Red Cross Society in the United States. On August 22, 1881, it was formally established at her beloved Dansville. Standing on the platform to address the 57 original members, Miss Barton seemed much taller than her actual height. Her face was wonderfully expressive, her dark eyes flashed. She wore a black silk dress, with the beautiful amethyst pansy given by the Grand Duchess of Baden at her neck. The old confidence and power had returned. "The good Lord be praised," she said, "for giving me the strength to be busy once more."

The idea of local chapters was too good to be limited to little Dansville; the nearby cities of

Rochester and Syracuse soon formed groups. Hardly had this action been taken when the American Red Cross was put to its first disaster test in the white pine forest of eastern Michigan. On September 4, papers reported clouds of dense smoke above Sanilac County. The next day strong winds from Lake Huron fanned the flames, and a Detroit headline screamed: HALF OF MICHIGAN ABLAZE. Homes, barns, fences, crops were soon charred ruins; 5,000 were homeless.

The new Red Cross chapters at Dansville, Rochester, and Syracuse swung into action. The white and scarlet flag unfurled over the Dansville chapter was the first display of the Red Cross flag in America. Soon crates of food and clothing were on trains en route to Michigan. Clara Barton volunteered her own money to help with the relief work, reflecting that intensity of feeling and crisis that always brought out the best in her.

"Our skies grew murky and dark and our atmosphere bitter with the drifting smoke that rolled over from the blazing fields," she wrote. "Living thousands fled in terror, dying hundreds writhed in the embers, the dead blackened in the ashes of their hard-earned homes. Instantly we felt the help and strength of our organization, young and untried as it was."

With Julian Hubbell heading one of the six areas through which the Port Huron Relief Committee functioned, America's first Red Cross venture and first field relief work was dramatically successful. But with the wounded President still clinging to life, no action took place on the treaty pending in Washington. Garfield's death on September 19 took from the scene one of Clara Barton's staunchest supporters.

His successor, Chester A. Arthur, recommended the signing of the Geneva treaty in an official message to Congress. But with all the confusion and adjustment that comes with a new administration, more pressing items got priority. Back to her old routine of office visits, pleas, and promptings went Clara Barton. One Saturday she called on an influential woman won over by the relief work in Michigan. Clara's heart sank when she saw, on the woman's desk, literature of an opposing relief organization, with an invitation to join.

This single episode plunged Clara Barton back into the dark emotional despair that she had fought so hard to conquer. Menacing spirits again hovered over her pathway. She confided to her diary: "I am very low-spirited. I am cold, alone, surrounded by harmful spirits. All the society people of the city and country seem to be arrayed in arms against me, with only my single hand, sore throat, and silent tongue to make my way against misrepresentation, malice, and selfish ambition."

"Laus Deo!"

Still she found somewhere inside herself the strength to keep going; a little dynamo would not turn off, no matter how many people or problems opposed her. Thus the spring of 1882 found Clara Barton working ceaselessly for the passage of the treaty. Almost 10 years had passed since she had returned from Europe, and still her great goal eluded her. Rival organizations, like the "real and original" Red Cross, the Blue Anchor, and even the White Cross, had appeared.

Then suddenly Clara Barton was called to the office of the new Secretary of State, Frederick Frelinghuysen. He asked if she would like to see the treaty—and brought out the document, an unbound book of parchment some 14 inches square, and put it in her hands.

On March 1, 1882, President Arthur signed the treaty. On March 16 Senator E. S. Lapham wrote a note to Miss Barton that read: "I have the gratifying privilege of informing you of the ratification by the Senate of the Geneva Convention; of the full assent of the United States to the same, by the action of the Senate this afternoon. I had the injunction of secrecy removed so that it could be published at once. The whole is in print, and if I get time I will send you some copies in the morning . . . *Laus Deo!*" Clara, too, gave praise to God—then noted (feeling too weak for joy), "I laid down

---

A SIGNIFICANT WORKING PARTNERSHIP

Of Dr. Hubbell and of Clara's methods of recruiting Red Cross workers, her biographer Ishbel Ross has written:

"This was the beginning of Clara's most significant working partnership. As Field Agent for the Red Cross, Dr. Hubbell gave years of devoted service to her and her cause. He supported her in every move, went out to the field as her advance agent, and applied his specialized knowledge of agriculture to the various disaster areas. Dr. Hubbell grew old in Clara's service. His benign manner, his straggling Dundrearies, his scarlet scarf, his violin and kindly solicitude for Mamie [his nickname for Clara] all became an inseparable part of her ménage. Her own most revealing tribute to him was that he was 'a patient man.'

"From this point on she deliberately built up a following of young men and women who could be useful to her in her work. As Dr. Appia had warned her, she would need 'feet for running, to go, to come, to collect, to buy, to make multitudes of visits. . . .' Clara did a little of everything herself, and expected her helpers to do the same.

"But she always kept the reins firmly in her own hands and made the top decisions herself. When a real obstacle arose, Clara was the one who could surmount it. But as her organization grew her corps of workers increased. Some were brilliantly effective in the aid they gave her. Many were unselfish, industrious volunteers, but she was usually saddled with a few lame ducks and she made some disastrous choices.

"When her agents betrayed her and damaged her cause, Clara was reluctant to abandon them or think ill of their motives. Her volunteer service was an important part of her early work, and a basic principle of the Red Cross. The day would come when 1,650,000 volunteers would work the year around in the United States, and 8,200,000 would function in one year of the First World War."

---

the letter, and wiped my tired eyes."

Negotiations in Switzerland followed. Finally, on July 26, 1882, the Treaty of Geneva was proclaimed the law of the land. When news of America's action reached Europe, there was wide rejoicing. From Geneva, President Moynier of the Red Cross sent out an official bulletin, noting that "without the energy and perseverance of this remarkable woman, Clara Barton, we should not for a long time have had the pleasure of seeing the Red Cross received into the United States."

Frederick Frelinghuysen (above) and his predecessor as Secretary of State, James Blaine (below), urged President Arthur to join the Geneva pact (left).

Clara herself, by this late-July date, was back at her home in Dansville, relaxed and "content" as she tended to her garden with her feet on "the soft green earth." She did pause long enough in in her summer vacation to observe:

"Our adhesion to this treaty has changed our articles of war and our military hospital flag. We have no longer the old faded yellow flag, but a bright Red Cross at every post, and the same sign to be worn by all military surgeons and attendants if the orders of the War Department have yet reached them. We are today . . . not only in full accord with the International Treaty of Geneva but are considered one of the strongest pledged nations within it."

But in her native land—still isolated by oceans and obsessed with internal reconstruction—little attention was paid to the event. Only one paper, the Washington *Evening Star*, mentioned it—and the space given was only four lines.

"No personal distinction had been bestowed," Miss Barton wrote, "no one politically advanced, no money of the Government expended; like other things of like nature and history, it was left in obscurity to make its own way and live its own hard life." Her Red Cross not only would survive and live, but would expand and triumph. Men and women still unborn would be praising it long after her own death.

Chapter 5
RESOURCEFUL RELIEF FOR CIVILIAN DISASTERS

POLITICIANS can control the fate of treaties, but no man can stay the mighty blows of nature. The American land, straddling a whole continent, is a power immense in grandeur and terrible in wrath. This land, with its range of extremes from hot searing sun to cold blue wind, has naturally called forth myths such as those of Paul Bunyan's strength, Casey Jones's daring, and John Henry's defiance. It is an awesome land, one that human beings can never completely tame—mighty as the Mississippi, white as Cape Cod sand, black as West Virginia coal pits, dry as Death Valley, often too steep even for Rocky Mountain goats.

Yet the plain facts of this land are even more remarkable and inspiring than the myths. American landscape and history are part of the same fabric, interwoven and inseparable. And a Clara Barton can accomplish still more in actuality than a Paul Bunyan can in legend. The saga of her Red Cross is a story of repeated struggle against rampaging nature and warring mankind.

As Clara Barton had foreseen, the most formidable enemies confronting her fledgling organization were fire, wind, water, and famine. Every spring great rivers pushed beyond their banks, bringing devastation and despair. The 1883 floods along the Mississippi, particularly severe, were followed by a fearful cyclone.

To meet such emergencies, the Red Cross drew up in 1883 five general regulations or principles that became guideposts for years to come: (1) Never to solicit relief as such; (2) Never to pay salaries to officers, but only to those employed to perform manual labor and special services; (3) To have money in readiness to start a relief operation, day or night, weekday, Sunday, or holiday; (4) To evaluate problems by firsthand observation, and make immediate and reliable reports to the country through the Associated Press, so that people could then contribute to the Red Cross relief work if they wished; (5) To acknowledge directly every contribution, and to carry out directions and employ materials in the wisest, swiftest way possible that was also consistent with sound management.

Such principles allowed maximum action with minimum red tape and delay. By putting her own money on immediate call—she kept several thousand dollars in cash on hand at all times—Clara Barton proved that she meant to lead the way. So she did.

When news of major floods on the Ohio River reached Washington in March, 1884, Clara Barton and the general field agent, Dr. Julian Hubbell, hurried west to Cincinnati. They found the city afloat, with many inhabitants being fed from boats through third-story windows. There was 400 miles of such distress along the river—and rain was still falling. To make matters worse, a cyclone struck, uprooting houses and trees, leaving thousands without home, food, or fire. On the railroad tracks were freight cars with tons of relief supplies—but what good would they do the marooned victims?

Zigzag aid by boat

"At eight o'clock in the morning I chartered my first boat," Clara wrote on March 18, 1884 —and thus opened a new chapter in Red Cross history. That boat, the *Josh V. Throop*, was the first Red Cross relief boat ever seen on American waters. Moving diagonally down the Ohio, from side to side and village to village, it unloaded fuel and supplies wherever a group of people huddled together.

Reaching Cairo five days later, the boat reloaded, returned, and resupplied victims on the way. By now the Mississippi River had begun to rise; the "Barton Brigade" went to Saint Louis, chartered the steamer *Mattie Bell*, and undertook another waterborne expedition.

This time Clara's old Civil War friend General Amos Beckwith, of the Quartermaster Corps, joined them. He personally supervised the distribution of rations and other government sup-

General Amos Beckwith, who aided Clara in the Mississippi floods, had also been her colleague in the Civil War.

plies, as well as clothing, corn, oats, salt, and hay. The hungry were fed, the naked clothed, and the dead buried. With heads, hearts, and hands, the relief workers struggled on, day and night. The angry waters finally subsided.

Then people could return to the places where once their homes had stood. Unwilling to leave them in such a plight, Clara devised a novel plan. She reloaded the *Josh V. Throop* with pine lumber, precut doors and windows, groceries, tools, and utensils. Hiring a skillful team of carpenters, she explained her idea. At designated spots they would go ashore, erect a one-room house, provision it, and move quickly to another site. Nature had not taken long to destroy men's homes—now men must not take long to rebuild them.

Imagine the scenes that followed hour after hour, day after day. A strange ship steams up the river, with a big iron cross, painted brilliant red, hung high between its smokestacks. The ship halts, turns, and draws up to the nearest landing. A half dozen men leave the ship with building materials and begin putting up a small house. While they work, following Clara's carefully established procedures, others bring furniture ashore.

Then follow bed and bedding, clothing, table and chairs, dishes, candles, a small stove, cooking utensils, a plow, rake, axe, hoe, shovel, spade, hammer, and nails. Finally a generous supply of meat, meal, and groceries is brought for the table. Then the ship backs away from the landing and disappears down the river. To many families, it must have been like a storybook miracle.

"The Little Six"

Behind this effort was Clara Barton's genius for creating a fairly small, tight-knit organization—and her generous heart. The combination won friends and supporters of every age, in every state. She could lead (and manage) a relatively few people in handling a quite large and difficult task for the Red Cross, so long as it was kept rather specific. And she could make Americans far and near realize the nature of an emergency—and respond wholeheartedly to it.

The letters in her daily mail proved the point. One dated March 24, 1884, came from Waterford, Pennsylvania, and described a public benefit for the flood sufferers; it was signed "The Little Six—Joe Farrar, twelve years old; Florence Howe, eleven years old; Mary Barton, eleven years old; Reed White, eleven years old; Bertie Ainsworth, ten years old; Lloyd Barton, seven years old."

The total amount the children had raised was not large: $51.25. But it represented the kind of

---

"THE BEST PRINCIPLES OF SOCIAL SCIENCE"

Clara, who had a keen sense of what is now called public relations, was most cooperative with journalists who covered her work. Many newspaper men and women journeyed on the two ships she chartered during her 1884 flood-relief activities, or reported from points ashore on the Red Cross work along the riverbanks in that period. All of them were vividly briefed by her on the new organization's aims.

The following editorial, which appeared on March 31, 1884, in the Chicago *Inter-Ocean,* was based on firsthand reporting and shows how knowledge of what she was accomplishing soon spread widely throughout the land:

"The day is not far distant—if it has not already come—when the American people will recognize the Red Cross as one of the wisest and best systems of philanthropic work in modern times. Its mission is not accomplished when it has carried the generous offerings of the people to their brethren who have met with sudden calamity. It does not stop with the alleviation of bodily suffering and the clothing of the destitute— blessed as that work is, when wisely done so as not to break down the manly spirit of self-help.

"The Red Cross has become a grand educator, embodying the best principles of social science, and that true spirit of charity which counts it a sacred privilege to serve one's fellowmen in time of trouble. The supplying of material wants—of food, raiment and shelter—is only a small part of its ministry in its work among suffering humanity.

"When fire or flood or pestilence has caused widespread desolation, the Red Cross seeks to carry to people's hearts that message which speaks of a universal brotherhood. It is all the time and everywhere sowing the seed of brotherly kindness and goodwill, which is destined in time to yield the fruits of world-wide peace. Once let the love of doing good unto others become deeply rooted and practiced as an international custom, and arsenals and ironclad navies will give way to the spirit of equity."

This contemporary news drawing of the 1884 floods shows a break in the levee, with workers rushing to stem the torrent.

grass-roots support and sacrifice that was more precious to Clara Barton than massive bars of gold. The children's note asked her to use the money "where it would do the most good."

A month later the *Josh V. Throop* spotted a tall, tattered woman and her daughter at a desolate spot known as Cave-in Rock, on the Illinois side of the Ohio River. The boat landed nearby and the shore party met the woman, Mrs. Plew. Her husband, a river pilot, had died during an earlier flood, leaving her with six children ranging in age from three to fifteen.

They had eked out an existence with two horses, three cows, chickens, and hogs. Then came the flood. The horses and cows were lost. Cholera claimed most of the hogs. When the house was destroyed in a windstorm, the Plews moved into an old log corncrib, along with their few surviving chickens. But the place was spotless, and the family was determined to hold on.

The Red Cross workers looked silently on the pitiful scene. Here was misfortune, poverty, and sorrow; but it was mixed with fortitude, courage, and endurance.

Miss Barton asked Mrs. Plew if she would like to return to her "childhood home in Indiana."

"No," Mrs. Plew said tenderly. "My husband lived and died here. He is buried here, and I would not like to go away and leave him alone. . . . I reckon we will stay here, and out of the wreck of the old house which sticks up out of the mud, we will put up another little hut, higher up on the bank out of the way of the floods . . . and make our crop this year."

Six children here, thought Miss Barton—and the Little Six! She told Mrs. Plew about the gift from the Waterford children, offered to bring the sum of $51.25 up to $100 with Red Cross money, and asked if the Plews could then

The disastrous floods of 1884, as depicted in this panorama drawn by an artist for "Frank Leslie's Illustrated Newspaper," inundated

make a new start. "At length," Clara's account of the episode continues, "with a struggling, choking voice she managed to say: 'God knows how much it would be to me. Yes, with my good boys I can do it, and do it well.' " The money was left and the boat steamed on.

Mrs. Plew named her new house "The Little Six," and for years thereafter people passing on the river could see, high on the bank where the Plews lived, a well-lettered cross board, with a painted sign reading "Little Six Red Cross Landing."

Finally, the Herculean task of river relief was finished. Clara Barton discharged the empty boat at Pittsburgh, bade her volunteer friends goodbye, and took the train for Washington. Of the task, she later wrote: "We had covered the Ohio River from Cincinnati to Cairo and back twice, and the Mississippi from St. Louis to New Orleans, and return—four months on the rivers—traveled over 8,000 miles, distributed in relief, of money and estimated material, $175,000—gathered as we used it."

Feeling the old searing head pains, and fearing a relapse, Clara Barton hurried back to her home. There she found notification of the 1884 International Red Cross meeting to be held at Geneva in September. A few days later she was requested to visit the office of Secretary of State Frelinghuysen. He too had received word of the Geneva meeting, and suggested that Clara Barton be America's chief delegate.

"No, Mr. Frelinghuysen," she later reported their dialogue. "I cannot go. I have just returned from field work. I am tired and ill. Furthermore, I have not had time to make a report of our work."

The Secretary of State answered: "There is no one else who sufficiently understands the Red Cross. . . . We cannot make a mistake in

much of the city of Cincinnati (center) and also drowned out large parts of Newport and Covington in Kentucky (right).

the matter of delegates to this first conference in which our Government shall participate. As to the report, have you not acknowledged the contributions to all those who have sent?"

"Oh yes; every dollar and every box of goods where the donor was known."

"Has anyone complained?"

"No; not a single person, so far as is known. We have had only thanks."

"Then to whom would you report?"

"To you, Mr. Secretary, or to such person or in such manner as you shall designate."

"I don't want any report," Mr. Frelinghuysen said. "Our Government relief boats have reported you officially, and all the country knows what you have done and is more than satisfied. Regarding your illness—you have had too much fresh water, Miss Barton. I recommend salt—and shall appoint you."

So he did; in the autumn of 1884, Miss Clara Barton was on hand to serve as the first official representative of the United States at an International Conference of the Treaty of Geneva. It was one of her triumphant moments.

The Johnstown Flood

During late May of 1889, it rained steadily in Pennsylvania. By Memorial Day, the Conemaugh River and Stony Creek were above their banks. A reservoir not far above Johnstown, Pennsylvania, reached its crest that night. Water poured over the top of the earthen dam. Old-timers were worried. They wished the discharge pipes had not been removed and the conduit plugged. What would happen if the pressure continued and the dam gave way?

By then the structure was almost half a century old, having been built before the Civil War to supply water for the Pennsylvania Canal. Its mass of earth fill was 70 feet high and about 900 feet long at the top. When the canal was abandoned in 1857, the Pennsylvania Railroad bought the site, but found no use for it. Leakage developed around the discharge pipes at the dam's base; repairs were neglected.

In 1879 a group of wealthy Pennsylvania businessmen bought the reservoir and surround-

KEYS TO HER SUCCESS

Some of the key characteristics of Clara Barton that help explain her great success in developing the Red Cross from 1881 onward were graphically described by William E. Barton:

"While extremely modest, Clara Barton was far from being a prude. She was never terrified by . . . gossip. . . . In 1884, when she was on her steamboat, *Josh V. Throop*, assisting in the Ohio River floods, the boat one night tied up at a landing, and a goodly number of people came on board. Among the rest were two young women. One of the prominent ladies of the town found opportunity to whisper to her that these were young women whose social standing was not above question. 'Then they will need help all the more,' she said; and she gave those two girls an hour of her evening. Such warnings she often received, and . . . she invariably reacted in the other direction.

"She never undertook any work without first carefully thinking it through in an effort to discover just where it was to end and how it was to be provided for. She had no sympathy with people who start good movements for other people to support when their well-meant but poorly reckoned endeavor fails. 'They get hold of a log they can't lift,' she said, 'and they make a great call for some one to come and lift it for them.' That was never the way in which she did things. She thought them through in advance.

"Clara Barton worked slowly. While she formed her decisions promptly in emergencies, she formulated them carefully and with painful precision. It was not by doing things easily she accomplished so much, but by rising early and working late and keeping constantly at the thing she wanted to do. . . . She coveted the ability to work more rapidly. She admired that ability, and perhaps overvalued it, in others. She once wrote to me: 'Where do you find time to do so many things? One of the griefs of my life is to see other persons getting things done— really *done*—and I accomplish so little. I don't see how they do it.' No more could they see how she did it; but she did it by working with an industry and devotion that never found an easy way of accomplishing results.

"A friend of hers was deeply interested in a movement for which he wished the endorsement of Clara Barton. . . . He became very desirous of having her commendation in time for a particular use;

and his wife invited Clara Barton to their home to dine. . . . After dinner . . . the man produced a typewritten statement of some length which he had prepared, endorsing his work. This he read to her, and she liked it. But when she understood that he had prepared this for her to sign, she was shocked. She refused to sign it. Her friend could not at first understand her scruples. Did she not believe in this work? She did. Had she not listened to his reading of this very statement with expressions of hearty approval? She had. Was there anything in it she would like to change? . . . No . . . except that she cared to change everything in it.

"He assured her that he was asking nothing of her which men of the highest honor did not do con-

Rescue work in the 1884 floods

stantly. . . . She understood . . . but she could not do what he asked of her. . . . There was nothing in the document to which she could object; but it was not hers. . . .

"Clara Barton had many devoted and loyal friends. . . . There were others who . . . betrayed her most sacred confidences. . . . Yet here was one of the finest triumphs of her nature. She never cherished permanent resentment. One time a friend recalled to her a peculiarly cruel thing that had been done to her some years previously, and Clara Barton did not seem to understand what she was talking about. 'Don't you remember the wrong that was done you?' she was asked. Thoughtfully and calmly she answered, 'No; I distinctly remember

forgetting that.' Friends deserted Clara Barton, but she never deserted a friend. . . .

"In every field in which she labored, she was flooded with volunteer workers who wanted to help. Some of them were competent; more were not. I recently talked with my longtime friend, Father Field, sometime head of the [Episcopal] Cowley Fathers, and learned that he was at the Johnstown Flood, and saw much of Clara Barton. They rode together in a buggy over a road filled with trees and house roofs and he feared she would be thrown out, but she told him to drive on; she had driven over worse roads, and with bullets besides. He said that her greatest difficulty as he saw it there was the number of people of good impulse but little discretion who rushed into Johnstown to help. . . . Assistance she must have, and must take what was offered. But the handling of this untrained force was a matter which called for the greatest tact as well as executive ability. . . .

"Nothing that came of her association with men —and rough men at that—made her anything less than a woman and a lady. . . . She had her own way of ignoring any incident occurring in her presence at which she might have been expected to be shocked. . . . Conventionalities meant little to her in the presence of human need. But on her return to home life, she was gentle, ladylike, and a stickler for proprieties. . . . People who expected to meet in her a big, aggressive female with a long stride and a heavy voice and a domineering attitude were amazed. She was a little, undemonstrative gentlewoman of the old school.

"One of Clara Barton's most outstanding quallities was her almost complete disregard of precedent. . . . She always had faith in the possibility of something better. It irritated her to be told how things always had been done. She knew that a very large proportion of things that have been done since the Creation have been blunderingly done and . . . having once decided upon a course that defied the tyranny of precedent, she held true to her declaration of independence, and saw her experiment through.

"In this she was not reckless or iconoclastic. She simply forbade herself the cheap luxury of a closed mind. If no better way presented itself, she was content with the old way of doing. But she was eager for any new thing that might improve upon the past. Hers was preeminently a forward-looking mind and a soul with face ever toward the sunrise."

ing land for a hunting and fishing preserve. They removed the discharge pipes, plugged the conduit, and installed wire-mesh fishguards. After all, this was the way to improve the fishing.

The dam broke on May 31, 1889. A solid wall of water, 30 to 40 feet high, rushed down the valley like a moving mountain, at an extraordinary speed of 22 feet per second. In 45 minutes the reservoir was empty, having discharged at an average rate of nearly 200,000 cubic feet per second.

Soon the wave hit Johnstown, which because of the earlier flooding was already marooned under 7 to 10 feet of water. Every tree en route, all houses, animals, telegraph poles, locomotives, and railroad track (including ties) were swept forward, forming a hugh 30-acre jumble of debris when caught by the stone-arch bridge in Johnstown. The jam caught fire, and many of those who had not been drowned were burned to death. Most of the victims—nearly 5,000 before the day of horror ended—were drowned, however. It was the worst dam-break disaster in American history—and one of the worst single catastrophes this nation has ever endured.

Looters appear on the scene at nearly every great disaster. Here two such robbers are fired at as they row off.

That same day Clara Barton and a picked Red Cross team left Washington by train for Johnstown. Despite washed-out ties and broken tracks, they arrived 48 hours later. This, in her words, is what they found: "Scarcely a house standing that was safe to enter, the wrecks piled in rubbish 30 feet high, 4,000 dead in the river beds, 20,000 foodless but for Pittsburgh bread rations, and a cold rain which continued unbroken by sunshine for 40 days."

There was only one thing to do: get to work. For five months the Red Cross workers lived amidst the destruction and desolation, sometimes in tents, sometimes in temporary shelter. On a dry-goods box set up as a makeshift desk, Red Cross officials transacted financial affairs totaling nearly $500,000.

"I shall never lose the memory of my first walk on the first day," Clara wrote. "The wading in mud, the climbing over broken engines, heaps of iron rollers, broken timbers, wrecks of houses; bent railway tracks tangled with piles of iron wire . . . dead animals, and often people being borne away."

Dazed and crushed, the surviving citizens of Johnstown dug in the muddy banks for their dead. Americans heard what had happened; money and material began to roll in from all parts of the nation. The Red Cross, Miss Barton said, played its "single fife among the grand chorus of relief of the whole country"—but that clear shrill fife could be heard above the whole band.

One mammoth Red Cross tent served as a general warehouse. As the situation improved, six "Red Cross Hotels" were erected—wooden barracks 100 feet long and 50 feet wide. Afterward, 3,000 single dwellings were erected and furnished either by gifts or by material purchased from Red Cross funds.

Two railroads, having repaired their tracks, brought in supplies. A large crew of men and seven two-horse teams ran daily for four months in the distribution. The paths of charity, as Clara Barton had good reason to know, are over roadways of debris and ashes. She trod that path with unflinching devotion.

In a final report on Johnstown, the Flood Finance Committee appointed by Governor Beaver of Pennsylvania wrote: "In this matter of sheltering the people, as in others of like importance, Miss Clara Barton, President of the Red Cross Association, was most helpful. . . . She made her own organization for relief work in every form, disposing of the large resources under her control with such wisdom and tenderness that the charity of the Red Cross had no sting. Its recipients are not Miss Barton's dependents, but her friends."

Such words pleased her, just as had the praise she had won earlier as a schoolteacher, nurse, overseas worker, and political lobbyist for good causes. Not a single case of unrelieved suffering was reported in the Johnstown area. Not a single person who contributed a dollar reported not having it acknowledged. The efficient little lady from New England liked that kind of operation. It made her wanted, welcomed, and acclaimed. In giving unstintingly to others, she was able to find inner consummation for herself.

Chapter 6
AID FOR SUFFERING RUSSIANS AND ARMENIANS

WITHIN a decade of its founding, the American Red Cross, led by Clara Barton, was known and supported throughout America. The national mood had come full circle since the grim days of Fredericksburg, Antietam, and Appomattox. If the 1860's had been sad, the early 1890's were ebullient. Once great fortunes were acquired and America's industrial might was fully recognized, a mood of splendor and extravagance swept the land.

The Vanderbilts, Rockefellers, Goulds, and Harrimans came into their own. Some called such millionaires moguls, after the resplendent rulers of medieval India. Others called them robber barons, after the powerful nobles of medieval Europe who levied toll on travellers who fell into their clutches. Diamond Jim Brady, who even had diamonds set in his teeth, epitomized the new opulence. J. P. Morgan, the leading man on Wall Street, personified the new financial power. Brownstone mansions sprang up in New York. Imitation French châteaus dotted the eastern seaboard. A new generation remembered no old war, and anticipated no new one. Of course, the Cuban problem was a thorn in America's side—but hardly a dagger in the heart. These were the "Gay Nineties," when boys and girls rode bicycles built for two, and when many tables of the nation sagged with good things even after depression struck in 1893.

Not so in Czarist Russia, laboring with century-old problems and ancient tyrannies. In 1889 and 1890, news reports told of massive Russian crop failures extending from Moscow north and south, and east beyond the Ural Mountains into Siberia. In 1891, crops were almost a total failure in a vast region. The granaries were empty, and 35,000,000 people were facing inevitable famine.

To most Americans of that generation, Russia was an unknown land, conjuring up images of Cossacks, onion-shaped domes, Orthodox priests with long black beards, and boatmen singing doleful songs on the Volga. Russian society was far more stratified than that of western Europe. Less than 5 per cent of the people lived in cities; 95 per cent were peasants. The vast, mysterious territory veered between autocracy and revolution.

Czar Alexander II (1855–1881) tried to liberalize policies; he paid for his efforts by being assassinated. Alexander III adopted more repressive measures, and widespread ignorance and illiteracy continued unchecked. Men like Pobedonostsev, procurator of the Holy Synod, and Plehwe, director of police, exercised thought control and the ruthless curbing of any opposition.

To democratic Americans, such policies and practices of the Czars were an unfathomable enigma—but hunger was something Americans understood and opposed. Though relatively few of them had direct ethnic or cultural ties with the Slavic world, Americans in the 1890's were anxious to help the hungry and the suffering anywhere on the globe. Moreover, they were *able* to help, since their rich land had yielded crops and wealth undreamed of in the Old World.

In the census of 1890 it was impossible to trace a continuous line of frontier in the United States. A steady stream of homesteaders had opened up vast stretches of agricultural country between the Mississippi and the Pacific. Other Americans had built an internal transportation system to handle the expansion, developed the Lake Superior iron-ore regions and various similarly rich mineral resources, and planned huge industrial empires to match the general need. From a position of inferiority in 1860, the United States had marched to a position of tremendously impressive economic strength.

Population almost doubled from 1870 to 1900. The annual production of petroleum increased twelve-fold; of coal, nearly nine-fold; of pig iron, more than eight-fold. This dramatic growth affected all aspects of American life, including the Red Cross. It provided money, influence, and power undreamed of in the rustic Jacksonian America in which Clara Barton had grown up.

Colored eggs and Tolstoi

As reports grew of suffering in Russia brought about by the famine of 1891 and 1892, Miss Barton probed into the problem to see what might be done even before the famine "had attracted general attention." The Russian Chargé d'Affaires in Washington found out that Russia would gladly receive shipments, and would

The yearning for display widespread among America's rich in the 1890's characterizes this "breakfast room."

even send ships for any food that might be offered. The United States government would not permit this. The Senate did vote an appropriation to take food to Russia, but the House defeated the measure.

Undaunted, Clara sought private support. The Order of Elks in Washington made an initial contribution; others quickly followed. Philadelphia chartered a ship, as did the state of Minnesota. But the largest impetus came from Iowa. That one midwestern state raised and sent by rail 225 carloads of corn and flour. In New York this was loaded on the British ship *Tynehead*, chartered by the Red Cross for $12,500, and sent to Riga in Russia. Other ships were also loaded and sent. The reluctance of Congress to act in no way dampened the enthusiasm or effectiveness of Clara Barton. After all, human beings were starving.

Her close friend and confidant, Dr. Julian B. Hubbell, went to Russia to oversee the distribution. On the Riga dock he found 250 peasants, who had waited two days for the ship to land so that they could have the honor of unloading the American gift. Once the *Tynehead* was tied up, the Russians worked night and day, without rest, determined to unload the entire cargo without help. Twelve women worked alongside the men, sewing up rips in the bags to prevent waste. These peasants refused any pay—they had labored for their starving brethren on the steppes.

The thanks that Clara Barton prized most came not from a high official, but from a peasant of Samara, who sent a crude note and three colored Easter eggs to America. "North Americans!" he wrote. "May the Lord grant you a peaceful and long life, and prosperity to your

During the Russian famine, a Cossack patrol near Kazan prevents hungry peasants from leaving their village.

land, and may your fields be filled with abundant harvest—Christ is risen!"

Dr. Hubbell saw that the American grain was shipped to 82 famine districts, some as far away as the Ural Mountains. The value of the material so distributed was put at over $800,000. The American ambassador estimated that it supported 700,000 people for a month. Soup kitchens and breadlines operated throughout the vast sprawling empire. No one could say how many thousands of lives were thus saved.

Russians of all ranks and stations, including the great novelist Leo Tolstoi, expressed their gratitude. Dr. Hubbell visited Tolstoi, slept in his library, and answered his many questions about the American Red Cross. Tolstoi told him, "From what I have heard of Miss Barton, I feel that she must be a very near relation. Please give her my love." Thanks to Clara and others like her, the United States of America was not only a powerful nation; it was one of the most generous the world had ever known.

Massacres in Armenia

People to the south of Russia, in the old Ottoman Empire, were soon to discover this fact for themselves. The "Sick Man of Europe," as diplomats called the tottering empire centered on Turkey, had been dying for years—and was indeed kept alive largely by diplomacy. Having reached great heights in the Middle Ages, the Moslem world had failed to adapt to the scientific and industrial revolution, and suffered from decay, corruption, and backwardness.

In 1876 the new sultan, Abdul Hamid II, began his regime by proclaiming a liberal Western type of constitution; but a series of events altered his policies. The constitution was suspended while Abdul Hamid set out on so bloody a policy of repression and persecution that he won the nickname "Red Sultan." A group of young Turks, affected by French revolutionary ideas, challenged his tyranny, and a series of insurrections and assassinations ensued.

The persecution of Christians, and civil war with Balkan nationalists, continued unabated. The slaughter of thousands of helpless Arme-

In Russia in 1902, Clara and her aide B. F. Tillinghast were presented to the Czar by his chamberlain (right).

nians in 1895 and 1896 shocked the world. Reports told of hundreds of towns and villages that had not been heard from since the bloodbaths; only the Red Cross could hope to reach them. Turkey had signed the Red Cross treaty—though as a Moslem, not a Christian, nation it later insisted on using the symbol of the Red

75

Crescent—and trained field workers could be dispatched there. The butchered would not be brought back to life, but the starving, orphaned, and helpless might be cared for. On this point Red Cross officials everywhere agreed.

A major barrier to any such relief plan loomed up. The reactionary Turkish government, suspicious of outside interference, announced that no foreign groups would be allowed to enter. Changing that order, and getting the workers in, would require a person gifted with the utmost tact, skill, and persuasion. An international Red Cross committee asked Clara Barton to undertake the mission. She was seventy-four now, and her health was poor. But what did that matter, with a critical assignment like this? She went to Constantinople.

After various delays and setbacks, she got an audience with Tewfik Pasha, the Turkish Minister of Foreign Affairs. "We have brought only ourselves," the slim, stout-hearted American visitor told him. "No correspondent has accompanied us, and we shall have none, and shall not go home to write a book on Turkey. Nothing shall be done in a concealed manner. All dispatches which we send will go openly through your own telegraph. . . . I shall never counsel or permit a sly or underhand action with your government, and you will pardon me, Pasha, if I say I shall expect the same treatment in return—such as I give, I shall expect to receive."

"And you shall have it," the Pasha replied. "We honor your position and your work."

The Sultan granted the freedom of the empire to Clara Barton, as a celebrated nurse and philanthropist. Dr. Hubbell, Clara's chief assistant, led one of the field parties; Clara herself stayed at the helm in Constantinople for the necessary liaison work with the Turkish government. Caravans were assembled to carry goods in all directions. Dr. Ira Harris, hero of epidemic control in the East, was employed to fight the numerous outbreaks of typhoid, typhus, dysentery, and smallpox. Repairing, replanting, and resettling were the order of the day.

"Unheard-of toil, care, hard riding day and

FLORENCE NIGHTINGALE

During her time in Turkey, Clara saw some of the sites where, during the Crimean War, her great English contemporary Florence Nightingale had done her notable work. The two ladies well repay a searching comparison—which William E. Barton provides:

"Florence Nightingale was a lady, born and bred; but vitriol was mild compared to some of her outbursts. Clara Barton was a lady to her very fingertips; and she had had enough of experience in Washington among officials and men of influence so that she knew how on occasion to be much more diplomatic and gracious than most other women with her responsibilities. Moreover, she shrank from giving pain, and was careful of her words. But she had as strong a will as had Florence Nightingale, and, while she was as a rule more amiable than that lady in her more violent moods, she got things done.

"People sometimes found [Clara] arbitrary, impatient, and obstinate; had she been less so, it had gone hard with the interests which she cherished. She . . . required that things should move, and move in the direction of her decision; but she was at heart, and on most occasions in her demeanor, quiet, gentle, affectionate, and calm. . . . Clara Barton was a self-willed woman. . . . So, most emphatically and uncomfortably for those who withstood her, was Florence Nightingale. . . .

"Like Florence Nightingale, [Clara] had opportunities of marriage in her youth, and resolutely turned to other work under force of a strong conviction, and that conviction had mighty impelling power. Lytton Strachey, in his remarkably penetrating sketch, says: 'Everyone knows the popular conception of Florence Nightingale. The saintly, self-sacrificing woman . . . the Lady with the Lamp, gliding through the horrors of the hospital at Scutari . . . is familiar to all. But the truth was different. . . . A Demon possessed her. Now demons, whatever else they may be, are full of interest. . . . In the real Miss Nightingale there was more that was interesting than in the legendary one; there was also less that was agreeable.'

"The disposition of Florence Nightingale lacked much of being angelic. When she encountered the stupidity of official red tape or the brutality and indifference of army surgeons, her words blistered. . . . But when she arrived in Scutari 42 wounded men out of every 100 were dying, and when she left them her hospitals showed a death rate of 22 out of every 1,000 [casualties brought to them].

"Clara Barton had a tongue less sharp than Florence Nightingale's, but she had a will no less inflexible. Both women had soft voices, which they never raised. Men fled from the soft tones and vitriolic words of Florence Nightingale. When Clara Barton grew angry, she lowered her voice. Instead of a woman's shrill falsetto, men heard a deep and determined tone quietly affirming that the thing was to be done in this way and in no other. Few men withstood that tone.

"Some . . . have been shocked to read the opinion of Dr. [Henry] Bellows of the [Civil War] Sanitary Commission concerning the uselessness and worse

Miss Florence Nightingale

of the ordinary woman nurse in war hospitals. That opinion was shared . . . by Clara Barton, and to an even greater degree by Florence Nightingale. Not very long after Florence Nightingale had reached Scutari with her 38 nurses, and about the time when she was having to ship some of them back, her official friends in England thought to win her eternal gratitude by sending to her 46 additional nurses. . . . She refused to . . . have these 'women scampering through the wards' and upsetting all her regulations. 'They are like troublesome children,' she said. Even the religious ones were given to what she called 'spiritual flirtations' with the soldiers; and, as for those who had not the fear of God . . . there were drunken orderlies and dis-

solute officers and unmarried chaplains to be considered. . . .

"Clara Barton, I believe, would have set them to emptying slops and scrubbing floors till she found the few out of whom she could make nurses. She would not have written the kind of letters about them which Florence Nightingale wrote. She would have scolded a little in her diary, and have written the committee who had sent them a letter of thanks, requesting them not to send any more until she asked for them, and meantime to send her some bandages and some lemons. But she would have felt much as Florence Nightingale felt. . . .

"Many interesting parallels suggest themselves between the work of Clara Barton and that of Florence Nightingale. They were contemporary in a remarkable degree. . . . Miss Nightingale was born May 12, 1820, and died August 13, 1910; Clara Barton was born December 25, 1821, and died April 12, 1912. They faced the question of marriage in much the same fashion, and each one gave herself in much the same spirit to her life task.

"They were not unlike in their religious faith and in its practical expression. The long, confidential letters of Florence Nightingale, written painfully when she ought to have been in bed, remind us of the detailed epistles which Clara Barton found time to write, mostly late at night. Each had a love of humor which stood her in good stead; Miss Barton's had less sting in it than that of Miss Nightingale, but otherwise it was not unlike, and it was a great help to both of them. . . . Each protested to the end of her life that her real work was not that of the popular imagination, that of personally administering to any considerable number of sick or wounded soldiers, but a work of direction and organization; and neither [could make] the public believe it.

"Not long before her death, Clara Barton relieved her mind in her diary concerning the sort of newspaper article which invented fairy tales of this sort. 'Oh, these women reporters!' she said in her diary. 'They never get anything right. They are forever telling and inventing the same old kind of gush!' Florence Nightingale also had a profound distrust of the limitations of members of her own sex; but also she knew, as did Clara Barton, the brutality, the stupidity, and the inefficiency of men. Miss Nightingale often wondered if there were in all the army enough officers of sympathy and conscience to have saved Sodom. Sometimes she doubted if there was one."

Tewfik Pasha, Foreign Minister of Turkey

Clara was kept so busy in Constantinople that one of the few trips she found time to take in Turkey was to Scutari, where she had been invited to address Miss Patrick's School for Girls, a missionary institute close to the hospital in which Florence Nightingale had performed her remarkable nursing feats in 1854.

At this school, young women from six nations were being trained as teachers before they returned to help raise the educational standards of their own lands. Clara was happy to feel that the students were absorbing the inspiration of Miss Nightingale, which still lingered at Scutari.

In paying tribute to her illustrious predecessor in the area, Clara said that when Florence Nightingale and her party "sailed from the shores of England, it meant more for its future history than all the . . . munitions of war and regiments that had sailed before her in that vast campaign! This little unarmed pilgrim band of women that day struck a blow . . . at the barbarities of war. . . . This work went on until the hospitals of the entire British armies in the Crimea, from awful depths of wretchedness, became types."

Clara also meekly observed: "To bring my tame story of hackneyed, everyday life, to lay beside this altar of history is a thought at which my whole being shrinks into nothingness." However, she had no slightest need thus to abase herself. She put the work she was then directing in a truer perspective at just about the same time, when she wrote her nephew Stephen, "We are doing so much for humanity that no one else could do."

After six months in Turkey, Clara Barton left the Near East in August, 1896, to return home via England. An elaborate banquet (with the tables arranged to form red crosses) and lavish praise awaited her once she was back in Washington. For years she had gotten little support, and relatively little praise, in this city. Now that she had a world reputation and following, the friendships she had so long coveted were there in abundance. Life is strange, Clara Barton mused in her diary—a matter of too little or too much.

night, with risk of life were all involved," wrote Miss Barton. Some routes were so dangerous that brigand chiefs were hired as escorts. Ambushes and raids persisted, but the work went steadily forward. One by one the expeditions made their way through hostile back country, then eventually returned to Sivas and Samsun.

The area around Arabkir, north of Harput, was ravaged with virulent fevers. Dr. Hubbell diverted major supplies there and checked the pestilence in five weeks. To do all this, the relief teams had risked every danger of an uncivilized world, faring and sharing with their beasts of burden, out of touch but never out of danger.

"They knew we had taken our lives in our hands to come to them with no thought of ourselves," Clara Barton wrote to explain their warm reception in the wilds of Turkey. The Red Cross, guided by American hands, was becoming a worldwide symbol of mercy and good will, admired by all who saw it in action.

Chapter 7
FRONTLINE ACTION AGAIN IN WAR-TORN CUBA

FEBRUARY 15, 1898, was a hard day for Clara Barton. In her seventy-seventh year, she was in poor health, far from home, and on an island ravaged by bitter insurrection. Having worked until late at night, she was about to go to bed. "The house had grown still; the noises on the street were dying away," she later wrote. At least she might hope for a good night's sleep.

"Suddenly the table shook," her account continues. "The great glass door opening on to the veranda, facing the sea, flew open; everything in the room was in motion or out of place —the deafening roar was of such a burst of thunder as perhaps one had never heard before, and off to the right, out over the bay, the air was filled with a blaze of light, and this in turn filled with black specks like huge specters flying in all directions."

The United States battleship *Maine* had just blown up in Havana harbor. Now a Spanish-American crisis over Cuba was inevitable.

The causes of that explosion have never been fully explained. But *Remember the Maine!* became a national war cry, and there was no turning back. On April 11, President William McKinley sent a message to Congress requesting authority "to secure the establishment of a stable Cuban government capable of maintaining order and observing its international obligations."

Eight days later Congress passed a resolution

The "Maine" passes Morro Castle as it enters Havana harbor. When it sank, 260 of the 350 seamen on it died.

directing and empowering the President "to use the entire land and naval forces of the United States, and to call into the actual service of the United States the militia of the several states, to such extent as may be necessary to carry these resolutions into effect." President McKinley proclaimed a Cuban blockade on April 22. The next day he called for 125,000 volunteers. On April 25, Congress announced that war with Spain had existed since April 21.

We were in it! And Clara Barton, not surprisingly, had been in it—on an errand of mercy—even before the *Maine* exploded. She had already visited the troubled Caribbean island, having gotten President McKinley's permission in January to go there and distribute food and medical supplies to the Cuban civilians who were being so grossly mistreated by the Spanish military forces during Cuba's struggle for liberation against Spain. American citizens were

ordered to leave Cuba, but Clara wanted to return with more food for the Cubans.

"They do not regard me as an American merely," she wrote to Admiral William T. Sampson on May 2, "but as the national representative of an international treaty to which they themselves are signatory and under which they act." The United States navy had orders to blockade Cuba. The admiral replied that "Under these circumstances it seems to me unwise to let a ship-load of such supplies be sent to the *reconcentrados* [the term for Cuban civilians put in concentration camps], for, in my opinion, they would be distributed to the Spanish army."

Miss Barton tried to get the decision reversed in Washington. Although the President and the Cabinet read her message "with moistened eyes" (according to her nephew and Washington spokesman, Stephen E. Barton), they did not reverse Admiral Sampson's order. The Red Cross steamer *State of Texas* would have to wait in Key West, Florida, until the military invasion took place.

"A splendid little war"

Impatient to get to work, Miss Barton turned her boundless energy to the problem of helping the hordes of Cuban refugees and the crews of impounded Cuban ships in Florida. She distributed supplies from the *State of Texas*, and arranged to have Red Cross chapters send additional material to fill up the empty spaces in the ship. Not until June 20 did the rescue vessel weigh anchor and head for the open Caribbean. How much had happened since as a volunteer nurse she rode supply wagons into Virginia almost 40 years earlier—and yet, how much was still basically the same!

The Rough Riders, under Colonel Leonard Wood and Lieutenant Colonel Theodore Roosevelt, had already gone ashore near Santiago. There was about them, and indeed the whole conflict, a romantic haze—a sort of excitement and enthusiasm that is often associated with Boy Scout outings. John Hay, soon to be Secretary of State, called it "a splendid little war."

The Spanish governor in Cuba, General Valeriano Weyler, was a picture-book villain, sparing neither gun nor whip, herding women and youngsters into concentration camps, defying mercy and justice.

The dream of *Cuba Libre* (a free Cuba) was enticing. Humanitarians saw the war as a blow for democracy and self-rule; politicians, as a chance to put the Monroe Doctrine to work and to get Spain out of the Western Hemisphere; journalists, as a sensational field for news; businessmen, as an opportunity to make sweet profits out of lucrative island sugar crops. All in all, it was as strikingly varied a combination of militant forces as one could imagine.

Clara Barton shared the general enthusiasm for America's "mission." She was genuinely concerned for the abused natives, and realistic about what could be done to help them. But when it came to Teddy Roosevelt, her heart melted. "It is the Rough Riders we go to," she wrote in her diary, "and the relief may also be rough, but it will be *ready*! A better body of helpers could scarcely be gotten together."

Later Clara described her encounter with "the gallant leader of the Rough Riders." Early one morning Colonel Roosevelt emerged from the bush, with a red bandanna handkerchief hanging from his broad-brimmed hat.

"I have some sick men with the regiment who refuse to leave it," the colonel said. "They need such delicacies as you have here, which I am ready to pay for out of my own pocket. Can I buy them from the Red Cross?"

Teddy Roosevelt (in light-colored uniform) and some of his Rough Riders are photographed in 1898.

"Not for a million dollars!" Dr. Joseph Gardner, one of Miss Barton's associates, replied.

"But my men need these things," the colonel said. "I think a good deal of my men. I am proud of them."

"And we know they are proud of you, Colonel. But we can't sell Red Cross supplies."

"Then how can I get them? I must have proper food for my sick men."

"Just ask for them, Colonel."

Teddy Roosevelt smiled broadly, and asked for malted milk, condensed milk, oatmeal, corn-meal, canned fruits, dried fruits, rice, tea, chocolate, and bully beef.

Dr. Gardner said the Red Cross had all these, and asked when to send them.

"Lend me a sack and I'll take them right along!" the colonel thundered. A few minutes later the future President was slinging the big sack over his shoulder, and striding off into the jungle. It was a bully performance.

"Send...anything"

But let no one think that the fighting during those blistering summer weeks was mere play-acting. General William R. Shafter, the 300-pound American commander, sent his troops against the Spanish on July 1 at the battles of San Juan Hill and El Caney. Medical preparations on the invaders' part were woefully inadequate.

Red Cross nurses worked with the surgeons for 30 hours straight, taking only short rest periods for food and coffee. On the second day of the San Juan battle, a messenger dashed up with an urgent message to Clara from General Shafter: "Send food, medicines, anything. Seize wagons from the front for transportation."

The Red Cross staff worked all night getting supplies from the holds of the *State of Texas* and floating them in on two dilapidated flatboat pontoons rigged up as a lighter. Such an amphibious operation, with poor equipment and inexperienced men, was extremely difficult; but it was accomplished with minimum loss. On shore Clara and three companions begged a ride on a wagon loaded with bales of hay. Four hours later they reached Shafter's headquarters.

Clara summed up conditions at the nearby hospital grounds as "indescribable." The level land with no drainage was covered with puddles and long, tangled grass. A few tattered small tents were up, sheltering men wounded in the

With its Red Cross flag, Clara's ship heads for Cuba.

A hospital tent provides some shelter for the wounded.

field. Flies were everywhere. Those who had come from the operating table, where their clothing had been removed for surgery—or as too wet, muddy, or bloody to be kept—were entirely nude, lying on the stubble grass with the tropical sun blazing down on them. For about 800 men, there was a pitiful field kitchen consisting merely of two kettles of soup and a small frying pan with some meat in it. The rain, which had alternated all day with the sun, increased. No wonder General Shafter's note had shown desperation.

The lady veteran of scores of battle scenes took over. Supplies were taken from the wagons, and tarpaulins put up to protect them. An adequate camp kitchen was built, a large fire started, and the cooking commenced. "I found the way into the bags and boxes of flour, salt, milk, and meal," Miss Barton wrote. "I had not thought ever to make gruel again over a campfire. I cannot say how far it carried me back in the lapse of time, or really where, or who I felt that I was. I did not seem to be me, and still I seemed to know how to do it."

There, and at other spots set aside for the wounded and dying, American visitors and correspondents saw sights they would never forget.

One of them, George Kennan, described a young Cuban, shot through the body, who was half crouching, half kneeling on the ground, his hands pressed to his loins. In deepest torment he could only repeat, over and over, "*O mi madre*" —oh, my mother. All around were buzzing flies, stench, splotches of half-dried blood, and groans.

Nearby, Kennan saw an American soldier naked to the waist. His whole right side, from the armpit to the hip, was purplish-blue from the bruising blow of a shell. Blood from a head wound completely covered his swollen face and closed his eyelids with a dull-red mask. On this there was a swarm of flies, which he was too weak to brush away, or in too much pain to notice.

Surgeons in the primitive hospitals did what they could. Every single abdominal operation attempted in the field resulted in death. None were performed after the first day, since the heat, dampness, and difficulty in giving patients proper care made recovery next to impossible.

"The day waned," Clara Barton wrote later of July 2. "Darkness came, and still the men were unsheltered, uncovered, naked, and wet— scarcely a groan, no word of complaint—no man

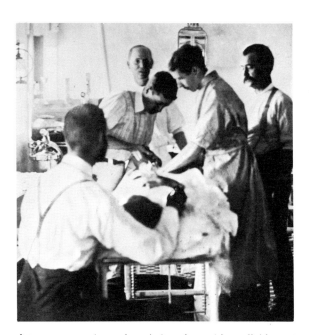
A surgeon operates, using what equipment is available.

A Cuban village thought to contain yellow fever is burned.

A volunteer nurse in Cuba, Miss Janet Jennings, wrote the following letter to a Chicago newspaper on July 8, 1898, about the work after San Juan Hill:

"Above hospital tents Red Cross flags are flying, and here is the real life—the suffering and heroism. . . . It all came at once—a quick blow—with little or no preparation to meet it. . . . It is not strange that surgeons were desperate and nurses distressed. The force of each was wholly inadequate. . . . The medical department of the army had failed absolutely to send hospital supplies. . . . The surgeons turned to the Red Cross ship 'State of Texas' for help, and the supplies originally intended for the starving Cubans were sent ashore for our wounded.

"Miss Barton had been urged and advised to wait until the army opened and made the way safe to land supplies for *reconcentrados* and refugees. But she had foreseen the situation . . . and followed the army as quickly as possible—to wait for the emergency, rather than have the emergency wait for her. . . . Four Red Cross sisters, trained nurses, assisted the surgeons. . . . Their knowledge of surgery, skill, and nerve were a revelation to the army surgeons. These young women, all under thirty, went from one operating table to another, and, whatever was the nature of the wound or complication, proved equal to the emergency. . . . A striking feature of the first day's engagement was the number of men wounded in the head, arms, and upper part of the body. . . .

"The courage that faces death on the battlefield or calmly awaits it in the hospital is not a courage of race or color. Two of the bravest men I ever saw were here, almost side by side on the little porch—Captain Mills and Private Clark—one white, the other black. They were wounded almost at the same time, and in the same way. The patient suffering and heroism of the black soldier was fully equal to that of the Anglo-Saxon. . . . They received precisely the same care; each fed like a child, for with their bandaged eyes they were as helpless as blind men. When the ice-pads were renewed on Captain Mills's eyes the same change was made on Private Clark's eyes. There was no difference in their beds or food. Neither uttered a word of complaint. . . .

"When told who his nearest neighbor was, Captain Mills expressed great sympathy for Private Clark and paid a high tribute to the bravery of the colored troops and their faithful performance of duty."

After a long sick leave, Private Clark returned to his regiment. Captain Mills became a general and was later superintendent of the United States Military Academy at West Point.

said he was not well treated. . . . It grew cold—for naked men bitter cold—before morning. We had no blankets, nothing to cover them, only the strips of cotton cloth."

Yellow fever; starvation

As horrible as were conditions for the Americans, they were matched or surpassed by those that the Cubans suffered. "I saw the survivors of the Johnstown Flood when the horror of that disaster was still plainly written in their eyes," wrote Richard Harding Davis in *Cuba in War Time.* "But they were in better plight than those fever-stricken, starving Cubans."

All around were blackened ruins, and buildings with no roofs, their broken windows staring pathetically like blind eyes. Both the Spaniards and the Cuban insurgents destroyed property and life indiscriminately. Thousands of people were herded into seaport towns where there were no houses, no food, and no doctors to care for them. Cholera, yellow fever, and smallpox spread unchecked.

The Cuban fighting from 1895 to America's entry in 1898 had reduced the island's population by at least one eighth, its wealth by two thirds. Children roamed homeless, living like wild animals. Many adults lay dying in homes and institutions. Food was scarce, prices were inflated, and agriculture was at a standstill.

Piles of mango skins, ashes, bones, rags, dung, and kitchen refuse filled town and city streets, attracting buzzards and rats. Water trickled into the open gutters from kitchens and cesspools of adjoining houses. Rotting organic matter stuck in many crevices. When the sea breeze died down at night, crowded areas took on a sickly, indescribable odor of corruption and decay. Into places like this, American troops must now move—and the Red Cross would, as in many other instances, move in with them.

When Clara Barton entered Siboney in late June, for example, the entire town was burned and a yellow fever colony was huddled on the outskirts. Because of this, army officials (fearing contamination) would not let her deliver food to starving Cubans at nearby Guantánamo.

Miss Barton (rear right) visits an orphanage in Cuba she set up for children who lost their parents in the war.

"Our supplies could not be received," Miss Barton wrote bitterly. "We took them away, leaving the starving to perish."

The fighting on land was brutal, bloody, and gruelling; but two of the engagements that especially caught the world's imagination were fought on water. The first of these occurred half a world away from Cuba. On May 1, American Commodore George Dewey sailed with his fleet into Manila Bay in the Spanish-held Philippines. Holding fire until he had the enemy well within range, the admiral turned calmly to his captain and said, "You may fire when you are ready, Gridley."

Gridley fired. Ten Spanish warships were destroyed, and all effective Spanish resistance anywhere in the Philippines was over.

The decisive New World battle against the Spanish navy came just outside Cuba's Santiago harbor. On the morning of July 3, the lookout on the flagship *New York* shouted: "Smoke in the harbor!" The Spaniards were preparing to slip past the American blockade.

Out steamed Admiral Cervera's flagship, the *Maria Teresa*, followed by the *Viscaya*, *Colon*, and *Oquendo*. Behind the four cruisers came Spanish destroyers. The big guns of the *Iowa*, *Texas*, *Indiana*, *Oregon*, *Brooklyn*, and *Gloucester* boomed out. The American war vessels ignored the shore batteries, and pursued the Spanish ships, massed together now less than a mile away. Flash followed flash. Within hours, every Spanish vessel had run aground, blown up, or surrendered to the triumphant Americans.

Food before pomp

After Santiago itself capitulated, a pilot from the *New York* came aboard the Red Cross relief ship, *State of Texas*, to take it into the harbor of the shattered city. Clara and her cohorts were soon gliding past the stone fort of Morro Castle with the wrecks of Spanish ships nearby. A Sabbath stillness covered the scene—the silence was oppressive as the vessel moved forward with hardly a ripple. The *State of Texas* was allowed to enter Santiago first, even ahead of the conquering warships, for food and drugs were more needed than pomp and military precedence.

"Is there any one here who will lead the Doxology?" Miss Barton asked as Santiago's spires came into view. One of her helpers, Enola Gardner, did so. Then the little group sang "My country! 'tis of thee," and anchored near one of the damaged wharfs.

The next day, as supplies were being carried ashore, Admiral Sampson and Admiral Schley came aboard and watched the cargo move briskly. "You need no directions from me," Admiral Sampson said, "but if any one troubles you let me know." There was no trouble, but there were thousands of empty mouths to feed.

The 30,000 residents of Santiago had fled to the little village of El Caney when the naval battle erupted. The first day 10,000 were summoned back, the second day 20,000 more. "In two days," Clara noted happily, "all were called back and fed." A general committee was formed. The city was districted into sections, and order was gradually restored. After four days of continuous work, the ship's cargo was discharged. And for five weeks, Clara stayed to aid in the salvaging of lives.

Clara had found Cuba a hard field, full of heartbreaking memories. She called it "such effort as one would never desire to repeat," and sensed that she would never be called upon to do so. Despite some testy moments, the cooperation between the government and what she liked to call "its supplemental handmaiden, the Red Cross," had been successful.

Any doubt of this fact was officially dispelled by President McKinley's December 6, 1898, message to Congress, in which he said: "It is a pleasure for me to mention in terms of cordial appreciation the timely and useful work of the American Red Cross, both in relief measures preparatory to the campaigns, in sanitary assistance at several of the camps of assemblage, and, later, under the able and experienced leadership of the president of the society, Miss Clara Barton, on the fields of battle and in the hospitals at the front in Cuba."

At the peace tables in Paris, Spain and the United States signed a treaty giving Cuba its freedom and the United States the Spanish possessions of Puerto Rico, Guam, and the Philippines. Spain received $20,000,000 for public property in the Philippines. The United States got "stepping stones" across the Pacific and a more direct opportunity to participate in Far Eastern affairs.

Despite strong objections of "anti-imperialists," who felt that America was overstepping its bounds, the United States also annexed the Hawaiian Islands that same year. The Senate approved the peace treaty by a margin of only one vote on February 6, 1899. This, in turn, gave the United States what President McKinley called "a high and sacred obligation to give protection for property and life, civil and religious freedom, and unselfish guidance in the paths of peace and prosperity."

Winning the Spanish-American War gave the nation effective control of the Caribbean Sea. But from the standpoint of its security, the United States needed something additional. In order to bring the battleship *Oregon* to the Cuban scene, that ship (stationed in San Francisco) had to go all the way around South America. A canal across the Isthmus of Panama would solve that problem. A few years later the United States was busily constructing such a canal, with Theodore Roosevelt, then President, photographed on the scene, at the controls of a giant steam shovel.

With that war won, and that canal built, America was, in fact as well as theory, a major world power, with imperial opportunities and obligations all over the globe. With such vistas, the Republic that had almost been rent asunder by civil war in the mid-nineteenth century strode confidently into the twentieth.

Miss Barton, her back to camera, plays ring-around-a-rosy with children at the Cuban orphanage she organized.

Chapter 8

BITTER ARGUMENTS, GALVESTON, AND GOODBYE

IF AMERICA came into a second springtime around 1900, Clara Barton moved into her Indian summer. Eighty years old now, she had helped shape American history through three generations. Her enduring monument was the American Red Cross. Born at her insistence, nourished by her fortitude, and matured through her service, it was, by 1900, a national institution. Clara knew it was time to pass control on to others—but like a person holding a charged electric wire, she seemed utterly unable to let go.

She had demanded more of herself than others could possibly give, so who could replace her? Those who tried to ease her out merely infuriated her. The last years of her presidency were the bitterest of her long life.

They were spent at a new house (named "Red Cross") at Glen Echo, Maryland, eight miles from the Capitol in Washington. Built from lumber originally used in the Johnstown Flood disaster, the house strove for utility, not beauty or appearances. Covered with Victorian embellishments and buttressed by two cone-shaped towers, "Red Cross" seemed to some more like a boat than a house.

From the central porch, which Miss Barton called her "main deck," one looked up to the "upper deck" and the "boat deck." On the interior walls hung Clara's diplomas and testimonials from all over the world. In deep closets were stored blankets, malted milk, canned goods, and emergency supplies—ready to be used at a minute's notice. "Red Cross" was not only a home, but a storehouse, a place of refuge for the needy, and an organization headquarters.

The heart of the home was Clara's sitting room at the south of the house, overlooking the Potomac canal. There she worked late at night, and made daily entries in her detailed diary. Close by was her narrow bed, a soldier's cot. Beside it on the table was a candle, pad of paper, and pencil. A lifelong victim of insomnia, she often lighted her candle, propped herself up in bed, and wrote for hours. Nevertheless she arose at five every morning to begin the daylight routine.

Even members of her own clan, such as her cousin and biographer William E. Barton, confessed to "a certain chill and sinking of heart" at the drab, camplike interior at Glen Echo. "But Clara gloried in those undecorated board walls as if they had been palatial," he wrote. She also took pride in being able to manage the vast house with its innumerable chores. As late as 1910, in her eighty-ninth year, she could write in her diary for February 11: "At night I fold the wash of Monday for ironing tomorrow. Up at six: commenced ironing and continued till all was done, at one o'clock. At night took the clothes from the frames and put them in place, and felt that for once one thing was done as it should be. 'Twas finished before leaving."

Clara's house at Glen Echo, on a wooded hillside above the Potomac, is 45 feet wide and 88 feet long, with 38 rooms and 36 closets. Its many mementoes of her include the landscape (below) she drew of Switzerland.

The Lone Eagle

On June 6, 1900, the American National Red Cross was incorporated by Congress, giving more power to the board and its executive committee. (The incorporations of 1881 and 1893 had been under the laws of the District of Columbia.) Having been centered on Clara Barton for 19 years, the focus of the Red Cross was to shift. At first she was willing to accept the new system. "The Board has full power," she wrote, "and will exercise it. I shall never come into a show of discord before the people of this country."

But that is just what she did do, as her outlook became in turn suspicious, critical, and finally hostile. Unhappily the quarrels sometimes sank to a matter of personalities, petty questions of privileges, and charges of misappropriated funds. Two "ways of life" were in

Miss Barton used this sturdy stone structure as her headquarters in Galveston after its 1900 disaster.

the United States: "Let me say then for your satisfaction and my own that after such announcement I must leave the country not to return, and I beg you to understand that I do this in good faith and patriotic loyalty. If disturbing elements will be more at rest and act in better harmony in my absence than with me present, it may be my duty to go."

Friends persuaded her to omit this passage from the letter she actually mailed to the President, and she did not leave the country. But she did continue to fight for what she wanted. On December 31, 1903, she wrote in her diary: "This ends this hard and terrible year. . . . All the scurril of the press has been poured over me like the filth of a sewer." Self-pity, which had marred the development and career of the young girl, overtook the old woman.

An event that had perceptibly helped to exhaust her was one of the most nightmarish and unsavory relief missions in Red Cross history. This occurred in 1900, when a huge tidal wave overwhelmed the coastline of Texas, leaving the city of Galveston in shambles. "The tale is all too dreadful to recall," Miss Barton wrote from the scene. "The uncoffined dead of the fifth part of a city lay there . . . lifeless bodies festering in the glaring heat of a September sun."

Bridges had been swept away, sandbars thrown up, all communication severed. For several days only one little ferryboat plied the course between Galveston and the mainland. Going on it, Miss Barton commented, was the kind of trip Dante might have imagined when he wrote of passing through Inferno. Corpses dumped by the bargeload into the Gulf of Mexico came floating back to menace the living. There was nothing to do but burn them. Against the night skies were flames from incinerators in which human bodies were "piled like cordwood, black and white together, irrespective of age, sex, or previous condition," Miss Barton reported. "That peculiar smell of burning flesh, so sickening at first, became horribly familiar within the next two months, when we lived in it and breathed it, day after day."

conflict. Clara was a Lone Eagle, eager to lead but unwilling to follow.

All her life she had answered only to herself, and now was too old to answer to others. Woe unto the young official or bureaucrat who stood in her way! "He needs someone to knock the wind out of his vain corporosity," she said of one critic. With unmatched prestige and legendary following, she could not be easily overruled. Even President Theodore Roosevelt (who did not maintain his high place in Miss Barton's esteem despite his high office) had trouble controlling her. So he informed her that he and his Cabinet could no longer be the Board of Consultation for the Red Cross.

Feeling that he had misconstrued her cause, she asked for an interview. When he refused it, she drafted a letter to President Roosevelt, on January 27, 1903, stating that she would leave

Exoneration and resignation

Exhausted and unnerved by the physical and mental strain she had undergone for months in this city of rotting flotsam and corpses, Clara Barton lost the control of herself that so long had enabled her to control and to lead the Red Cross. She was infuriated by official probings into what she had done, and by questions as to why her records were incomplete. She was so sick for a while after Galveston that she could not attend Red Cross board meetings—and the board acted without her. "I am disgusted with the way my life is being spent with this miserable 'Control' treadmill," she said. Mustering all her strength, she decided to fight back.

Her strategy was to have the Red Cross by-laws amended so as to increase the power of her office as president. These changes that she desired were put through over strong opposition at the December 9, 1902, annual meeting; Clara Barton was elected president for life. *That* would show everyone where the power lay!

But the strategy of an ailing old lady over-reached itself. Instead of quieting the disaffection, this action merely enlarged it. Even Clara soon admitted that her move was "perhaps not quite wise, in view of ugly remarks that may be made." This was all too true—for the amendments led President Roosevelt to notify Miss Barton that he could no longer serve as an officer of the Red Cross in the condition of unrest that had developed.

Early in 1904 a minority report from the Red Cross board embodying the protest against Clara Barton's presidency was introduced to Congress and printed as House Document 340. The ensuing congressional investigation was dropped when no real irregularities were found. Clara Barton had not kept the most perfect of accounts; the "Red Cross Park" in Indiana had been unfortunately managed; Clara had sometimes trusted unfit aides too far. But there was no slightest stain on her character. In this way Miss Barton was exonerated. She had inaugurated an expanded National Red Cross program in 1903, and on May 14, 1904, she presented her resignation. Soon afterwards the new officers

---

READING HEARTS AS OTHERS READ BOOKS

Mrs. Fannie B. Ward, one of the Red Cross workers who hurried to Galveston in 1900, wrote of it:

"We found ourselves stranded at Texas City, on the mainland opposite Galveston Island, waiting for transportation across the six-mile stretch of water. . . . The only method of communication between the mainland and Galveston was one poor little ferryboat, which had to feel her now dangerous way very cautiously, by daylight only.

"She had also to carry nearly a quarter of her capacity in soldiers to prevent her being swamped by waiting crowds of people, frantic to learn the fate of their friends on the island. Each trip to the mainland, the boat came filled with refugees from the city of doom . . . many with fearful bodily injuries inflicted by the storm, and others with deeper wounds of grief--mothers whose babies had been torn from their arms, children whose parents were missing, fathers whose entire families were lost—a dazed and tearless throng. . . .

"Of Texas City . . . nothing remained but heaps of bricks and splintered wood . . . not a standing habitation within miles. . . . What was our dismay when told that here we must remain at least 24 hours, for the return of the boat! However, we were better off, even physically, than most. . . .

"As a special courtesy to Miss Barton, the railway company left a car to shelter her during the night. . . . This was the shabbiest of day coaches, equipped with few 'modern conveniences.' But this was no time to think of comfort, on the threshold of so much misery; and who could murmur when the head of our little company set such a heroic example of patience. I have seen her in many trying situations, that threatened the fortitude and endurance of the strongest—and have yet to hear [a] complaint from her. . . .

"The most we could do for the grief-stricken survivors was to mitigate in some degree their bodily distress. . . . None of us will ever forget the grand-niece of an ex-President of the United States—a handsome and imposing woman of middle age. . . . She called one day at headquarters, and although she did not ask for aid, the truth came out in a heart-to-heart talk with Miss Barton that she had lost all in the storm and had not where to lay her head, nor food for the morrow; even the clothes she wore were not her own.

"Nobody living could put this lady on the pauper list, and none with a spark of human feeling could wish to wound her pride. Our honored president, who reads hearts as others do open books, clasped this unfortunate sister's hand—and left in it a bank note—I do not know of what denomination, but let us hope it was not a small one. The look of surprise and gratitude that flashed over that woman's face was worth going far to see."

After addressing the graduating class of nurses at Philadelphia's Blockley Hospital about 1902, Clara was photographed with the group. In 1903, as part of an enlarged program for the Red Cross, she introduced the earliest first aid kit to be used in the United States. With her own money, she distributed sample kits. She also had classes started in many cities and in September 1903 signed and mailed 40 first aid diplomas, writing: "These are the first diplomas that go out. It is like commencing anew after 20 years' work." One of her many posthumous honors is this stamp, issued in 1948, in which laurel leaves flank her portrait.

dropped her 1903 program on the grounds that it was too expensive.

Her resignation put the society under the board of control with a strong executive committee; the President of the United States would serve as nominal president. In December, 1904, Congress passed a new bill reincorporating the Red Cross, and bringing it more directly under government supervision.

Being Clara Barton, incapable of admitting defeat, the dynamic former president of one organization decided it was her duty to found another independent one. She called it the "National First Aid Association of America," incorporated under the laws of the District of Columbia, with general offices in Boston. She hoped there would be chapters in every American town and city; lecture courses; and first aid charts, reflecting "the highest standard of authority upon first aid methods of treatment known to the world."

Still strong enough to do some traveling and speaking, she told audiences that a "wise providence" had permitted her to leave the Red Cross so she might found the new group. She greeted crowds "from a heart tried as by fire," and ended with words that summed up her own life and work: "Your joy will be the joy of those you serve, and minister to; your reward the success you achieve. It is a search for the Holy Grail; in God's mercy may you find it."

Her plans and projects for first aid are another prime example of her pioneering vision—she lived long enough to see the Red Cross itself include just such work in its program, and smilingly noted the fact in her diary. She wished the Red Cross well in this endeavor too—and first aid has indeed thrived even beyond her dreams.

Sharp and vigorous

In her twilight years Clara Barton was fascinated by pseudoscience in the forms of astrology, horoscopes, seances, and palm readings. Her 1904 diary begins: "January 1. I may as well commence this day by saying that the astrologer Keys, of Chicago, told me in taking

RATHER INFORMAL ACCOUNTING METHODS

Miss Mabel T. Boardman, one of the Red Cross leaders whose objections led to the 1904 congressional investigation, and who for many years thereafter was a guiding light of the Red Cross, has written of Clara's rather informal accounts:

"After its first field of relief work in the Ohio and Mississippi floods, surprise was expressed that no statement as to the receipts and expenditures was made public. When the Pennsylvania State Committee for relief at Johnstown prepared a general report a request was made of the president of the Red Cross for an account of its receipts and expenditures, which was refused. . . .

"At the time of the Russian famine in 1892, when an appeal signed by Chief Justice Fuller and Cardinal Gibbons asked that contributions be sent to the Red Cross, no financial report was made. The Armenian Relief Committee, which raised funds for its relief work, obtained after delay a report of receipts and expenditures which it did not regard as satisfactory.

"In the many reports of the Cuban and Spanish War relief work there are on file the various committee treasurers' financial statements, but no statement of the funds received by the president of the Red Cross, who was also its treasurer. . . . After the Galveston disaster dissensions arose over certain expenditures that were not approved by all of the members of the Executive Board. . . .

"The 'Remonstrants,' as those were called who disapproved . . . laid certain facts before [the congressional investigating] committee, which decided to have a Treasury expert audit the books of the Society. . . . He found no records save one of the Russian famine, which showed some $45,000 received, but not more than $15,000 expended. Evidence was given before the committee showing that certain moneys contributed for this famine relief were deposited in western banks and a portion expended in the purchase and improvement of a farm, later called the 'Red Cross Park,' and which, in an officially printed circular of the Red Cross, was announced as a gift to the organization.

"The year following the Johnstown disaster, 1890, nearly $30,000 worth of land was purchased in Washington, the titles of which stood in the personal name of the president of the association. At the time that certain portions of this land were purchased, a balance of Red Cross funds for Johnstown relief that had been sent directly to a Washington bank was drawn upon for the amount paid. . . .

"Mr. Spencer Trask, who was chairman of the executive committee of the National Armenian Relief Committee . . . testified to the unsatisfactory organization of the Red Cross . . . and to the serious lack of business management."

my horoscope that he saw nothing dangerous to my life or limb until about 1904. The date is here. The fulfilment of the prophecy waits." She exulted when palm readers told that her lifeline was "almost endless," and she toyed with the idea of spiritualism.

If her thoughts sometimes wandered to other worlds, she kept clear and sharp contacts with this one too. During one illness, Miss Barton's physician told her nephew Stephen that she could live only a few hours. Overhearing the prediction, Clara called Stephen over and whispered to him: "I shall not die. Don't let them frighten you!" And she didn't.

Instead she lived on to take up tree-grafting and typewriting at eighty-nine; to rejoice in the progress of woman suffrage (which she thought would be a blessing, but a mixed blessing); to rediscover the power and profundity of thinkers like Socrates and Demosthenes, whom she began reading in English translations.

In 1910 she was vigorous enough to travel alone to Chicago, and go through a round of teas, dinners, and receptions. She spoke in churches and auditoriums, and shook hands daily with thousands of people. On the evening of the second Sunday of May, 1910, Clara spoke from the pulpit of the Congregational Church at Oak Park, Illinois. Its pastor was her cousin the Reverend William E. Barton. "I got my revenge [i.e., for his assigning her the normally less popular Sunday evening period] by having a larger audience than he did in the morning," she wrote.

Soon after that she stopped by Boston to check on the progress of her National First Aid Association. Once back at Glen Echo, she resumed work on her autobiography (which she never finished).

"Peace and goodwill"

On May 21, 1911, Clara Barton made her will. From that time on, she gradually relinquished life. Physicians found every bodily organ sound but her pulse slowly weakening. Still she was strong enough to send a cheerful word to the press on her ninetieth birthday—

"LOW FARE, HARD WORK"

Many people who knew Clara well during the last two decades of her life have testified that she changed very little in that time, and never grew truly old. The single best firsthand account of her person and personality by one who knew her closely in the last phase of her life is the detailed analysis by William E. Barton:

"At the beginning of her public career, Clara Barton was short of stature and slender as she was short. Her form rounded out in middle life, but she never exhibited any approach to stoutness. . . . The author measured her in her later years, and she was [then] exactly five feet tall without her shoes. Her carriage was erect, except for a slight stoop in the shoulders. . . . Her spine below the shoulders was carried to the end of her life as erect as in youth. As she stood or sat, she never had the bearing of an old person. When seated, she commonly kept her back well away from the back of the chair, depending upon nothing external to assist her in maintaining her erect bearing.

"She walked quietly, deliberately, and flat-footedly. She put her whole foot down at once. There was a certain firmness in her gait which indicated strength of character and resolute purpose. She did not dart or rush or drift or flutter; she walked, and her walk was of moderate speed and of marked decision. Her hair was brown, and in her younger days she had great wealth of it. . . . While there was less of it in her later years, it retained its fine texture. . . . Her eyes were brown, and in some lights appeared black. . . .

"Her features were regular. Her nose was prominent and straight. Her mouth was large, and very expressive. Her features were remarkably mobile. Her forehead was both high and wide, and . . . her chin was a very firm chin. . . . She said to the writer, 'Every true Barton knows how to possess an open mind and teachable disposition with a firmness that can be obstinate if necessary, and no one can be more obstinate than a Barton.' Obstinate she certainly could be, but she was reasonable to a marked degree. No one who saw her shut her mouth when she had made a decision could cherish any doubt of her tenacity of purpose. . . .

"She did not stare, but she had a habit of fixing her eyes upon an object or a person which did not put arrogance or pretense at ease. She could, on occasion, look through a person as if she discerned his inmost thoughts. But ordinarily her look into one's face was gentle and companionable and sympathetic. . . .

"She had no intention of growing old. She said to me that she did not see why people should be so curious about anybody's age; what did it matter? So far as she was concerned, there was no secret about it; but when people had learned the date of her birth, how could they know whether she was old or young? She did not greatly like to be asked for her 'latest photograph.' The photograph which she liked best, the one which she had framed and which the author has just as it stood on her desk, was the familiar Civil War portrait [*by Mathew Brady; see page 102*]. On December 30, 1910, she

Miss Barton in her eighties

wrote in her diary, concerning her friend, Julia Ward Howe, whose death she mourned and whose biography she had read with keen interest:

"'I notice a strife over the placing of Mrs. Howe's portrait in Fanueil Hall. The art committee object to it. . . . I wonder at the idea of people having their pictures taken after time and age have robbed them of all their characteristic features. I regard this as a mistake. I want the last picture of the friends I love to show them in their strength and at their best. Mrs. Howe's picture as now painted would have shocked even herself in strong middle life. Why not show the world the writer of the "Battle Hymn of the Republic" as she was when she wrote it? . . . I wish the art committee would

insist on a picture of Mrs. Howe at the age of forty years.'

"When Clara Barton was in her eighties, she often, as was her custom, would sit upon the floor, à la Turk, with her work spread around her. When her work was finished, she would rise, with the suppleness of a girl, without touching her hands to the floor. . . . She carried through life a pulse ten beats slower to the minute than that of an ordinary woman of her years, but her pulse beat steadily and reliably. A half-cup of coffee stimulated her almost to the point of intoxication, and a child's dose of medicine was too much for her.

"So simply did she live that when she died in her ninety-first year there was not a physical lesion, not a diseased organ in her body. Her physician, who for 30 years had been her almost daily companion, Dr. Julian B. Hubbell, declared that, barring accident, or some acute attack, such as that which actually caused her death, she could easily have lived to be one hundred years of age and still not have been technically old.

"There was nothing about her voice or manner that suggested a really aged person. Senility was further removed from her at ninety than from most women at sixty. A California octogenarian was compiling a book of personal testimonies by aged people and wrote to her asking for the secret of her long life. Her answer was contained in four words, 'Low fare, hard work.' If to this she had added anything, it should have been a self-forgetful purpose, a serene spirit, and an upholding faith. . . .

"A lady who was about to undertake a long journey by rail spoke to Clara Barton of her dread of it. Railway travel, she said, always tired her out and made her sick. Miss Barton said, 'Travel rests me.' Her friend asked her how she managed it. She replied: 'I delegate to the conductor and the engineer the full responsibility for the running of the train. . . . When I think of something I want to remember, I jot it down; when I see something that interests me, I make note of it. I read as long as I enjoy reading; and when I grow tired of that, I close my eyes and rest, and let the train go on.' . . .

"In her young womanhood . . . she was loved and did not return the affection of the men who loved her. . . . There were times when Clara Barton felt keenly her isolation. But, in 1911, she recorded in her diary some of the domestic trials of her friends, and added, 'After all, *Aloneness* is not the worst thing in the world.' "

Christmas Day, 1911: "Please deliver for me a message of peace and goodwill to all the world for Christmas. I am feeling much better today, and have every hope of spending a pleasant and joyful Christmas."

She longed for the rebirth of spring: for sticky green buds, chirping bluejays, views of the Virginia hills alive again with leaves. Whenever possible, she liked to sit on one of her porches: straight, keen-eyed, self-contained. And what memories the tiny old lady could conjure up! They stretched back to rural New England in the days before Jackson came to power; came forward in time to the second decade of the twentieth century; and out in space to the far corners of the world.

The young girl who had tried to command attention in a small country schoolhouse had matured to be applauded by kings and emperors. In her own land she had known, and dealt effectively with, every President from Abraham Lincoln to Theodore Roosevelt. But the center of her life had not been political conferences. It was in the field, on the sharp-cutting edge of disaster, that she was at her best.

Not even to mention her work as a teacher, on Civil War battlefields, or in the Franco-Prussian War, but just to name her major operations for the Red Cross is to conjure up stirring chapters of the American epic: the 1881 Michigan forest fires, the perennial Ohio and Mississippi river floods, the 1883 tornadoes, the Texas famine of 1885, the 1886 Charleston earthquake, the Illinois cyclone and Florida yellow fever epidemic of 1888, and the Johnstown Flood of 1889. Along with hurricanes and tidal waves, there was the 1898 Cuban *reconcentrado* relief, followed by the Spanish-American War.

The new century brought the 1900 Galveston storm, the 1904 Pennsylvania typhoid fever epidemic, as well as an annual parade of natural disasters. Wherever and whenever they came, the Red Cross followed. And as long as she was physically able, Clara Barton was on hand herself to direct operations.

In addition to her frequent personal gifts to the Red Cross, no one knew how many individuals she had helped anonymously. Her whole life had been a matter of giving to others.

Francis Atwater, who visited Miss Barton on her ninetieth birthday, reported on her sharp memory and vision. "She knew she had but a short time to live," he noted, "but if her strength would not permit of further usefulness, she was ready to go."

In the spring of 1912 an old enemy, double pneumonia, closed in. Always a fighter, Clara lingered on, counting the days to Palm Sunday and Easter. To her doctors' amazement, she made Easter. Towards the end of the struggle, her mind reverted to Civil War days.

On April 10, 1912, two days before the end, she opened her eyes and said: "I saw death as it is on the battlefield. . . . I saw the surgeons coming, too much needed by all to give special attention to any one. Once again I stood by them and witnessed those soldiers bearing their soldier pains, limbs being sawed off without opiates being taken, or even a bed to lie on. I crept around once more, trying to give them at least a drink of water to cool their parched lips, and I heard them at last speak of mothers and wives and sweethearts, but never a murmur or complaint."

Clara Barton's last request came quietly and quickly two days later, soon after sunrise; it was quietly and quickly obeyed. "Let me go, let me go!" she gasped. Then she died.

FINAL ECHO OF A FAVORITE POEM

She often pasted into scrapbooks verses that struck her fancy for any reason from comic to tragic. In Europe during the Franco-Prussian War Clara so pasted some stanzas by the Reverend John Purves in memory of John Pitt, who died at Woodbury, Connecticut, on August 1, 1870. The poem was entitled "The Old Soldier":

"Loose me, loose me, and let me go,"
  The old man faintly cried,
His face was pale, but all aglow
  For Christ unseen was by his side.

. . . . .

"Loose me," he cried, "and let me go!"

PICTURE PORTFOLIO

Miss Barton's portrait, by Charles Stevenson, includes wounded soldiers, a Civil War cannon, and a Red Cross.

YOUNG TEACHER

TEACHING in a one-room, multi-grade
school required a juggler's dexterity, a
train dispatcher's sense of timing, and a general's skill at command—along with knowledge and the ability to impart it. Six-year-
olds away from home for the first time,
rugged farm boys bigger than the teacher,
and children of all the sizes in between had to
be kept busy learning, simultaneously but
separately, the whole range of the curricu-
lum, from ABC's to ancient history. In Clara
Barton's first schoolroom, which probably
resembled Winslow Homer's "The Country
School" (above), the seventeen-year-old
teacher with the merry brown eyes and the
thick brown ringlets quickly demonstrated
all these skills. At recess, she won her pupils'
affection by joining such games as Homer
depicted in "Snap the Whip" (left.)

Clara Barton at eighteen, in an 1840 photograph

LADY OF STYLE

CLARA BARTON'S poise and daring in the saddle tested the horsemanship and courage of Civil War cavalry officers with whom she galloped in the dawn at Hilton Head along roads festooned with Spanish moss. Like the genteel creature in the fashion plate at the left, she always sat sidesaddle (though she considered the practice rather absurd). Switching from a bay to a jet-black mount, she had difficulty deciding whether to wear navy blue or black. Like most women of her time, she followed the styles in *Godey's Lady's Book* (below and lower left). She made her own first straw bonnet out of green rye stalks that she cut, bleached, and braided herself. In her mid-fifties, when the photograph at the upper right was taken, she looked quite spendid in a green velvet gown with a long plush train.

ANGEL IN BATTLE

CLARA BARTON'S courage and compassion impelled her, at almost forty, out of the obscurity of the Patent Office and into a fame that was to become worldwide. Both virtues shone on her face when Mathew B. Brady, the great Civil War photographer, took the picture at the right. She demonstrated them again and again on the battlefield, along with indomitable determination, a fine capacity for organization, and a flair for publicizing real needs which brought her proper support.

Early in the war, she wrote her father: "We are ready to bind the wounds or bear them of our own, if necessary. I shall remain here while anyone remains, and do whatever comes to my hand. I may be compelled to *face* danger, but *never fear it,* and while our soldiers can stand and *fight,* I can stand and feed and nurse them." At Culpeper a captain said, "Miss Barton, this is a rough and unseemly position for you, a woman, to occupy." She replied, "Is it not as rough and unseemly for these pain-racked men?" She bathed and staunched the wounds of everyone — Northern and Southern, white and Negro — and was especially moved by the

Clara's voluntary tasks included writing for the sick and wounded in the manner depicted in Eastman Johnson's "Letter Home." She nursed the casualties of the 22nd Colored Infantry in her hospital after their charge near Petersburg (top right), but often worked in the primitive conditions of such battlefields as Marye's Heights, shown in photograph at lower right.

heroism of such troops as the 22nd Colored Infantry.

To her own heroism she gave no thought, though often death was mere inches away. At Antietam (below), where she was the only woman present: "A man lying upon the ground asked for a drink; I stopped to give it, and having raised him with my right hand, was holding him. Just at this moment a bullet

Armory Square Hospital in Washington (above) was one of the hospitals where Clara busied herself when not at the front. Its ill-equipped wards were jammed with men like the casualties of Richmond (below).

sped . . . between us, tearing a hole in my sleeve and found its way into his body. He fell back dead."

Untrained medically, she operated in the field with a penknife to remove a ball from a soldier's cheek. Later, in an improvised hospital in a barn, she administered chloroform for the surgeons, who were using green corn leaves for dressings. No supplies would be brought up until the battle was over, lest they would fall into enemy hands. But in the wagon in which she had come, Clara had linen for bandages and other medical necessities.

"That was the point I always tried to make," she wrote later, "to bridge that chasm and succor the wounded until the medical aid and supplies should come up. I could run the risk; it made no difference to anyone if I

ANGEL IN BATTLE

were shot or taken prisoner."

Clara did "whatever comes to my hand," from scrounging and cooking food for hungry troops to charming or browbeating a senator powerful enough to make the army improve its care of the wounded. But the front needed her often. At Fredericksburg, despite the peril and the bitter cold, she unhesitatingly sped through heavy fire to the side of a doctor who wrote her a bloodstained note: "Come to me. Your place is here." For her, even Appomattox did not end the war or what she deemed her duty. In unmarked mass graves lay thousands of Northern soldiers who had died in Andersonville's prison camp. Aided by a prisoner who had kept a secret record, Clara established Andersonville Cemetery and provided decent burial.

Nervous, inexperienced reserves about to go into action at Fredericksburg (below) saw amputations at a crude field hospital while covered wagons went off to gather more casualties. Primitive treatment made fatalities high, and Homer's "A Trooper Meditating Beside a Grave" (right) was both tragically real and a common sight. At Andersonville (lower right), the dead were buried by their fellows.

PUBLIÉ PAR LE COMITÉ INTERNATIONAL
à l'occasion du 25ème Anniversaire de la fondation de la Croix-Rouge.
1863 ✦ GENÈVE ✦ 1888

DÉVELOPPEMENT DE L'OEUVRE DE LA CROIX-ROUGE

The Red Cross "Tree" at left celebrates its first 25 years of development dating from the original conference of 1863. The Geneva Convention itself was signed in 1864; the left branch of the tree shows the shields of the nations that ratified it and the year they did so, from France in 1864 onward. Thanks to Clara's persistence, Etats-Unis (United States) appears opposite 1882.

Among Clara's numerous medals are the nine at right. The top row, left to right, shows a decoration of 1896 from the Prince of Jerusalem, Cyprus and Armenia for her labors after the Armenian massacres; an 1898 Spanish award for relief work in Cuba; a Red Cross insignia commemorating her Armenian labors above a German-awarded brooch; a gold and diamond medal of 1886 from the Grand Army and its Women's Relief Corps. The lower row shows a silver medal conferred in 1885 by the Empress of Germany; a Turkish decoration bestowed in 1897 by Sultan Abdul Hamid with a request that if America wanted to give his country further help, it should send "missionaries of humanity" like Miss Barton; an 1892 award from the Belgian Red Cross; a medal from the Cuban Red Cross, inscribed "Inter inimicos charitas" (Charity among foes).

WORK AND REWARDS ABROAD

THE doctor's orders that sent Clara to Europe in the summer of 1869 specified "three years of absolute rest." She sampled several spots, from Britain to Corsica, hoping they would prove restful. Eventually she chose Geneva. There she first encountered the Red Cross. Several of its high officials visited her to ask why America had never ratified the Geneva Convention. Many other countries had done so—as indicated on the "family tree" at left. Geneva was not ideal for convalescence. Clara said, "Switzerland has pretty days and her snow-capped peaks are grand, but even in a July evening they remind you of their power to bite and pierce."

Before her first year of "rest" was completed, the Franco-Prussian War broke out in 1870. Red Cross representatives urgently asked her to help. Thus began a career abroad that earned for her more foreign medals than any American, perhaps, had then received.

Clara had planned to work for the French. But when the war's developments put her within the German lines, she nursed their wounded just as gladly. In German-held Strasbourg, her fine work brought two notable decorations (below, right). The uppermost is the Gold Cross of Remembrance conferred by the Grand Duke and Duchess of Baden. The lower medal is the Iron Cross of Germany, bestowed by Emperor Wilhelm I. Both were awarded in "recognition of Miss Barton's services for humanity."

Clara entered Strasbourg two days after

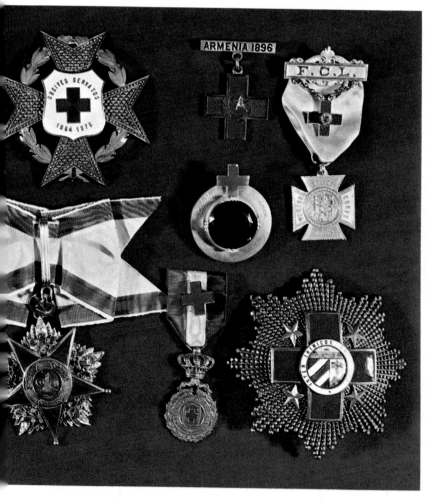

WORK AND REWARDS ABROAD

its fall. She found it a smoking shambles, with women comprising half the wounded (left) as a result of the furious siege (below). Speedily, she organized emergency relief. Then, having fed the hungry and established a workshop, she headed for Metz to succor its "famishing, fevered population," returned to Strasbourg for a winter of toil, and finally delivered 40,000 garments and other supplies to chaos-ridden Paris. In time of crisis, her strength never failed. After this crisis, she became half-blind, and in 1872 sought recovery in Italy. Pope Piux IX received her—a Protestant—in Rome, and she strolled beneath the Arch of Titus, which had been painted (right) the year before by her fellow-American G. P. A. Healy. But her longest and gravest nervous and physical collapse was now about to commence.

THE COLLEAGUE OF PRESIDENTS

C LARA BARTON heard Abraham Lincoln deliver his first inaugural address "in a loud fine voice" and received "a delightful invitation" to the inaugural ball, though a cold kept her from attending. Thereafter, as long as she lived, her work was to associate her with Presidents and the White House. In the last month of his life Lincoln wrote for her the note that was to expedite her search for missing soldiers.

When Lincoln was shot, General Grant considered her so important that he posted sentries at her door for three days, in fear that the assassins would make her a target, too. Though she and Grant admired one another, Grant as President annoyed her by his failure to commit America to the Geneva Convention. She got Grant's successor, Rutherford B. Hayes, to request the State Department to hear her arguments — but thought Mrs. Hayes shrewder than her husband.

Clara campaigned for James A. Garfield— who considered her a comrade and once said, "We fought together in the Civil War, didn't we?" His support made ratification of the Geneva Convention possible. Chester A. Arthur signed the treaty even before the Senate voted for it, telling Clara she need not "expect him to go back on humanity."

Grover Cleveland and Benjamin Harrison both made her chief U.S. delegate to International Red Cross conferences—as Theodore Roosevelt also did when she was almost eighty-one. Before the Spanish-American War broke out, Clara conferred with President McKinley about her taking an active personal part in relief operations in Cuba. Though she was seventy-six, he assured her: "You need no looking after. You will stand without hitching." And when her freewheeling methods of operation evoked criticism once the war began, McKinley stood loyally by her. After his assassination, she wrote: "Our good President has gone. All the world mourns with us . . . What it is to have lived through the slaying of three Presidents."

James A. Garfield
Chester A. Arthur
Grover Cleveland

Benjamin Harrison
William McKinley
Theodore Roosevelt

ANGEL OF HELP AMID DISASTER

THE Geneva Convention had not yet been ratified and the first chapter of the American Red Cross was only a few days old when monumental tragedy befell four counties of Michigan in 1881. Feeding on drought-stricken forests and farms—and whipped on by a gale—flames consumed 1,800 square miles. While thousands of human beings fled, or tried to flee, the fire's heat boiled trout in their streams, downed birds seeking refuge over Lake Huron, and put orchards miles away into untimely bloom.

Clara was among the first to organize re-lief, dispatching Red Cross field workers with money and supplies. Years before, Henri Dunant, founder of the International Red Cross, had suggested that "these societies ... could also render great service at the time of epidemics, floods, great fires and other ... catastrophes." Miss Barton transformed Dunant's vision into reality, inspiring Red Cross groups everywhere to peacetime rescue missions of every conceivable kind. This earned her a distinction rarely conferred by modern humanity on its contemporaries: inclusion in stained-glass windows, such as the one below.

An engraving (left) done at the time for "Frank Leslie's Illustrated Newspaper" vividly records "the moment of despair" during Michigan's terrible fire of 1881.

A stained-glass panel in St. Thomas' Episcopal Church on New York City's Fifth Avenue shows Clara wearing a Red Cross badge as she starts her nursing task.

The Johnstown Flood of 1889 was one of the most dreadful disasters in America's history. In it, 20 million tons of water broke through the 90-foot-thick Lake Conemaugh dam and, in a towering wall, raced 18 miles in 17 minutes down a narrow valley to obliterate the city of Johnstown, Pennsylvania.

The deluge swept with it men, women, children, animals, houses, giant trees, and bridges. It demolished a large brick roundhouse, and tossed one of its 85-ton locomotives almost a mile. It battered swimmers to death against tree trunks. Compounding the horror, it piled the debris, tangled with household goods and miles of wire from ruined mills, against the piers of a bridge in Johnstown. The debris caught fire, apparently from a stove in a still floating house. Survivors of the waters burned to death in the flaming trap.

This "Harper's Weekly" drawing records a "Scene at the Bridge." Soon afterwards, Clara and a Red Cross field force arrived to help. Miss Barton stayed five months, and won even warmer acclaim than she usually received.

BACK TO BATTLE

IN Cuba on a relief mission even before the Spanish-American War broke out, Clara was also there throughout the fighting and stayed on after the Spanish surrender. Charles Johnson Post, a soldier in the war, depicted her there in the watercolor at the left—never before reproduced.

Post described the picture thus: "Incident depicted in Santiago, Cuba after the surrender. The artist was on special detail in that city unloading regimental stores and was taking delirious yellow fever cases to the army hospital . . . Miss Barton is describing the canned 'beef stew' to Capt. Malcolm A. Rafferty, 71st Infantry. The artist remembers that Miss Barton was telling the captain that the beef stew was made from the left-over after beef-extract was made and was no more than sawdust as food."

The two other Post paintings on these pages show scenes of a kind with which Clara Barton, then a seventy-six-year-old veteran of three wars, was all too familiar.

During the fighting at San Juan Creek (left), the mortally wounded Colonel Charles A. Wikoff is carried off in a chair. Other American casualties (above) take shelter behind the San Juan blockhouse, while their comrades continue to fire at the white-clad Spanish.

HER LAST HOME

CLARA, like most people whose work demands travel afar, was a homebody. She always wanted a place where she could be both mistress and generous hostess. In 1897, at seventy-five, she built a refuge in sylvan Glen Echo, Maryland, handy to Washington. It was hardly the cozy cottage of which many homebodies dream. Long, huge, and multichimneyed, it bizarrely blended the Victorian externally with steamboat Gothic internally (left). Her neighbors whispered, "She is more for comfort than looks."

It served not only as a home but also as Red Cross headquarters and warehouse. Into it she packed vast quantities of emergency *materiel*, the trophies of a lifetime, including the bust below, and—reluctantly—a piano. (No music lover, she found piano playing distracting to her work, but finally yielded for her guests' sake.) On her acre and a half she kept horses, chickens, and pets. In March of 1905 she wrote: "All winter I was home in Glen Echo because it was home."

A portrait of Tommy (the steak-for-breakfast cat), painted by Clara's friend Antoinette Margot, hangs above the Glen Echo piano to which Miss Barton long refused houseroom. The pansy carved from amethyst (left) and the settee below were gifts from the Grand Duchess of Baden. The side table came from "the people of France" as thanks for Clara's efforts to relieve their misery in the Franco-Prussian War.

Have you answered the Red Cross Christmas Roll Call?

World War I posters like that at the left, showing a beautiful girl in a nurse's uniform, helped the Red Cross raise $120 million for its wartime relief work. Some posters, with a girl holding a wounded soldier's head in her lap, à la Clara Barton, gave a misleading idea of the organization's function, and were abandoned. But the Red Cross did perform vital work among American and Allied troops and with displaced civilians. The French marshal Pétain declared that the war had no more brilliant chapter "than that of the American Red Cross in France. Nothing has contributed more to the morale of my soldiers." General Pershing felt likewise.

HER LEGACY

WHEN Clara Barton died in 1912, the Detroit *Free Press*, in one of the thousands of tributes paid to her, said: "She was perhaps the most perfect incarnation of mercy the modern world has known. She became the founder of the most significant and wide-spread philanthropic movement of the age, a movement that already has become an intrinsic part of world civilization."

In two world wars, in countless peacetime disasters, and in everyday life, the American Red Cross has carried on and even broadened Clara Barton's work, albeit not always in a style she would have approved. Before America entered World War I, the Red Cross already had ambulance units in service overseas. When America entered, the Red Cross dispatched six base hospitals to serve with the British, established low-priced canteens to feed French soldiers and civilian refugees, like those in the background of the painting at right, and, along with other volunteer organizations, provided a variety of services for the American fighting man typified by Harvey Dunn's "The Sentry" at top right.

On the home front, local units all over America rolled bandages and used 15 million pounds of wool to knit sweaters (of somewhat debatable need) for the troops. The Red Cross also ran lunchrooms, showers, information centers, and first-aid stations for

HER LEGACY

soldiers in transit, and assisted soldiers' needy families. In World War I, too, the Junior Red Cross (poster at top right), which aids fund and membership drives (and by 1964 boasted 18 million members), was organized.

Between wars, the Red Cross distinguished itself in the Barton tradition in such disasters as the great Mississippi flood in 1927 (above), which took 250 lives, destroyed

9,000 homes, and damaged 88,000 more in 170 counties from Illinois to Louisiana. The Red Cross rushed in 383 nurses to cope with the emergency. One of them is at work above in John Steuart Curry's painting "Hoover and the Flood," which records a visit by the then Secretary of Commerce to a Red Cross relief post. When the flood subsided, the Red Cross financed the destitute in rebuilding their homes, and provided seed, livestock,

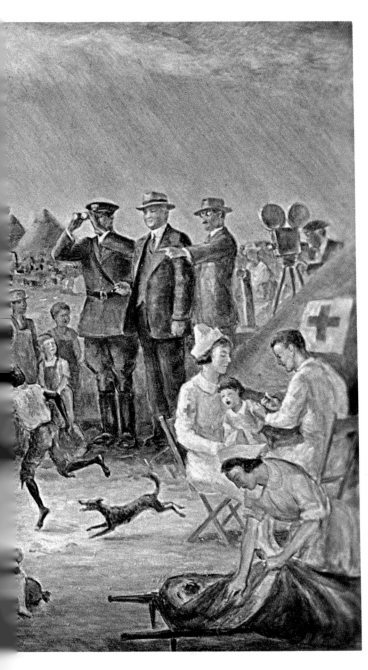

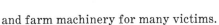

and farm machinery for many victims.

The between-wars years also saw the Red Cross experiment with a number of special services, not all of them successful. Among those that survived were the Gray Ladies (who help in hospitals) and the courses in disease prevention and care of the sick at home (described in middle poster at the right). These courses supplemented the training in first aid to the injured that Clara pi-

HER LEGACY

It's time to roll up *your* sleeve...

GIVE BLOOD NOW

CALL YOUR RED CROSS TODAY!

NATIONAL BLOOD PROGRAM

oneered—and virtually forced the Red Cross to adopt.

In World War II, one major Red Cross contribution was to organize a national blood program. Blood from some six million volunteers was converted into plasma to treat the wounded (right). "Six thousand units of plasma went ashore at Tarawa," one naval surgeon reported from the Pacific, "and 4,000 of them came back in the veins of wounded Marines. At least half of the seriously wounded owe their lives to plasma." Clara Barton would have approved the program—but not the fact that in many collecting centers the blood of white and Negro donors was segregated.

As in World War I, the Red Cross sent field workers overseas to cheer the troops as they boarded trains from transports (lower left) and to follow them as they went into combat at such places as Omaha Beach (shown in Aaron Bohrod's painting below). Not all Red Cross workers were Clara Bartons. Many devoted far more time to officers than they did to enlisted men. But the soldier

HER LEGACY

with troubles at home could generally get assistance from the Red Cross, and the soldier recuperating from combat could find some relaxation at a Red Cross club.

An organization of human beings, the Red Cross has its human failings. But in one single recent year, it conducted more than 400 major relief operations following floods, storms, earthquakes, fires, and like disasters. The hand in John Falter's poster below is indeed outstretched in emergencies. The Red Cross probably comes as close as any organization of human beings could to keeping alive the vision of Clara Barton.

JOHN FALTER

...aying that I possess the entire

...very one of them, For the Officers,

...

HER OWN WORDS

...ear unreasonable, and must be

...tiently, ~~though~~ sorrowfully, but;

... I beg to subscribe myself

...est Respect –

Yours d.

Clara H. Barton

HER EARLY CHILDHOOD

Clara Barton was almost two and a half years old, with "the lilacs in bloom" at the farm where her family lived. There came "the first moment of my life that I remember":

■ I must have been enjoying a ramble by myself in the grass-green dooryard, with the broad hand-hewn doorstep and the traditional lilacs on either side. Suddenly my resounding cries brought the whole family to the door in alarm. My wailing took the form of a complaint expressed with my best linguistic ability: "Baby los' 'im—pitty bird—baby los' 'im—baby mos' caught him—pitty bird—baby mos' caught 'im."

At length they succeeded in inducing me to listen to a question, "But where did it go, Baby?" Among my heart-breaking sobs I pointed to a small round hole under the doorstep. The terrified scream of my mother remained in my memory forever more. Her baby had "mos' caught" a snake.

Her second recollection came when she was about four, and was left in the charge of her older brother David, during which period "some outside duty called him from the house":

■ A sudden thunder shower came up; massive rifts of clouds rolled up in the east, and the lightning darted among them like blazing fires. The thunder gave them language and my terrified imagination endowed them with life. Among the animals of the farm was a huge old ram, that doubtless upon some occasion had taught me to respect him, and of which I had a mortal fear. My terrors transformed those rising, rolling clouds into a whole heaven full of angry rams, marching down upon me. Again my screams alarmed, and the poor brother, conscience stricken that he had left his charge, rushed breathless in, to find me on the floor in hysterics. . . .

In these later years I have observed that writers . . . in a friendly desire to compliment me, have been wont to dwell upon my courage, representing me as personally devoid of fear, not even knowing the feeling. However correct that may have become, it is evident I was not constructed that way, as in the earlier years of my life I remember nothing but fear.

When Miss Barton was born, on Christmas Day in 1821, her sisters Dorothy and Sally were seventeen and ten, respectively, and her brothers Stephen and David were fifteen and thirteen. "I had no playmates, but in effect six fathers and mothers," she subsequently observed. At eighty-six, Miss Barton wrote of some of the results:

■ I have no knowledge of ever learning to read, or of a time that I did not do my own story reading. The other studies followed very early. . . . Stephen was a noted mathematician. He inducted me into the mystery of figures. Multiplication, division, subtraction, halves, quarters and wholes, soon ceased to be a mystery, and no toy equalled my little slate. . . . My father was a lover of horses, and one of the first in the vicinity to introduce blooded stock. He had large lands, for New England. He raised his own colts. . . . Of my brother, David, to say that he was fond of horses describes nothing. . . . He was the Buffalo Bill of the surrounding country, and . . . it was his delight to take me, a little girl five years old, to the field, seize a couple of these beautiful young creatures, broken only to the halter and bit, and gathering the reins of both bridles firmly in hand, throw me upon the back of one colt, spring upon the other himself, and catching me by one foot, and bidding me "cling fast to the mane," gallop away over field and fen, in and out among the other colts in wild glee like ourselves. . . . This was my riding school. I never had any other, but it served me well. . . . Sometimes, in later years, when I found myself suddenly on a strange horse in a trooper's saddle, flying for life or liberty in front of pursuit, I blessed the baby lessons of the wild gallops among the beautiful colts.

Stephen Barton, Clara's father, was born in 1774 and enlisted at nineteen for the young nation's Indian wars in what later became the states of Ohio and Michigan. He served three years and became a noncommissioned officer (he was subsequently known as "Captain" but the rank was honorary). He may well have been the greatest single force in shaping his daughter's destiny. She listened endlessly, and with utter fascination, to his military tales, and later testified that she "early learned that next to Heaven, our highest duty was to love and serve our country and honor and support its laws." Here are some of her recollections of her father:

■ When a little child upon his knee he told me that as he lay helpless in the tangled marshes of Michigan the muddy water oozed up from the track of an officer's horse and saved him from death by thirst. And that a mouthful of a lean dog that had followed the march saved him from starvation. When he told me how the feathered arrow quivered in the

A chilly Christmas Day in 1821 saw the birth of Clarissa Harlowe Barton in this sturdy frame house near North Oxford in Massachusetts. The house still stands. Clara was born in the ground-floor room whose windows are at left rear in the photograph. Her father and mother, then respectively forty-seven and thirty-eight, are here seen as much older people— photography was not a practical invention until Miss Barton was well into her teens.

flesh and the tomahawk swung over the white man's head, he told me also with tears of honest pride of the great and beautiful country that had sprung up from those wild scenes of suffering and danger. How he loved those new States for which he gave the strength of his youth! . . .

His soldier habits and tastes never left him. Those were also strong political days—Andrew Jackson days—and very naturally my father became my instructor in military and political lore. I listened breathlessly to his war stories. Illustrations were called for, and we made battles and fought them. Every shade of military etiquette was regarded. Generals, colonels, captains and sergeants were given their proper place and rank. So with the political world; the president, cabinet and leading officers of the government were learned by heart, and nothing gratified the keen humor of my father more than the parrot-like readiness with which I lisped these often difficult names, and the accuracy with which I repeated them upon request.

My elder sister, with a teacher's intuition, mistrusting that my ideas on these points might be somewhat vague, confidentially drew from me one day my impressions in regard to the personages whose names I handled so glibly, and to the amusement of the family found that I had no conception of their being men like other men, but had invested them with miraculous size and importance. I thought the president might be as large as the meeting house, and the vice-president perhaps the size of the school house.

And yet I am not going to say that even this instruction had never any value for me. When later, I . . . was suddenly thrust into the mysteries of war, and had to find and take my place and part in it, I . . . never addressed a colonel as captain, got my cavalry on foot, or mounted my infantry.

From her mother, Sarah Stone Barton, who had married at seventeen, Clara learned the arts of cooking and homemaking, which were as useful to her as nursing on Civil War battlefields and later in Red Cross missions to disaster areas. Clara never forgot the "mother's watchfulness that neither toil could obscure, nor mirth relax." As for Mrs. Barton's part in her education, Clara recalled:

■ My mother, like the sensible woman that she was, seeming to conclude that there were plenty of instructors without her, attempted very little, but rather regarded the whole thing as a sort of mental conglomeration, and looked on with a kind of amused curiosity to see what they would make of it. Indeed, I heard her remark many years after, that I came out with a more level head than she would have thought possible.

By the time she was eight, Clara was so shy that her parents decided to send her to a nearby boarding school run by Colonel Richard Stone:

■ I was what is known as a bashful child, timid in the presence of other persons, a condition of things found impossible to correct at home. In the hope of overcoming this . . . it was decided to throw me among strangers.

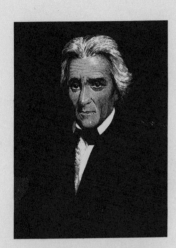

Thanks to her father's tutelage, Miss Barton's first political idol was Andrew Jackson, who served as President from the time she was seven until she was fifteen. During his two terms, Jackson displayed the powers of the presidential office more fully than any man who had held the post before him.

... There were probably 150 pupils daily in the ample school rooms, of which I was perhaps the youngest, except the colonel's own children. My studies were chosen with great care. I remember among them, ancient history with charts. . . . I found difficulty both in learning the proper names and in pronouncing them, as I had not quite outgrown my lisp. One day I had studied very hard on the Ancient Kings of Egypt, and thought I had everything perfect, and when the pupil above me failed to give the name of a reigning king, I answered very promptly that it was "Potlomy" [Ptolemy—tol-e-mee]. The colonel checked with a glance the rising laugh of the older members of the class, and told me, very gently, that the P was silent in that word. I had, however, seen it all, and was so overcome by mortification for my mistake, and gratitude for the kindness of my teacher, that I burst into tears and was permitted to leave the room.

I am not sure that I was really homesick, but the days seemed very long, especially Sundays. . . . My studies gave me no trouble, but I grew very tired, felt hungry all the time but dared not eat, grew thin and pale. . . . Finally at the end of the term a consultation was held between the colonel, my father and our beloved family physician . . . and it was decided to take me home until a little older, and wiser, I could hope. My timid sensitiveness must have given great annoyance to my friends. If I ever could have gotten entirely over it, it would have given far less annoyance and trouble to myself all through life.

To this day, I would rather stand behind the lines of artillery at Antietam, or cross the pontoon bridge under fire at Fredericksburg, than to be expected to preside at a public meeting.

SOMETHING OF A TOMBOY

The next effort to cure Clara's shyness was more successful; she even became something of a tomboy. Since her older brothers and sisters were now all living elsewhere, the Bartons set up house with a widowed relative and five children fairly near Clara's age.

■ From never having had any playmates, I now found myself one of a very lively body of six—three boys and three girls. . . . The territorial domain comprised something over 300 acres. We knew it all. . . . Old "Rocky Hills," so high, so steep, so thickly wooded that a horse would never attempt them, were no strangers. We knew where the best chestnuts were. We explored the "Devil's Den," in spite of the tradition that it was an abode for the tempter of Eve. The "French River" . . . spread itself out in lazy rest, after its rugged leaps, as it meandered through the broad, beautiful meadows. . . . A long hewn log or pole stretched across it in its narrowest, deepest place. . . . It could not have been more than 14 inches wide, and swayed and teetered from the moment the foot touched till it left it. The waters glided still and black beneath. It was there as a convenience for the working men in crossing from one field to another; but if

A hero of the American Revolution, General "Mad Anthony" Wayne commanded the troops with whom Clara's father served in the 1790's along the young nation's western frontier. Wayne's most spectacular victory came in the battle of Fallen Timbers, close to what is now Toledo, which routed the Indians and decisively ended their power in that area.

ever a week day passed that we did not cross it several times, we knew one duty had been neglected. The only saw-mill in that section of the town was a part of my father's possessions. The great up-and-down saw cut its angry way through the primeval forest giants from morning till night, and . . . the long saw-carriage ran far out over the raceway at the rear end. How were we to withstand the temptation of riding out over the rushing mill stream 20 feet below, and then coming quickly in as the sawn log was drawn back for another cut? Hurt? Never one of us. Killed? We knew not such a thing could be.

Nor was her brother David, who had taught her to ride when she was only five, neglecting "his rule of practical teaching":

■ I recall vividly the half impatient frown on his fine face when he would see me do an awkward thing, however trivial. He detested false motions; wanted the thing done rightly the first time. If I started to go somewhere, go, and not turn back; if to do something, do it. I must throw a ball or a stone with an under swing like a boy and not a girl, and must make it go where I sent it, and not fall at my feet and foolishly laugh at it. If I would drive a nail, strike it fairly on the head every time, and not split the board. If I would draw a screw, turn it right the first time. I must tie a square knot that would hold, and not tie my horse with a slip noose and leave him to choke himself. These were little things, still a part of the instructions not to be undervalued. In the rather practical life which has sometimes fallen

More heavily wooded in Miss Barton's girlhood than it is now, New England at that period was dotted with sawmills such as the one owned by her father, where she so enjoyed risking life and limb. This old engraving shows similar sawmills along the Penobscot River in Maine.

to me, I have wondered if they were not among the most useful, and if that handsome frown were not one of my best lessons.

At this period in the nineteenth century, phrenology—which attempted to analyze a person's character, and to foretell his aptitudes, by carefully examining the "bumps" on his head—was widely popular. In 1836 a leading phrenologist, L. N. Fowler, spent some weeks as a guest in the Barton home while he gave two courses of lectures in nearby Massachusetts towns. It was then that Fowler gave his advice about Clara to Mrs. Barton. Clara later felt this was the turning point in her life. And toward the end of her life, when she was asked what book had influenced her most, she wrote:

■ That which interests most, may influence little. Most books interest in a greater or less degree, and possibly have a temporary influence. . . . If it had read "interested" rather than "influenced," I should have made a wide range—"The Fables of Aesop," "Pilgrim's Progress," "Arabian Nights" . . . and mainly the mass of choice old English classics—for who can select? . . . How grateful I am for all this; and to these writers immortal! How they have sweetened life! But they really changed no course, formed no character, opened no doors, "influenced" nothing. . . .

I have explained my own [childhood] nature—timid, sensitive, bashful to awkwardness—and that at this period of a dozen years or so I chanced to make the acquaintance of L. N. Fowler, of the "Fowler Brothers". . . . Mr. Fowler placed in my hands their well-written book and brochures on Phrenology, "The Science of the Mind." This carried me to another class of writers, Spurzheim, and Combe—"The Constitution of Man." These became my exemplars and "Know thyself" became my text and my study. A long life has passed, and so have they, but their influence has remained. In every walk of life it has gone with me. It has enabled me to better comprehend the seeming mysteries about me; the course of those with whom I had to deal, or come in contact. . . . It has enriched my field of charitable judgment; enlarged my powers of forgiveness, made those things plain that would have been obscure to me, [or] easy that would have been hard, and sometimes made possible to endure, without complaint, that which might otherwise have proved unendurable. "Know thyself" has taught me in any great crisis to put myself under my own feet; bury enmity, cast ambition to the winds, ignore complaint, despise retaliation, and stand erect in the consciousness of those higher qualities that made for the good of human kind, even though we may not clearly see the way.

Phrenology has long since been discarded as a science, but in its time it did provide some clues to the human mind and spirit that were otherwise not readily available. A phrenologist such as Fowler was not necessarily a quack but—according to his best lights—taught those who listened to him how to search out their own full potentialities. Phrenology had that effect on Clara. She corresponded with Fowler, and nearly 40 years later met him again in England, when she happily wrote:

■ He is the same gentle, kind man he used to be so many years ago, gray now, stoops a little, but is wise, considerate and gentlemanly as he always must be. Mrs. Fowler is younger . . . and full of life and vivacity. She is a charming lady. They have three daughters. Of all the people in England I was most glad to find them. Mr. Fowler recollected father, and gave me directly his traits of character, even to minute characteristics. . . . They have done a most excellent work in England. Have been worth so much to the middle classes, given instruction as they would never get from other sources.

A TEACHER AT SEVENTEEN

The Bartons all basically agreed with Fowler that, "as soon as her age will permit," Clara should have "a school to teach." On May 5, 1839, when she was less than five months past her seventeenth birthday, she received her first teacher's certificate. Soon after, she "put down her skirts and put up her hair" to make herself seem as adult as possible, and began to teach near North Oxford, Massachusetts, at District School Number 9.

■ How well I remember the preparations—the efforts to look larger and older, the examination by the learned committee of one clergyman, one lawyer and one justice of the peace; the certificate with "excellent" added at the close; the bright May morning over the dewy, grassy road to the schoolhouse, neither large nor new, and not a pupil in sight.

On entering, I found my little school of 40 pupils all seated according to their own selection, quietly waiting with folded hands. Bright, rosy-cheeked boys and girls from four to thirteen, with the exception of four lads, as tall and nearly as old as myself. These four boys naturally looked a little curiously at me, as if forming an opinion of how best to dispose of me, as rumor had it that on the preceding summer, not being *en rapport* with the young lady teacher, they had excluded her from the building and taken possession themselves. . . .

Never having observed how schools were opened, I was compelled, as one would say, to "blaze my own way". . . . I said they might take their Testaments and turn to the Sermon on the Mount. . . . This opened the way for remarks upon the meaning of what they had read. I found them more ready to express themselves than I had expected, which was helpful to me as well. I asked them what they supposed the Saviour meant by saying that they must love their enemies and do good to them that hated and misused them? This was a hard question, and they hesitated, until at length a little bright-eyed girl [named Emily] with great earnestness replied: "I think He meant that you must be good to everybody, and mustn't quarrel nor make nobody feel bad, and I'm going to try." An ominous smile crept over the rather hard faces of my four lads, but my response was so prompt, and my approval so hearty, that it disappeared and they listened attentively but ventured no remarks. . . .

On the second or third day an accident on their outside field of rough play called me to them. They had been playing unfairly and dangerously and needed teaching, even to play well. I must have thought they required object lessons, for almost imperceptibly either to them or to myself, I joined in the game and was playing with them. My four lads soon perceived that I was no stranger to their sports or their tricks; that my early education had not been neglected, and that they were not the first boys I had seen. . . . [After that] no courtesy within their knowledge was neglected.

Their example was sufficient for the entire school. I have seen no finer type of boys. They were faithful to me in their boyhood, and in their manhood faithful to their country. Their blood crimsoned its hardest fields, and the little bright-eyed girl with the good resolve, has made her whole life a blessing to others, and still lives to follow the teaching given her. Little Emily has "made nobody feel bad."

My school was continued beyond the customary length of time, and its only hard feature was our parting. . . . When, in accordance with the then custom at town meetings, the grades of the schools were named and No. 9 stood first for discipline, I thought it the greatest injustice, and remonstrated, affirming that there had been no discipline, that not one scholar had ever been disciplined. Child that I was, I did not know that the surest test of discipline is its absence.

If the published school report, so misunderstood by me, had given me displeasure, it had also given me a local reputation, quite as unexpected. I soon found myself the recipient of numerous invitations to teach in the nearby towns, especially such schools as required the "discipline" so largely accredited to, and so little deserved by, me.

From 1839 to 1850, Clara taught various schools in Massachusetts, then decided she needed more schooling herself. "I broke away from my long shackles," she said, went to the Clinton Liberal Institute in upstate New York, and "got all the Institute could give me." Though she was only twenty-nine, she complained that her old pupils were "already calling me Aunt Clara!" Later she wrote of this period:

■ Hard, tiresome years were these, with no advancement for me. Some, I hoped, for others. Little children grew to be large, and mainly "well behaved." Boys grew to manhood, and continued faithfully in their work, or went out and entered into business, seeking other vocations. A few girls became teachers, but more continued at their looms or set up housekeeping for themselves, but whatever sphere opened to them, they were all mine, second only to the claims and interests of the real mother. And so they have remained. Scattered over the world, some near, some far, I have been their confidant, standing at their nuptials if possible, lent my name to their babies, followed their fortunes. . . .

Most of this transpired during years in which I should have been in school myself, using time and opportunities for my own advancement which could not be replaced. This thought grew irresistibly upon me, until I decided that I must withdraw and find a school, the object of which should be to teach *me* something . . . . I decided upon the "Liberal Institute," of Clinton, New York. . . . Clinton was also the seat of Hamilton College. The sisters and relatives of the students of Hamilton contributed largely to the personnel of the Institute . . . .

The difficulty to be met lay mainly in the assignment of studies. The prescribed number was a cruel limit. I was there for study. I required no rudiments, and wanted no allowance for waste time; I would use it all; and diffidently I made this fact known at the head, asking one more and one more study until the limit was stretched out of all reasonable proportions. I recall, with amusement, the last evening when I entered with my request. The teachers were assembled in the parlor and, divining my errand, as I had never any other, Miss Barker broke into a merry laugh—with "Miss Barton, we have a few studies left; you had better take what there are, and we will say nothing about it." This broke the ice, and the line. I could only join in the laugh, and after this studied what I would, and "nothing was said."

I would by no means be understood as crediting myself with superior scholarship. There were doubtless far more advanced scholars there than I, but I had a drilled rudimentary knowledge which they had never had, and I had the habit of study, with a burning anxiety to make the most of lost time. So true it is that we value our privileges only when we have lost them.

Clara became so absorbed in the courses she was taking and the new friends she had made at Clinton that she did not even go home during her school vacations. One lifelong friend she made there was Samuel Ramsey, then studying theology at Hamilton, who by some was thought to be the great romance of her life. In 1876 she scotched this rumor, asking her lawyer to

Miss Barton entered the "Female Department" of the Clinton Institute in December 1850; the building in which she so eagerly enrolled herself in every possible course of study is here depicted in a print of 1852.

collect a loan she had previously made to Ramsey and stating: *"My pecuniary affairs and my heart affairs are not at all mixed. My observation has not been favorable to such a course of procedure."* Meanwhile she was working hard on compositions and exercise papers, some of which, including one on *"Prejudice,"* survive:

■ Prejudice, if not altogether invincible, is perhaps the most difficult of all errors to be eradicated from the human mind; for by disguising itself under the respectable name of firmness it passes through the world without censure, whereas open vice would receive a severe reprimand.

One of the most intimate friends Clara made at Clinton was Mary Norton of Hightstown, New Jersey, who persuaded her "to try the Cedar Swamp School, near Hightstown, and be her companion at home." With characteristic energy and initiative, she even called on the parents of her pupils—"If I'm to help them, I must know them as they are." But the year 1852 saw one of the gray periods of melancholy and self-doubt that were to descend on her so often during the rest of her long life. The woman destined to found a great organization thought she was "badly organized" and grew weary of her very existence. Here are some entries in her diary from the early months of 1852:

■ Cannot see much in these days worth living for; cannot but think it will be a quiet resting-place when all these cares and vexations and anxieties are over, and I no longer give or take offense. I . . . have grown weary of life at an age when other people are enjoying it most. . . .

I have found it extremely hard to restrain the tears today, and would have given almost anything to have been alone and undisturbed. I have seldom felt more friendless, and I believe I ever feel enough so. I see less and less in the world to live for, and in spite of all my resolution and reason and moral courage and every thing else, I grow weary and impatient. I know it is wicked and perhaps foolish, but I cannot help it. There is not a living thing but would be just as well off without me. . . . True, I laugh and joke, but could weep that very moment, and be the happier for it. . . .

Grow dull and I fear selfish in my feelings and care less what is going on. . . . The whole world is false. This brings me to my old inquiry again, what is the use of living in it? I can see no possible satisfaction or benefit arising from my life; others may from theirs. . . .

I am thinking tonight of the future, and what my next move must be. Wish I had some one to advise me, or that I could speak to some one of it. Had ever one poor girl so many strange, wild thoughts, and no one to listen or share one of them, or even to realize that my head contains one idea beyond the present foolish moment? . . . I will not allow myself any more such grumbling! I know it is wicked. But how can I make myself happy and contented under such circumstances as I am ever placed in? . . .

Have kept no journal for a month or more. Had nothing to note, but some things are registered where they will never be effaced in my lifetime.

HER FIRST AMBITIOUS PROJECT

However gloomy her inner thoughts were, Clara completed the school term successfully—and even took a trip to Trenton, where she purchased herself a silk dress! And throughout these months she managed to keep a cheerful countenance toward those around her—as she frequently did during the next 60 years.

By now she had evolved a pattern of incessantly searching for the deepest possible meaning of her every thought and purpose so as to "know herself." But, now and later, this seldom stopped her from constructive and even daring action. Soon after the gloom-filled diary entries above, she optimistically embarked—over strong objections from others—on her most ambitious project to date. She began teaching school on a fee basis in Bordentown, near Hightstown, and then insisted on starting a free public school.

■ But the boys! I found them on all sides of me. Every street corner had little knots of them idle, listless, as if to say, what shall one do, when one has nothing to do? I sought every inconspicuous occasion to stop and talk with them. . . . They spoke of their banishment or absence from school with far less of bravado or boasting than would have been expected, under the circumstances, and often with regret.

"Lady, there is no school for us," answered a bright-faced lad of fourteen, as he rested his foot on the edge of a little park fountain where I had accosted him. "We would be glad to go if there was one." I had listened to such as this long enough, and, without returning to my hotel, I sought Mr. Suydam, as chairman of the School Committee, and asked for an interview . . . . I made known my desire to open a public school in Bordentown, teaching it myself.

Surprise, discouragement, resistance, and sympathy were all pictured on his manly face. He was troubled for terms in which to express the mental conflict, but in snatches something like this. These boys were renegades, many of them more fit for the penitentiary than school—a woman could do nothing with them. They wouldn't go to school if they had the chance, and the parents would never send them to a "pauper school." I would have the respectable sentiment of the entire community against me; I could never endure the . . . disgrace that I should meet. . . . A strong man would quail and give way under what he would be compelled to meet, and what could a woman—a young woman, and a stranger —do?

He spoke very kindly and appreciatingly of the intention, acknowledging the necessity, and commending the nature of the effort, but it was ill-timed, and had best be at once abandoned as impracticable.

With this honest effort, and wiping the perspiration from his forehead, he rested. After a moment's quiet and seeing that he did not resume, I said with a respect, which I most sincerely felt, "Thank you, Mr. Suydam, shall I speak?" "Certainly, Miss Barton," and with a little appreciative laugh, "I will try to be as good a listener as you have been."

I thanked him again for the evident sincerity of his objections, assuring him that I believed them drawn entirely in my interest, and his earnest desire to save me from what seemed to him an impossible undertaking, with only failure and humiliation as sure and logical results. A few of these I would like to answer, and . . . told him plainly that I was, and had been for years, a teacher of the public schools of New England. That was my profession and that, if entered in the long and honored competitive list of such, I did not suppose that in either capacity, experience, or success I would stand at the foot.

I had studied the character of these boys, and had intense pity for, but no fear of them. As for exclusion from society, I had not sought society, and could easily dispense with it, if they so willed; I was not here for that. As for reputation, I had brought with me all I needed, and that of a character that a bit of village gossip could not affect. With all respect for the prejudices of the people, I should try not to increase them. My only desire was to open and teach a school in Bordentown, to which its outcast children could go and be taught; and I would emphasize that desire by adding that I wished no salary.

I would open and teach such a school without remuneration, but my effort must have the majesty of the law, and the power vested in its offices behind it or it could not stand. If I secured a building and proceeded to open a school, it would be only one more private school like the score they already had; that the School Board, as officers of the law, with accepted rights and duties, must so far connect themselves with the effort as to provide quarters, the necessary furnishings, and to give due and respectable notice of the same among the people. In fact, it must stand as by their order, leaving the work and results to me.

I was not there for necessity. Fortunately I needed nothing of them—neither as an adventuress. I had no personal ambitions to serve, but as an

Joseph Bonaparte, Napoleon's brother and the ex-king of Spain, settled in Bordentown after Waterloo and developed an impressive estate there at the junction of Crosswicks Creek and the Delaware River. He died before Miss Barton came to Bordentown, but the estate was still there and she took long and enjoyable walks among its "miles of shrubs and flowers."

"I believe you are a maker of shoes"?

"Yes Miss Barton, I am".

"And you think you understand your profession"?

"I ought to, I am one of the oldest shoe-makers in Bordentown".

"M——— if I were to come into your shop to-morrow, with the purpose of directing and changing your methods of work in accordance with my ideas of proper shoe making, and you followed my suggestions, do you think you would make a better shoe than you do to-day"?

With the first smile I had seen on a face since they entered, he replied

"No Miss Barton, I do not."

"Neither do I M———. I think it would trouble you to find either a buyer or a wearer for that shoe."

Addressing the next—

"M——— I believe you are a tin smith and

This page from Miss Barton's diary, written shortly after she settled in Bordentown, tells of her struggles to persuade doubting adults in the community that she should open and teach a public school there. She left out the names of her opponents, a shoemaker and a tinsmith, but the excerpt shows her skill at persuading such opponents that she would not presume to teach them their trades so long as they did not try to tell her how to handle a school.

observer of unwelcome conditions, and, as I thought, harmful as well, to try, so far as possible, the power of a good, wise, beneficent, and established state law, as against the force of ignorance, blind prejudice, and the tyranny of an obsolete, outlived public opinion. I desired to see them both fairly placed upon their merits before an intelligent community, leaving the results to the winner. If the law, after trial, were not acceptable, or of use to the people serving their best interest, abolish or change it—if it were, enforce and sustain it. . . .

When he spoke again, it was to ask if I desired my proposition to be laid before the School Board? I surely did. He would speak with the gentlemen this evening, and call a meeting for tomorrow. Our interview had consumed two hours, and we parted better friends than we commenced.

The following afternoon, to my surprise, I was most courteously invited to sit with the School Board in its deliberations, and I made the acquaintance of two more, plain, honest-minded gentlemen. The subject was fairly discussed, but with great misgivings, a kind of tender sympathy running through it all.

At length Mr. Suydam arose, and, addressing his colleagues, said,

"Gentlemen, we feel alike, I am sure, regarding the hazardous nature of this experiment and its probable results, but situated as we are, officers of a law which we are sworn to obey and enforce, can we legally decline to accede to this proposition, which is in every respect within the law. From your expressed opinions of last evening, I believe we agree on this point, and I put the vote."

It was a unanimous yea, with the decision that the old closed school-house be refitted, and a school commenced.

This public school in Bordentown was a notable success from the start. Soon its quarters had to be greatly enlarged, and Clara had to hire assistant teachers, including her old friend Fannie Childs from North Oxford.

■ One bright morning I found myself there with six bright renegade boys (not a girl could be trusted with me) and the public school was commenced. I understood boys, and school teaching was my trade. We got on well and at the end of 12 months I stood in a new schoolhouse building, which had been built for me at the cost of $4,000 and my six pupils had grown to 600, a bright, loving, faithful phalanx among whom never a punishment had been administered.

Prejudice, as Clara had noted in her composition at Clinton, is difficult to eradicate. Even though she had been solely responsible for the success of the Bordentown school, it was almost impossible in 1853 for anyone to think that such a large institution should be headed by a woman. Against the desire of her pupils, a male principal was appointed for the new school building, with Clara simply kept in second place. For a few months she tried to continue, but the man made it as difficult as possible for her, and she had a nervous collapse with a complete failure of her voice. She wrote:

■ I could bear the ingratitude, but not the pettiness and jealousy of this principal, under whom I am set to work.

CRUCIAL YEARS IN WASHINGTON

So, early in 1854, she and Fannie Childs left Bordentown for Washington, D.C. Clara Barton was just thirty-two and, though she did not then realize it, would never teach school again. The first phase of her long and brilliant professional career was over. For the rest of her life the nation's capital would be her headquarters at crucial intervals. Meanwhile, Washington's warm climate soon restored her health, and the "copperplate style" of handwriting she had perfected as a young woman enabled her to join the Patent Office as one of the Federal government's first female clerks.

■ After some rest I was requested by the commissioner of patents to take charge of a confidential desk, with which he had found difficulty. The secrecy of its papers had not been carefully guarded. I accepted and thus became as I believe the first woman who entered a public office in the Departments of Washington in her own name drawing the salary over her own signature. I was placed equal with the male clerks at $1,400 per year. This called for some criticism and no little denunciation on the part of those who foresaw dangerous precedents.

In those days, long before the Civil Service Act of 1882 had given government employees some security of tenure, many of them lost their jobs whenever there was a change of administration, since the incoming officials used the "spoils system" to reward their political supporters with Federal jobs. Clara, a Republican, knew she might well have to yield her post in the Patent Office after the Democrat James Buchanan was elected President in 1856. At first her sheer efficiency saved her; in September 1857, she was able to write her brother David's wife, Julia:

■ I dare not ask you to excuse me for neglecting you so badly, but still I have a kind of indefinable hope that you will do so, when you remember how busy I am and that this is summer with its long weary days and short sleepy nights; and then the *"skeeters!"* Just as soon as you try to write a letter in the evening to anybody, they must come in flocks to "stick their bills".... My health [she had had malaria in the spring when she visited Massachusetts] is much better than when I was home.... The yellow has almost gone off of my forehead, else it has grown yellow all alike; but it looks *better*, let it be which way it may; it isn't so spotted....

I have written "a heap" since my return; let me see, seven large volumes, the size of ledgers, I have read all through and collected and transferred something off of every page—3,500 pages of dry lawyer writing is something to wade through in three months; and out of them I have filled a *great* volume almost as heavy as I can lift.... I begin to feel that my Washington life is drawing to a close, and I think of it without regret, not that I have not prized it, not that it has not on the whole been a great blessing to me. I realize all this, but if I could tell you in detail all I have gone through along with it, you would agree with me that it had not been *all* sunshine. I look back upon it as a weary pilgrimage which it was necessary for me to accomplish ... so it has been a sturdy battle, hard-fought, and I trust well won.

Near the end of 1857, she did finally lose her post to the "spoils system," and returned home for her first long period of rest in many years. By this time her elder brother, Stephen, had moved to North Carolina and established mills there, and in June 1858, her second brother, David, was visiting him there. David had written back to his wife, Julia, worrying whether he had left her and Clara "destitute" in his absence, and the tone of Clara's letter in reply shows that she was getting some amusement from her complete change of pace as she relaxed in the Massachusetts countryside.

James Buchanan of Pennsylvania, who won the White House for the Democrats in 1856, is here shown, in a campaign picture, eating a solitary meal and thus emphasizing the fact that he is the only President who never married. He had previously been an effective diplomat for the United States, but proved a rather ineffective President. The years immediately preceding the Civil War were far too troubled to let him succeed with his own rule: "Be quiet and discreet and say nothing."

■ Julia has discoursed considerably upon the propriety of that word "destitute" which you made use of. She says you left her with a barrel and a half of flour, a barrel and a half of crackers, a good new milch cow, fish, ham, dried beef, a barrel of pork, four good hogs in the pen, a field of early potatoes just coming on, a good garden, plenty of fowls, a good grain crop in and a man to take care of them, a good team, 30 cords of wood at the door and a horse and chaise to ride where she pleased. This she thinks is one of the last specimens of destitution. Can scarcely sleep at night through fear of immediate want—and besides we have not mentioned the crab apples. I shouldn't wonder if we have 50 bushels of them. . . . I forgot to tell you about the garden. Julia has hoed it all over, set out the cabbage plants, waters them almost every day; they are looking finely. . . .

Don't trouble to send long letters, it is hot work to write. Sleep all you can, don't drink ice water, be careful about grease, don't expose yourself to damp evenings or mornings if too misty, or you will get the chills. Love to Stephen. Will he ever write me, I wonder?

In the 1850's the movement for woman suffrage had barely begun, and few women in the United States were actively informed in political matters or taking a vigorous part in political discussions. Clara was one of the striking exceptions. In Washington she often attended major congressional debates and made it her business to understand the thinking of many key officials; in Massachusetts, New Jersey, and wherever else she chanced to live, she closely followed political developments.

In the tense years leading up to the Civil War, she took a moderate view and hoped both North and South would manage to do the same. Thus when, after John Brown's raid at Harpers Ferry in 1859, a Northerner who (like her brother Stephen) had been living in the Carolinas was driven away by his Southern neighbors, she wrote Stephen as follows:

In a matching picture to that of Buchanan in the 1856 campaign, the Republican candidate, John C. Frémont, is shown happily married to his wife, Jessie. She was a notable help to Frémont in many ways, not least in greatly improving the literary style of his accounts of the pioneering explorations in the Far West that made him known as "the Pathfinder." Miss Barton ardently supported Frémont in 1856 and on September 28 wrote her brother Stephen, "The Democrats are looking pale in this quarter."

■ I have not seen Mr. Seaver since his return, and regret exceedingly that there should have been any necessity for such a termination to his residence in the South. I should not have supposed that he would have felt it his *duty* to uphold such a cause as "Harpers Ferry," and if he *did* not, it is a pity he had the misfortune to make it appear so. . . . Occasionally we hear that *you* have been or will be requested to leave—this *amuses me*. It would be singular, indeed, if in all this time your Southern friends had not learned *you* well enough to tolerate you. It will be a strange pass when the *Bartons* get fanatical, and cannot abide by and support the laws they live under, and mind their own business closely enough to remain anywhere they may chance to be.

I am grieved and ashamed of the course which our Northern people have taken relative to the John Brown affair. . . . Their gatherings and speechifyings serve the purpose of a few loud-mouthed, foaming, eloquent fanatics. . . . It matters little to them that every rounded sentence which falls from their chiseled lips, every burst of eloquence which "brings down the house," drives home one more rivet in slavery's chain; if slavery be an evil, they are but helping it on. . . .

Nature, and cause and effect, are, I suppose, much the same the world over, and if our Southern neighbors clasp their rights all the firmer, when assailed, and plant the foot of resistance toe to toe with the foot of aggression, it is not for *us* to complain of it; what differently should we ourselves do? That slavery be an evil I am neither going to affirm nor deny . . . but allowing the affirmative in its most exaggerated form, could it *possibly* be equal to the pitiful scene of confusion, distrust and national paralysis before and around us at the present hour, with the prospect of all the impending danger threatening our vast Republic? Men talk flippantly of dissolving the Union. This may happen, but in my humble opinion never till our very horses gallop in human blood.

But I must hold or I shall get to writing politics to you, and you might tell me, as old Mr. Perry of New Jersey did Elder Lampson when he advised him to leave off drinking whiskey and join the Temperance Society. After listening long and patiently until the Elder has finished his remarks, he looked up very, very benignly, with "Well, Elder, your opinions are very good, and probably worth as much to yourself as anybody."

THE COMING OF THE CIVIL WAR

In 1860 Clara was recalled to a government clerkship in Washington; the Patent Office files had become badly confused, and her previous service had shown her skill at straightening them out. She was there when Lincoln was

Three of John Brown's sons took part in his raid at Harpers Ferry and two of them were killed. Here Brown cradles one of the mortally wounded raiders in his lap while those left in his little band gather around him. Troops sent from Washington and commanded by Robert E. Lee, who was still an officer in the Federal army in 1859, broke down the door of Brown's stronghold and forced his surrender.

elected President, and cheerfully attended his inauguration in March 1861. After Fort Sumter was fired upon, she knew the time for moderation and peaceful compromise was past, and wrote her niece:

■ I think the city will be attacked within the next 60 days. If it must be, let it come, and when there is no longer a soldier's arm to raise the Stars and Stripes above our Capitol, may God give strength to mine.

When President Lincoln asked for 75,000 volunteers after Sumter, Clara felt that even women should prepare themselves to be of use. She took target practice near the Washington Monument, "putting nine balls successively within the space of six inches at a distance of 50 feet." But after the 6th Massachusetts Regiment, which included some of her former pupils and neighbors, had to fight its way through Baltimore on the way to Washington, she decided to help the troops. On April 25 she wrote a friend:

■ The Massachusetts regiment is quartered in the Capitol. . . . Their baggage was all seized and they have *nothing* but their heavy woolen clothes— not a cotton shirt—and many of them not even a pocket handkerchief. We of course emptied our pockets and came home to tear up old sheets for towels and handkerchiefs, and have filled a large box with all manner of serving utensils, thread, needles, thimbles, scissors, pins, buttons, strings, salves, tallow, etc. etc.—have filled the largest market basket in the house and it will go to them in the next hour.

But don't tell us they are not determined—just fighting mad; they had just one Worcester "Spy" of the 22d, and all were so anxious to know the contents that they begged me to read it aloud to them, which I did. You

On March 4, 1861, Buchanan (left) and Lincoln ride toward the unfinished Capitol, where Lincoln took his oath of office and delivered his first inaugural address. One observer noted a striking contrast between Buchanan's "exhausted energies" and Lincoln's "vigorous strength."

would have smiled to see *me* and my *audience* in the Senate Chamber of the U. S. Oh! but it was better attention than I have been accustomed to see there in the old times. . . . God bless . . . the noble fellows who may leave their quiet, happy homes to come at the call of their country. So far as our poor efforts can reach they shall never lack a kindly hand or a sister's sympathy if they come.

The Southern victory in the first great battle of the Civil War—Bull Run in July 1861—made it clear that the North could never restore the Union quickly or easily. Clara saw the routed troops pouring back into Washington and wrote her father:

■ That the results amount to a *defeat* we are not willing to admit, but we have been severely repulsed. . . . It is certain that we have at length had the *"Forward Movement"* which has been so loudly clamored for, and I am a living witness of a corresponding *Backward* one.

In helping to provide supplies for poorly supplied soldiers, and in helping to nurse the wounded who were scandalously undernursed, Clara Barton in her fortieth year finally had for the first time a cause that could truly use all her talents and energy. Through Northern newspapers she appealed for supplies she could distribute among the troops tented around Washington—"trying a very poor hand at nursing up, and comforting as well as I could, any portion of 75,000 strange, ill-convened and homesick boys." At first she concentrated on those from the areas where she herself had lived.

■ The first regiment of troops, the old 6th Mass. that fought its way through Baltimore, brought my playmates and neighbors, the partakers of my childhood; the brigades of New Jersey brought scores of my brave boys, the same solid phalanx; and the strongest legions from old Herkimer brought the associates of my [Clinton] seminary days. They formed and crowded around me. What could I do but go with them, or work for them and my country? The patriot blood of my father was warm in my veins. The country which he had fought for, I might at least work for. . . . I would not draw salary from our government in such peril, so I resigned and went into direct service of the sick and wounded troops wherever found.

Supplies flooded in for her to dispense. And when the women who shipped them wrote to ask if she really needed additional supplies, Clara had an eloquent answer—as shown in this letter of December 1861 to the secretary of the Ladies' Relief Committee of Worcester, Massachusetts.

■ "Are our labors needed, are we doing any good, shall we work, or shall we forbear?" From the first I have dreaded lest a sense of vague uncertainty in regard to matters here should discourage the efforts of our patriotic ladies at home. . . . It is *said*, upon proper authority, that "our army is supplied". . . . It is said also, upon the same authority, that we

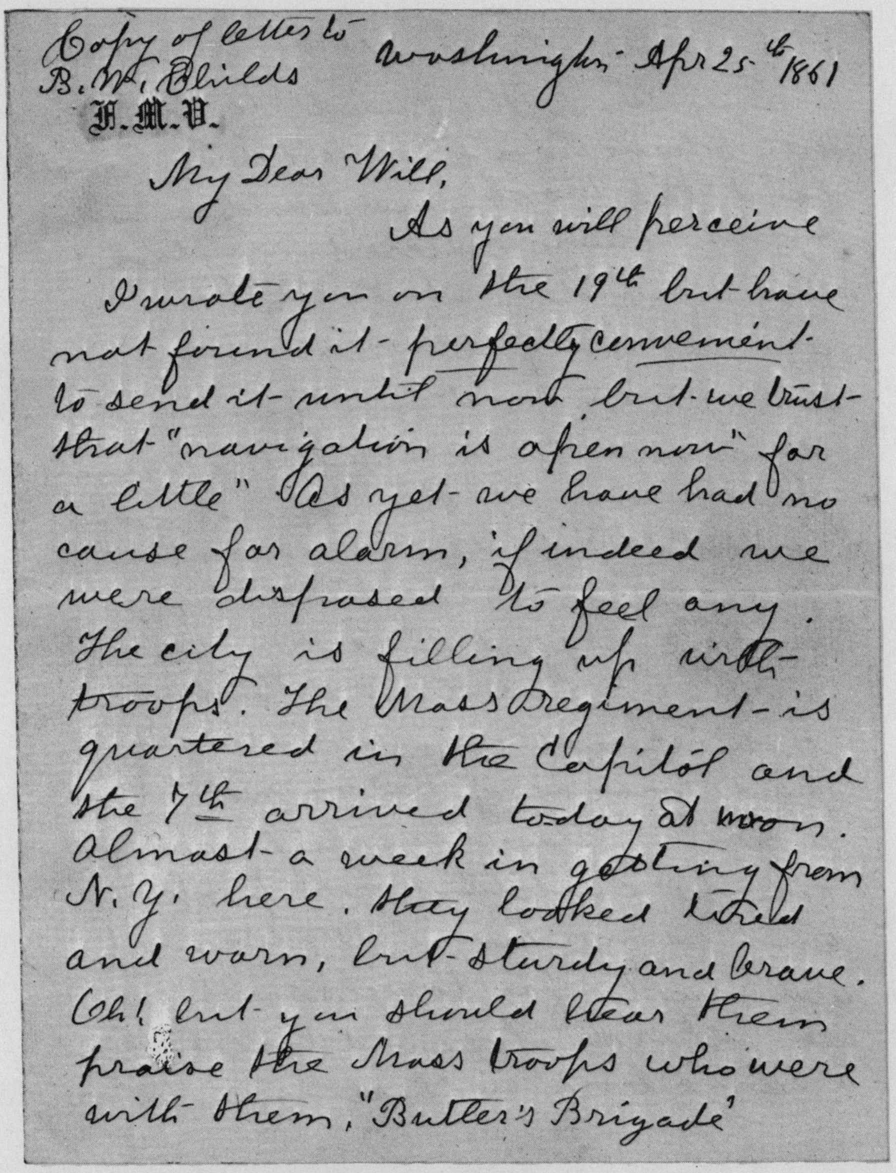

Copy of letter to
B. W. Childs
Washington. Apr 25th 1861
F.M.V.

My Dear Will,

As you will perceive I wrote you on the 19th but have not found it perfectly convenient to send it until now, but we trust that "navigation is open now" for a little" As yet we have had no cause for alarm, if indeed we were disposed to feel any. The city is filling up with troops. The Mass Regiment is quartered in the Capitol and the 7th arrived today at noon. Almost a week in getting from N. Y. here. They looked tired and worn, but sturdy and brave. Oh! but you should hear them praise the Mass troops who were with them, "Butler's Brigade"

In her own hand Miss Barton copied (apparently for her file) this letter to her friend B. W. Childs. She was to see much of "Butler's Brigade" and its general during the war. Later in this letter, she quoted other troops as saying that "the 'Massachusetts Boys' are equal to anything they undertake."

"need no nurses," either male or female, and none are admitted.

I wished an hour ago that you had been with me. In compliance with a request of my sister in this city I went to her house and found there a young Englishman, a brother of one of their domestics who had enlisted during the summer in a regiment of Pennsylvania Cavalry. They are stationed at Camp Pierpont; the sister heard that her brother was sick, and with the energetic habit of a true Englishwoman crossed the country on foot nine miles out to his camp and back the same day, found him in an almost dying condition and begged that he be sent to her.

He was taken shortly after in an ambulance, and upon his arrival his condition was found to be most deplorable; he had been attacked with ordinary fever six weeks before, and had lain unmoved until the flesh upon all parts of the body which rested hard upon whatever was under him had decayed, grown perfectly black and was falling out. . . . He had been neglected until he was literally starving. . . .

The surgeon of the regiment comes to see him, but had no idea of his condition; said that their assistant surgeon was killed and that it "was true that the men had not received proper care; he was very sorry." With the attention which this young man is now receiving, he will probably recover, but had it been otherwise? Ah me, all of our poor boys have not a sister within nine miles of them. And still it is said, upon authority, *"we have no need of nurses"* and *"our army is supplied"*. . . . I greatly fear that the few privileged, elegantly dressed ladies who ride over and sit in their carriages

This drawing of the Civil War period, by A. R. Waud, shows "lady clerks leaving the Treasury Department at Washington." Miss Barton, who had been one of the Federal government's pioneer female clerks in the 1850's, kept her job at the Patent Office through the Civil War, while hiring a substitute to do her work there. The war saw the first great influx of female employees into government offices, since so many men were in the armed forces.

to witness "splendid services" and "inspect the Army of the Potomac" and come away "delighted," learn very little of what lies there under canvas. . . .

Our army cannot afford that our ladies lay down their needles and fold their hands; if their contributions are not needed just today, they may be tomorrow, and *somewhere* they are needed today. . . . There is some truth in the old maxim that "what is everybody's business is nobody's business." . . .

A note just now informs me that our four companies of surgeons from Fort Independence, now stationed at the arsenal in this city (some two miles from me), in waiting for their supplies from Boston, were compelled to sleep in low, damp places with a single blanket and are taking severe

North Oxford. Mar. 20th 1862.

To His Excellency John A Andrew Governor.
of the Commonwealth of Massachusetts. —

Governor Andrew
will perhaps recollect the writer, as the Lady who waited
upon him in Company with Hon. Alex. DeWitt, to mention the existence of certain petitions from the Officers of the
Mass. Regts of Volunteers, relating to the establishment of an
Agency in Washington in the City of Washington

With the promise of your Excellency to "look after the
leak", came a "lessening of my fears," and the immediate discovery
of the truly magnificent rebel organization in Alexandria, and the
arrest of twenty five of the principal actors, including the purchas-
ing Committee, brought with it not only entire satisfaction,
but a joy I had scarce known in months. — Since September
I had been fully conscious in my own mind, of the existence of
something of this kind, and in October attempted to warn our
relief Societies, but in the absence of all proof, I must perforce
say very little.   I should never have brought the subject

colds and coughing fearfully. My ingenuity points no way of relief but to buy sacking, run up many ticks to be filled with hay to raise them from the drafts a little, and to this the remainder of my day must be devoted; they are far more exposed than they would be on the ground under a good tent. I almost envy you ladies where so many of you can work together and accomplish so much, while my poor labors are so single-handed.

The more Clara saw of the military muddle, the more she realized that the nearer to the front a soldier was the more his illness or wounds were neglected. This in turn made her the more eager to get to the front herself and do what she could there. But every propriety of the Victorian era forbade a "good" woman to go to an army's front lines—and the army's own regulations also forbade it. As she later wrote:

■ I struggled long and hard with my sense of propriety—with the appalling fact that I was only a woman whispering in one ear, and thundering in the other, the groans of suffering men dying like dogs, unfed and unsheltered, for the life of every institution which had protected and educated me! I said that I struggled with my sense of propriety and I say it with humiliation and shame.

BLOODY SCENES OF STRIFE

Early in 1862, while she was still in the midst of fighting her inner doubts and uncertainties, she heard that her father, in his eighty-eighth year, was dying. She hurried home to Massachusetts and, while nursing him in his final illness, told him her problem. "Go, if it is your duty to go," Captain Barton told her. "I know soldiers, and they will respect you and your errand" —and he gave her his Masonic emblem as a talisman.

After his death on March 21 she returned to Washington. It took her months of persistent effort to cut through almost endless objections, but finally she did succeed. After the battle of Cedar Mountain (also called Culpeper and Cedar Run) on August 9, 1862, when Stonewall Jackson defeated a Union corps under General Banks, she had all the passes needed for her to reach the scene—and the supplies to make herself effective.

■ When our armies fought on Cedar Mountain, I broke the shackles and went to the field. Five days and nights with three hours' sleep—a narrow escape from capture—and some days of getting the wounded into hospitals at Washington brought Saturday, August 30. And if you chance to feel that the positions I occupied were rough and unseemly for a *woman*—I can only reply that they were rough and unseemly for *men*. But under all, lay the life of the nation. I had inherited the rich blessing of health and strength of constitution—such as are seldom given to woman—and I felt that some return was due from me and that I ought to be there.

In the course of her early war work, Miss Barton uncovered some evidence of a Confederate spy ring near Washington. Her letter (opposite) to Governor Andrew of Massachusetts (above) expresses her joy that his following up her warning of a "leak" resulted in the arrest of 25 "of the principal actors." The letter was written while she was home tending to her dying father (he died the very next day) and in it she also successfully enlisted Governor Andrew's help in getting permission for her to work at the front. Part of the last page of this letter to Governor Andrew is reproduced on pages 8–9 and 129 of this book.

While still working with the survivors of Cedar Mountain in Washington, Clara "saw everybody going to the wharf." She hurried there herself, and found that the second battle of Bull Run was being fought with heavy casualties. With her helpers—Mrs. Ada Morrell, Mrs. Almira Fales, and Miss Lydia Haskell—she made ready to leave. A few days later she wrote her Cousin Lizzie an account of this experience, which she subsequently revised as a part of one of her public lectures on the war. No single account more fully illuminates why she was known as the "Angel of the Battlefield":

■ Our coaches were not elegant or commodious; they had no windows, no seats, no platforms, no steps, a slide door on the side was the only entrance, and this higher than my head. For my manner of attaining my elevated position, I must beg of you to draw on your own imaginations and spare me the labor of reproducing the boxes, barrels, boards, and rails, which, in those days, seemed to help me up and on in the world. We did not criticize the unsightly helpers and were only too thankful that the stiff springs did not quite jostle us out.

This description need not be limited to this particular trip or train, but will suffice for all that I have known in army life. This is the kind of conveyance by which your tons of generous gifts have reached the field with the precious freights. These trains, through day and night, sunshine and rain, heat and cold, have thundered over heights, across plains, through ravines, and over hastily built army bridges 90 feet across the rocky stream beneath.

At ten o'clock Sunday [August 31] our train drew up at Fairfax Station. The ground, for acres, was a thinly wooded slope—and among the trees, on the leaves and grass, were laid the wounded who were pouring in by scores of wagonloads, as picked up on the field under the flag of truce. All day they came, and the whole hillside was covered. Bales of hay were broken open and scattered over the ground like littering for cattle, and the sore, famishing men were laid upon it.

And when the night shut in, in the mist and darkness about us, we knew that, standing apart from the world of anxious hearts, throbbing over the whole country, we were a little band of almost empty-handed workers literally by ourselves in the wild woods of Virginia, with 3,000 suffering men crowded upon the few acres within our reach.

After gathering up every available implement or convenience for our work, our domestic inventory stood, two water buckets, five tin cups, one camp kettle, one stewpan, two lanterns, four bread knives, three plates, and a two-quart tin dish, and 3,000 guests to serve.

You will perceive, by this, that I had not yet learned to equip myself, for I was no Pallas, ready armed, but grew into my work by hard thinking and sad experience. It may serve to relieve your apprehension for the future of my labors if I assure you that I was never caught so again.

You have read of adverse winds. To realize this in its full sense you have only to build a camp-fire and attempt to cook something on it.

There is not a soldier within sound of my voice but will sustain me in the assertion that, go whichsoever side of it you will, wind will blow the smoke and flame directly in your face. Notwithstanding these difficulties, within 15 minutes from the time of our arrival we were preparing food and dressing wounds. You wonder what, and how prepared, and how administered without dishes.

You generous thoughtful mothers and wives have not forgotten the tons of preserves and fruits with which you filled our hands. Huge boxes of these stood beside that railway track. Every can, jar, bucket, bowl, cup or tumbler, when emptied, that instant became a vehicle of mercy to convey some preparation of mingled bread and wine or soup or coffee to some helpless, famishing sufferer, who partook of it with the tears rolling down his bronzed cheeks and divided his blessings between the hands that fed him and his God.

I never realized until that day how little a human being could be grateful for, and that day's experience also taught me the utter worthlessness of that which could not be made to contribute directly to our necessities. The bit of bread which would rest on the surface of a gold eagle [$10 gold piece] was worth more than the coin itself.

But the most fearful scene was reserved for the night. I have said that the ground was littered with dry hay and that we had only two lanterns, but there were plenty of candles. The wounded were laid so close that it was impossible to move about in the dark. The slightest misstep brought a torrent of groans from some poor mangled fellow in your path.

The gold eagle, a $10 coin, was fairly familiar to Americans until the nation went off the gold standard in the 1930's, and was often used for Christmas or graduation presents. Here the two sides of it are shown actual size. As Miss Barton notes in her battlefield account, a very small piece of bread could cover it.

Consequently here were seen persons of all grades, from the careful man of God who walked with a prayer upon his lips to the careless driver hunting for his lost whip—each wandering about among this hay with an open flaming candle in his hand.

The slightest accident, the mere dropping of a light, could have enveloped in flames this whole mass of helpless men.

How we watched and pleaded and cautioned as we worked and wept that night! How we put socks and slippers upon their cold damp feet, wrapped your blankets and quilts about them, and when we had no longer these to give, how we covered them in the hay and left them to their rest!

On Monday [September 1] the enemy's cavalry appeared in the wood opposite, and a raid was hourly expected. In the afternoon all the wounded men were sent off and the danger became so imminent that Mrs. Fales thought best to leave, although she only went for stores. I begged to be excused from accompanying her, as the ambulances were up to the fields for more, and I knew I should never leave a wounded man there if I were taken prisoner 40 times.

At six o'clock it commenced to thunder and lightning, and all at once the artillery began to play, joined by the musketry about two miles distant. We sat down in our tent and waited to see them break in, but Reno's forces held them back. The old 21st Massachusetts lay between us and the enemy and they would not pass.

God only knows who was lost, I do not, for the next day all fell back. Poor Kearny, Stephen, and Webster were brought in, and in the afternoon

Kearny's and Heintzelman's divisions fell back through our camp on their way to Alexandria. We knew this was the last. We put the thousand wounded men we then had into the train. I took one carload of them and Mrs. Morrell another. The men took to the horses. We steamed off, and two hours later there was no Fairfax Station.

We reached Alexandria at 10 o'clock at night, and, oh, the repast which met those poor men at the train. The people of the island are the most noble I ever saw or heard of. I stood in my car and fed the men till they could eat no more. Then the people would take us home and feed us, and after that we came home. I had slept one and one half hours since Saturday night and I am well and strong and wait to go again if I have need.

ANGEL OF THE BATTLEFIELD

Even more detailed—and equally vivid—is Clara's account of her work at the battle of Chantilly, which followed close upon the second battle of Bull Run. It includes these experiences:

■ The slight, naked chest of a fair-haired lad caught my eye, and dropping down beside him, I bent low to draw the remnant of his torn blouse about him, when with a quick cry he threw his left arm across my neck and, burying his face in the folds of my dress, wept like a child at his mother's knee. I took his head in my hands and held it until his great burst of grief passed away. "And do you know me?" he asked at length; "I am Charley Hamilton who used to carry your satchel home from school!" My faithful pupil, poor Charley. That mangled right arm would never carry a satchel again.

About three o'clock in the morning I observed a surgeon with his little flickering candle in hand approaching me with cautious step far up in the wood. "Lady," he said as he drew near, "will you go with me? Out on the hills is a poor distressed lad, mortally wounded and dying. His piteous cries for his sister have touched all our hearts, and none of us can relieve him, but rather seem to distress him by our presence."

By this time I was following him back over the bloody track, with great beseeching eyes of anguish on every side looking up into our faces saying so plainly, "Don't step on us."

"He can't last half an hour longer," said the surgeon as we toiled on. "He is already quite cold, shot through the abdomen, a terrible wound." By this time the cries became plainly audible to me.

"Mary, Mary, sister Mary, come—oh, come, I am wounded, Mary! I am shot. I am dying—oh, come to me—I have called you so long and my strength is almost gone—Don't let me die here alone. Oh, Mary, Mary, come!"

Of all the tones of entreaty to which I have listened—and certainly I have had some experience of sorrow—I think these, sounding through that dismal night, the most heart-rending. As we drew near, some 20 persons, attracted by his cries, had gathered around and stood with moistened eyes and helpless hands waiting the change which would relieve them all. And in the midst, stretched upon the ground, lay, scarcely full grown, a young man with a graceful head of hair, tangled and matted, thrown back from a forehead and a face of livid whiteness. His throat was bare. His hands, bloody, clasped his breast, his large, bewildered eyes turning anxiously in every direction. And ever from between his ashen lips pealed that piteous cry of "Mary! Mary! Come."

I approached him unobserved, and, motioning the lights away, I knelt by him alone in the darkness. Shall I confess that I intended if possible to cheat him out of his terrible death agony? But my lips were truer than my heart, and would not speak the word "Brother" I had willed them to do. So I placed my hands upon his neck, kissed his cold forehead, and laid my cheek against his.

The illusion was complete; the act had done the falsehood my lips refused to speak. I can never forget that cry of joy. "Oh, Mary! Mary! You have come? I knew you would come if I called you and I have called you so long. I could not die without you, Mary. Don't cry, darling, I am not afraid to die now that you have come to me. Oh, bless you. Bless you, Mary." And he ran his cold, blood-wet hands about my neck, passed them over my face, and twined them in my hair, which by this time had freed itself from fastenings and was hanging damp and heavy upon my shoulders.

He gathered the loose locks in his stiffened fingers and holding them to his lips continued to whisper through them, "Bless you, bless you, Mary!" And I felt the hot tears of joy trickling from the eyes I had thought stony in death. This encouraged me, and, wrapping his feet closely in blankets and giving him such stimulants as he could take, I seated myself on the

Miss Barton was not the only woman who nursed at night on the battlefield. Mrs. Mary A. ("Mother") Bickerdyke, also pictured on page 36, is here shown "groping among the dead . . . uneasy lest some might be left to die uncared for. She could not rest while she thought any were overlooked who were yet living."

ground and lifted him on my lap, and drawing the shawl on my own shoulders also about his I bade him rest.

I listened till his blessings grew fainter, and in 10 minutes with them on his lips he fell asleep. So the gray morning found us; my precious charge had grown warm, and was comfortable.

Of course the morning light would reveal his mistake. But he had grown calm and was refreshed and able to endure it, and when finally he woke, he seemed puzzled for a moment, but then he smiled and said: "I knew before I opened my eyes that this couldn't be Mary. I know now that she couldn't get here, but it is almost as good. You've made me so happy. Who is it?"

I said it was simply a lady who, hearing that he was wounded, had come to care for him. He wanted the name, and with childlike simplicity he spelled it letter by letter to know if he were right. "In my pocket," he said, "you will find mother's last letter; please get it and write your name upon it, for I want both names by me when I die."

"Will they take away the wounded?" he asked. "Yes," I replied, "the first train for Washington is nearly ready now." "I must go," he said quickly. "Are you able?" I asked. "I must go if I die on the way. I'll tell you why; I am poor mother's only son, and when she consented that I go to the war, I promised her faithfully that if I were not killed outright, but wounded, I would try every means in my power to be taken home to her dead or alive. If I die on the train, they will not throw me off, and if I were buried in Washington, she can get me. But out here in the Virginia woods in the hands of the enemy, never. I *must* go!"

I sent for the surgeon in charge of the train and requested that my boy be taken. "Oh, impossible, madam, he is mortally wounded and will never reach the hospital! We must take those who have a hope of life." "But you must take him." "I cannot"—"Can you, Doctor, guarantee the lives of all you have on that train?" "I wish I could," said he sadly. "They are the worst cases; nearly 50 per cent must die eventually of their wounds and hardships."

"Then give this lad a chance with them. He can only die, and he has given good and sufficient reasons why he must go—and a woman's word for it, Doctor. You take him. Send your men for him." Whether yielding to argument or entreaty, I neither knew nor cared so long as he did yield nobly and kindly. And they gathered up the fragments of the poor, torn boy and laid him carefully on a blanket on the crowded train and with stimulants and food and a kind-hearted attendant, pledged to take him alive or dead to Armory Square Hospital and tell them he was Hugh Johnson, of New York, and to mark his grave.

Although three hours of my time had been devoted to one sufferer among thousands, it must not be inferred that our general work had been suspended or that my assistants had been equally inefficient. They had seen how I was engaged and nobly redoubled their exertions to make amends for my deficiencies. Probably not a man was laid upon those cars who did not receive some personal attention at their hands, some little kindness, if it were only to help lift him more tenderly.

This finds us shortly after daylight Monday morning. Train after train of cars was rushing on for the wounded, and hundreds of wagons were bringing them in from the field still held by the enemy, where some poor sufferers had lain three days with no visible means of sustenance. If immediately placed upon the trains and not detained, at least 24 hours must elapse before they could be in the hospital and properly nourished. They were already famishing, weak and sinking from loss of blood, and they could ill afford a further fast of 24 hours.

I felt confident that, unless nourished at once, all the weaker portion must be past recovery before reaching the hospitals of Washington. If once taken from the wagons and laid with those already cared for, they would be overlooked and perish on the way. Something must be done to meet this fearful emergency. I sought the various officers on the grounds, explained the case to them, and asked permission to feed all the men as they arrived before they should be taken from the wagons. It was well for the poor sufferers of that field that it was controlled by noble-hearted, generous officers, quick to feel and prompt to act.

They at once saw the propriety of my request and gave orders that all wagons should be stayed at a certain point and only moved on when every one had been seen and fed. This point secured, I commenced my day's work of climbing from the wheel to the brake of every wagon and speaking to and feeding with my own hands each soldier until he expressed himself satisfied.

Still there were bright spots along the darkened lines. Early in the morning the Provost Marshal came to ask me if I could use 50 men. He had that number, who for some slight breach of military discipline were under guard and useless, unless I could use them. I only regretted there were not 500. They came—strong, willing men—and these, added to our original force and what we had gained incidentally, made our number something over 80, and, believe me, 80 men and three women, acting with well-directed purpose, will accomplish a good deal in a day.

Our 50 prisoners dug graves and gathered and buried the dead, bore mangled men over the rough ground in their arms, loaded cars, built fires, made soup, and administered it. And I failed to discern that their services were less valuable than those of the other men. I had long suspected, and have been since convinced, that a private soldier may be placed under guard, court-martialed, and even be imprisoned without forfeiting his honor or manliness; that the real dishonor is often upon the gold lace rather than the army blue.

At three o'clock the last train of wounded left. All day we had known that the enemy hung upon the hills and were waiting to break in upon us. . . . At four o'clock the clouds gathered black and murky, and the low growl of distant thunders was heard while lightning continually illuminated the horizon. The still air grew thick and stifled, and the very branches appeared to droop and bow as if in grief at the memory of the terrible scenes so lately enacted and the gallant lives so nobly yielded up beneath their shelter.

A typical military punishment of the Civil War is shown in the above sketch by Charles W. Reed, himself a Union soldier. Miss Barton, as she vividly describes on this page, was happy to use the front-line services of minor military offenders.

This was the afternoon of Monday. Since Saturday noon I had not thought of tasting food, and we had just drawn around a box for that purpose, when, of a sudden, air and earth and all about us shook with one mingled crash of God's and man's artillery. The lightning played and the thunder rolled incessantly and the cannon roared louder and nearer each minute. Chantilly with all its darkness and horrors had opened in the rear.

The description of this battle I leave to those who saw and moved in it, as it is my purpose to speak only of events in which I was a witness or actor. Although two miles distant, we knew the battle was intended for us, and watched the firing as it neared and receded and waited minute by minute for the rest.

With what desperation our men fought hour after hour in the rain and darkness! How they were overborne and rallied, how they suffered from mistaken orders, and blundered, and lost themselves in the strange mysterious wood. And how, after all, with giant strength and veteran bravery, they checked the foe and held him at bay, is an all-proud record of history. And the courage of the soldier who braved death in the darkness of Chantilly let no man question.

The rain continued to pour in torrents, and the darkness became impenetrable save from the lightning leaping above our heads and the fitful flash of the guns, as volley after volley rang through the stifled air and lighted up the gnarled trunks and dripping branches among which we ever waited and listened.

In the midst of this, and how guided no man knows, came still another train of wounded men, and a waiting train of cars upon the track received them. This time nearly alone, for my worn-out assistants could work no longer, I continued to administer such food as I had left.

Do you begin to wonder what it could be? Army crackers put into knapsacks and haversacks and beaten to crumbs between stones, and stirred into a mixture of wine, whiskey, and water, and sweetened with coarse brown sugar. Not very inviting you will think, but I assure you it was always acceptable. But whether it should have been classed as food, or, like the Widow Bedott's cabbage, as a delightful beverage, it would puzzle an epicure to determine. No matter, so it imparted strength and comfort.

The departure of this train cleared the grounds of wounded for the night, and as the line of fire from its plunging engines died out in the darkness, a strange sensation of weakness and weariness fell upon me, almost defying my utmost exertion to move one foot before the other.

A little Sibley tent had been hastily pitched for me in a slight hollow upon the hillside. Your imaginations will not fail to picture its condition. Rivulets of water had rushed through it during the last three hours. Still I attempted to reach it, as its white surface, in the darkness, was a protection from the wheels of wagons and trampling of beasts.

Perhaps I shall never forget the painful effort which the making of those few rods and the gaining of the tent cost me. How many times I

On the battlefield, Miss Barton was as much a cook and provider as she was a nurse. On this page she tells how she could even make something palatable out of the unpalatable army crackers. The soldiers normally hated this hardtack; one of their pet Civil War songs told of "dry mummies of hard crackers" and had as its chorus: "Hard crackers, hard crackers, come again no more! Many days have you lingered upon our stomachs sore."

fell, from sheer exhaustion, in the darkness and mud of that slippery hillside, I have no knowledge, but at last I grasped the welcome canvas, and a well-established brook, which washed in on the upper side at the opening that served as door, met me on my entrance. My entire floor was covered with water, not an inch of dry, solid ground.

One of my lady assistants had previously taken train for Washington and the other, worn out by faithful labors, was crouched upon the top of some boxes in one corner fast asleep. No such convenience remained for me, and I had no strength to arrange one. I sought the highest side of my tent which I remembered was grass-grown, and, ascertaining that the water was not very deep, I sank down. It was no laughing matter then. But the recollection of my position has since afforded me amusement.

I remember myself sitting on the ground, upheld by my left arm, my head resting on my hand, impelled by an almost uncontrollable desire to lie completely down, and prevented by the certain conviction that if I did, water would flow into my ears.

The best-known male nurse of the Civil War is probably the poet Walt Whitman, who worked tirelessly in hospitals of the Washington area. He chose this drawing of himself as the frontispiece for the first edition of his most famous book, "Leaves of Grass," in 1855.

How long I balanced between my desires and cautions, I have no positive knowledge, but it is very certain that the former carried the point by the position from which I was aroused at 12 o'clock by the rumbling of more wagons of wounded men. I slept two hours, and oh, what strength I had gained! I may never know two other hours of equal worth. I sprang to my feet dripping wet, covered with ridges of dead grass and leaves, wrung the water from my hair and skirts, and went forth again to my work.

When I stood again under the sky, the rain had ceased, the clouds were sullenly retiring, and the lightning, as if deserted by its boisterous companions, had withdrawn to a distant corner and was playing quietly by itself. For the great volleying thunders of heaven and earth had settled down on the fields. Silent? I said so. And it was, save the ceaseless rumbling of the never-ending train of army wagons which brought alike the wounded, the dying, and the dead.

And thus the morning of the third day broke upon us, drenched, weary, hungry, sore-footed, sad-hearted, discouraged, and under orders to retreat.

A little later, the plaintive wail of a single fife, the slow beat of a muffled drum, the steady tramp, tramp, tramp of heavy feet, the gleam of 10,000 bayonets on the hills, and with bowed heads and speechless lips, poor Kearny's leaderless men came marching through.

This was the signal for retreat. All day they came, tired, hungry, ragged, defeated, retreating, they knew not whither—they cared not whither.

The enemy's cavalry, skirting the hills, admonished us each moment that we must soon decide to go from them or with them. But our work must be accomplished, and no wounded men once given into our hands must be left. And with the spirit of desperation, we struggled on.

At three o'clock an officer galloped up to me, with "Miss Barton, can you ride?" "Yes, sir," I replied.

"But you have no lady's saddle—could you ride mine?"

"Yes, sir, or without it, if you have blanket and surcingle."

"Then you can risk another hour," he exclaimed, and galloped off.

At four he returned at a break-neck speed, and, leaping from his horse, said, "Now is your time. The enemy is already breaking over the hills; try the train. It will go through, unless they have flanked, and cut the bridge a mile above us. In that case I've a reserve horse for you, and you must take your chances to escape across the country."

In two minutes I was on the train. The last wounded man at the station was also on. The conductor stood with a torch which he applied to a pile of combustible material beside the track. And we rounded the curve which took us from view and we saw the station ablaze, and a troop of cavalry dashing down the hill. The bridge was uncut and midnight found us at Washington.

You have the full record of my sleep—from Friday night till Wednesday morning—two hours. You will not wonder that I slept during the next 24.

On Friday (the following), I repaired to Armory Square Hospital to learn who, of all the hundreds sent, had reached that point. I traced the chaplain's record, and there upon the last page freshly written stood the name of Hugh Johnson.

Turning to Chaplain Jackson, I asked, "Did that man live until today?" "He died during the latter part of last night," he replied. "His friends reached him some two days ago, and they are now taking his body from the ward to be conveyed to the depot."

I looked in the direction his hand indicated, and there, beside a coffin, about to be lifted into a wagon, stood a gentleman, the mother, and sister Mary!

"Had he his reason?" I asked.

"Oh, perfectly."

"And his mother and sister were with him two days?"

"Yes."

There was no need of me. He had given his own messages; I could add nothing to their knowledge of him, and would fain be spared the scene of

Three types of cannon used by the Union forces are shown in this sketch of a practice battery in Washington. From left they are: a Cochran's breech-loading gun, a Dahlgren gun, and a Dahlgren rifled gun.

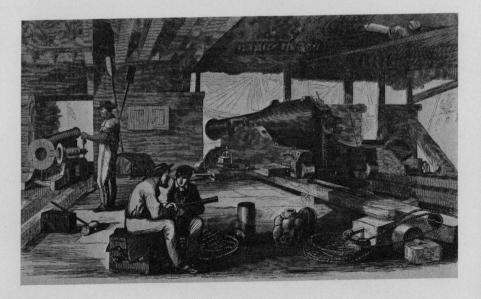

thanks. Poor Hugh, thy piteous prayers reached and were answered, and with eyes and heart full, I turned away, and never saw sister Mary.

These were days of darkness—a darkness that might be felt. The shattered bands of Pope and Banks! Burnside's weary legions! Reinforcements from West Virginia—and all that now remained of the once glorious Army of the Peninsula had gathered for shelter beneath the redoubts and guns that girdled Washington.

THE FEARFUL COST OF ANTIETAM

By now Clara knew quite well how she wanted to operate. She knew she could—and should—get to the front early, and what equipment was most useful. And the army was much more willing than at first to cooperate with her. In September of 1862 it provided a mule-drawn army wagon to take her and her supplies to what turned out to be the gory battle of Antietam.

■ I was to ride 80 miles in an army wagon, and straight into battle and danger at that. I could take no female companion, no friend. . . . I watched the approach of the long and high, white-covered, tortoise-motioned vehicle, with its string of little, frisky, long-eared animals, with the broad-shouldered driver astride. . . . My vehicle was loaded, with boxes, bags, and parcels, and, last of all, I found a place for myself and the four men who were to go with me.

I took no Saratoga trunk, but remembered, at the last moment, to tie up a few articles in my handkerchief. . . . Thus all day we rattled on over the stones and dikes, and up and down the hills of Maryland. . . . We were directly in the midst of a train of army wagons, at least 10 miles in length. . . . I busied myself as I rode on hour by hour in cutting loaves of bread in slices and passing them to the pale, haggard wrecks as they sat by the roadside, or staggered on to avoid capture, and at each little village we entered, I purchased all the bread its inhabitants would sell. . . .

I have already spoken of the great length of the army train, and that we could no more change our position than one of the planets. . . . The order of the train was, first, ammunition; next, food and clothing for well troops; and finally, the hospital supplies. Thus, in case of the battle the needed stores for the army . . . must be from two or three days in coming up. Meanwhile, as usual, our men must languish and die. Something must be done to gain time. And I resorted to strategy.

We found an early resting-place, supped by our camp-fire, and slept again among the dews and damps. At one o'clock, when everything was still, we arose, breakfasted, harnessed, and moved on past the whole train, which like ourselves had camped for the night. At daylight we had gained 10 miles and were up with the artillery and in advance even of the ammunition. All that weary, dusty day I followed the cannon, and nightfall brought us up with the great Army of the Potomac. . . . In all this vast assemblage I saw no other trace of womankind. I was faint, but could not eat; weary, but could not sleep; depressed, but could not weep.

So I climbed into my wagon, tied down the cover, dropped down in the little nook I had occupied so long, and prayed God with all the earnestness of my soul to stay the morrow's strife or send us victory. And for my poor self, that He impart somewhat of wisdom and strength to my heart, nerve to my arm, speed to my feet, and fill my hands for the terrible duties of the coming day. Heavy and sad I awaited its approach. . . .

Many of you may never hear the bugle notes which call to battle . . . but if, like us, you had heard them this morning . . . waking one camp from sleep to hasten to another, they would have lingered in your ears, as they do in mine tonight. . . . The battle commenced on the right and already with the aid of field glasses we saw our own forces . . . overborne and falling back. . . .

Thinking our place might be there, we [went] eight miles, turning into a cornfield near a house and barn, and stopping in the rear of the last gun. . . . A garden wall only separated us. The infantry were already driven back two miles, and stood under cover of the guns. The fighting had been fearful. . . . Around the old barn lay there, too badly wounded to admit of removal, some 300 thus early in the day, for it was scarce 10 o'clock.

We loosened our mules and commenced our work. The corn was so high as to conceal the house, which stood some distance to the right, but, judging that a path which I observed must lead to it, and also that surgeons must be operating there, I took my arms full of stimulants and

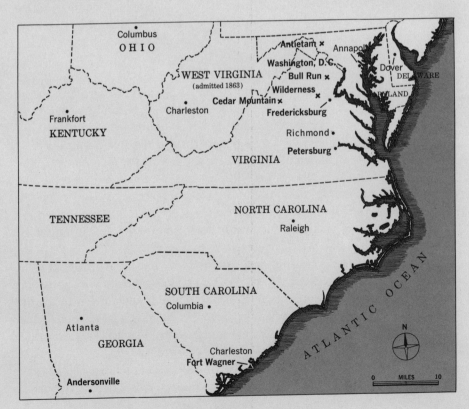

This map of the Civil War shows a number of places where Miss Barton did outstanding work. These include Washington, Cedar Mountain, Bull Run, Antietam, Fredericksburg, Fort Wagner, the Wilderness, Petersburg, and Andersonville. Readers will find page references to each of these in the index.

bandages and followed the opening. . . .

I found the dooryard of a small house, and myself face to face with one of the kindest and noblest surgeons I have ever met, Dr. Dunn of Conneautville, Pa. Speechless both, for an instant, he at length threw up his hands with "God has indeed remembered us, how did you get from Virginia so soon? And again to supply our necessities! And they are terrible. We have nothing but our instruments and the little chloroform we brought in our pockets. We have not a bandage, rag, lint or string, and all these shell-wounded men bleeding to death."

Upon the porch stood four tables, with an etherized patient upon each, a surgeon standing over him with his box of instruments, and a bunch of green corn leaves beside him. With what joy I laid my precious burden down among them, and thought that never before had linen looked so white. . . .

Thrice that day was the ground in front of us contested, lost, and won, and twice our men were driven back under cover of that fearful range of guns, and each time brought its hundreds of wounded to our crowded ground. . . . The smoke became so dense as to obscure our sight, and the hot, sulphurous breath of battle dried our tongues and parched our lips to bleeding. We were in a slight hollow, and all shell which did not break over our guns in front, came directly among or over us, bursting above our heads or burying themselves in the hills beyond.

A man lying upon the ground asked for a drink; I stopped to give it, and, having raised him with my right hand, was holding him. Just at this moment a bullet sped its free and easy way between us, tearing a hole in my sleeve and found its way into his body. He fell back dead. . . .

The patient endurance of these men was most astonishing. As many as could be were carried into the barn, as a slight protection against random shot. Just outside the door lay a man wounded in the face, the ball having entered the lower maxillary on the left side and lodged among the bones of the right cheek. His imploring look drew me to him, when, placing his finger upon the sharp protuberance, he said, "Lady, will you tell me what this is that burns so?" I replied that it must be the ball. . . .

"It is terribly painful," he said. "Won't you take it out?" I said I would go to the tables for a surgeon. "No! No!" he said, catching my dress. "They cannot come to me. I must wait my turn, for this is a little wound. You can get the ball. There is a knife in your pocket. Please take the ball out for me."

This was a new call. I had never severed the nerves and fibers of human flesh, and said I could not hurt him so much. He looked up, with as nearly a smile as such a mangled face could assume, saying, "You cannot hurt me, dear lady, I can endure any pain that your hands can create. Please do it. It will relieve me so much." I could not withstand his entreaty and, opening the best blade of my pocket-knife, prepared for the operation.

Just at his head lay a stalwart orderly sergeant from Illinois, with a face beaming with intelligence and kindness, and who had a bullet directly

Miss Barton prayed that those who listened to her lectures on the Civil War might "never hear the bugle notes which call to battle." In this drawing, a bugler of the time sounds a call. Of all the bugle melodies used from 1861 to 1865, the one that has become most famous is "Taps"

through the fleshy part of both thighs. He had been watching the scene with great interest and, when he saw me commence to raise the poor fellow's head, and no one to support it, with a desperate effort he succeeded in raising himself to a sitting posture, exclaiming as he did so, "I will help do that." Shoving himself along the ground he took the wounded head in his hands and held it while I extracted the ball and washed and bandaged the face.

I do not think a surgeon would have pronounced it a scientific operation, but that it was successful I dared to hope from the gratitude of the patient. I assisted the sergeant to lie down again, brave and cheerful as he had risen, and passed on to others. Returning in half an hour, I found him weeping, the great tears rolling diligently down his manly cheeks. I thought his effort had been too great for his strength and expressed my fears. "Oh! No! No! Madam," he replied. "It is not for myself. I am very well, but," pointing to another just brought in, he said, "this is my comrade, and he tells me that our regiment is all cut to pieces, that my captain was the last officer left, and he is dead."

Oh, God! what a costly war! This man could laugh at pain, face death without a tremor, and yet weep like a child over the loss of his comrades and his captain.

At two o'clock my men came to tell me that the last loaf of bread had been cut and the last cracker pounded. We had three boxes of wine still unopened. What should they do? "Open the wine and give that," I said, "and God help us."

The next instant an ejaculation from Sergeant Field, who had opened the first box, drew my attention, and, to my astonished gaze, the wine had been packed in nicely sifted Indian [corn] meal. If it had been gold dust it would have seemed poor in comparison. I had no words. No one spoke. In silence the men wiped their eyes and resumed their work. Of 12 boxes

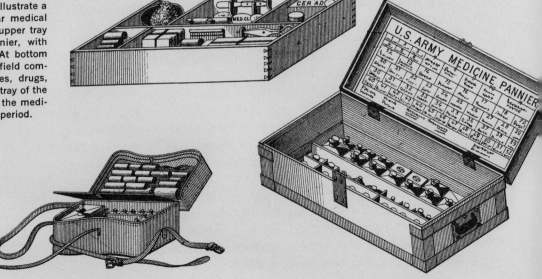

These three drawings illustrate a characteristic Civil War medical kit. At top left is the upper tray of the medicine pannier, with sponge, scalpel, etc. At bottom left is the "surgeon's field companion," with bandages, drugs, etc. At right, the lower tray of the pannier has bottles of the medicines used during that period.

of wine which we carried, the first nine, when opened, were found packed in sawdust, the last three, when all else was gone, in Indian meal.

A woman would not hesitate long under circumstances like these. This was an old farmhouse. Six large kettles were picked up and set over fires, almost as quickly as I can tell it, and I was mixing water and meal for gruel.

It occurred to us to explore the cellar. The chimney rested on an arch, and, forcing the door, we discovered three barrels and a bag. "They are full," said the sergeant, and, rolling one into the light, found that it bore the mark of Jackson's army. These three barrels of flour and a bag of salt had been stored there by the rebel army during its upward march.

I shall never experience such a sensation of wealth and competency again, from utter poverty to such riches.

All that night my 30 men (for my corps of workers had increased to that number during the day) carried buckets of hot gruel for miles down the line to the wounded and dying where they fell. This time, profiting by experience, we had lanterns to hang in and around the barn, and, having directed it to be done, I went to the house and found the surgeon in charge, sitting alone, beside a table, upon which he rested his elbow, apparently meditating upon a bit of tallow candle which flickered in the center. Approaching carefully, I said, "You are tired, Doctor."

He started up with a look almost savage, "Tired! Yes, I am tired, tired of such heartlessness, such carelessness!" Turning full upon me, he continued: "Think of the condition of things. Here are at least 1,000 wounded men, terribly wounded, 500 of whom cannot live till daylight, without attention. That two inches of candle is all I have or can get. What can I do? How can I endure it?"

I took him by the arm, and, leading him to the door, pointed in the direction of the barn where the lanterns glistened like stars among the waving corn. "What is that?" he exclaimed. "The barn is lighted," I said, "and the house will be directly." "Who did it?" "I, Doctor." "Where did you get them?" "Brought them with me." "How many have you?" "All you want—four boxes."

He looked at me a moment, as if waking from a dream, turned away without a word, and never alluded to the circumstances, but the deference which he paid me was almost painful. . . .

Through the long starlit night we wrought and hoped and prayed. But it was only . . . in the hush of the following day . . . that we learned at what a fearful cost the gallant Union army had won the battle of Antietam.

Antietam! With its eight miles of camping armies, face to face; 160,000 men to spring up at dawn like the old Scot from the heather! Its miles of artillery shaking the earth like a chain of Etnas! Its 10 hours of uninterrupted battle! Its thunder and its fire! The sharp, unflinching order, "Hold the bridge, boys—always the bridge." At length, the quiet! The pale moonlight on its cooling guns! The weary men, the dying and the dead! The flag of truce that buried our enemies slain, and Antietam was fought, and won, and the foe turned back!

GRIM DAYS AT FREDERICKSBURG

The more she served at the actual fighting front, the more Clara became convinced that only this sort of work could truly satisfy her yearning to be of full, practical use in the war. By now she knew from ample firsthand experience that the wounded often died on the battlefield for lack of the most elementary treatment. Each moment of delay between a soldier's injury and the time succor reached him was a moment that could well mean the difference between life and death. Previously, when she had helped take care of wounded soldiers brought slowly back to hospitals in the Washington area, she had seen dirt and blood "caked on their sore wounds till they were like the hard shells of turtles."

By then, even the best of care was frequently far too late, while even rather skimpy care often sufficed if it came at the earliest possible moment. Nor was such care necessarily, or even primarily, through nursing. In her phrase, she must "follow the cannon" and then administer every sort of relief in the places of greatest need and danger. As she put it, "I can save some of those poor fellows, whose lives may be lost but for me."

These individualistic methods of Clara drew some criticism at this period as well as later in the Civil War. Yet as she observed: "If I have by practice acquired any skill, it belongs to me to use untrammeled, and I might not work as efficiently, or labor as happily, under the direction of those of less experience than myself. It is simply just to all parties that I retain my present position."

Thus Major Rucker, who supplied the army wagons with which she went to the front, told her (Clara herself reported): "No other woman could stand what I would and she would become helpless on my hands and cause me more trouble instead of less." A month after Antietam, on getting advance warning of another possible major battle, she hurried off again—with none of her usual helpers, but in command of an ambulance and six mule-drawn army vehicles, all provided by Major Rucker. Clara later devoted part of a lecture to this particular trip:

■ There may be those present who are curious to know how eight or ten rough, stout men, who knew nothing of me, received the fact that they were to drive their teams under the charge of a lady. This question has been so often asked in private that I deem it proper to answer it publicly.

Well, the various expressions of their faces afforded a study. They were not soldiers, but civilians in government employ. Drovers, butchers, hucksters, mule-breakers, probably not one of them had ever passed an hour in what could be termed "ladies' society" in his life. But every man had driven through the whole Peninsular campaign. Every one of them had taken his team unharmed out of that retreat, and had sworn an oath never to drive another step in Virginia.

They were brave and skillful, understood their business to perfection, but had no art. They said and looked what they thought; and I understood them at a glance. . . . As early as four o'clock, they turned into a field, formed a circle, and prepared to camp. I sent for the leader and inquired his purpose. With some surplus of English he assured me that: "He wasn't going to drive in the night."

I replied that he could drive till night, and he would find it for his interest to do so, and I said no more. By some course of reasoning he seemed to arrive at the same conclusion. For after a few minutes of consultation with the men, who stood grouped about their wagons, cracking their long whips, as a kind of safety valve to their indignation, they drew their teams out into the road, and moved on at a speed by no means retarded by their late adventure. And with full measure of human perversity they not only drove till night, but far into it. But as they were moving in the right direction, and working off their surplus energy, I did not interfere with them.

They evidently wanted to drive a little after they had been told to stop. But I was not disposed to gratify them, and about nine o'clock getting weary of their fun, they halted beside a field, and announced their intention of camping for the night. They had eight days' dry rations of meat and bread in their feed boxes, upon which they expected to subsist cold, and with little cooking.

While they were busy with their animals, with the aid of my ambulance driver, a fire was kindled (these were the days when fence rails suffered) and I prepared a supper, which I now think would grace a well-spread table. But as I had no table, I spread my cloth upon the ground, poured the coffee, and sent my driver to call the men to supper. They came, a little slowly, and not all at once, but as I cordially assigned each to his place, I took my seat with them, and ate and chatted as if nothing had happened.

They were not talkative but respectful, ate well, and when through, retreated in better order than they came. I washed my dishes and was spending the last few moments by the broad bed of coals, for it was chilly, when I saw this whole body of men emerge from the darkness and come toward me. As they approached I received them graciously, and invited them all to sit by the fire.

They halted, reminding one of a band of brigands, with the red glare of the embers lighting up their bare, brown faces, and confronted me in the silence, awaiting their spokesman, George, who was, of course, their leader, and whose coal-black hair and eyes would well befit the chief of banditti. As they waited, I again invited them to sit by the fire.

"No, thank you," George replied. "We didn't come to warm us, we are used to the cold. But"—he went on slowly, as if it were a little hard to say—"but we come to tell you we are ashamed of ourselves."

I thought honest confession good for the soul, and did not interrupt him.

"The truth is," he continued, "in the first place we didn't want to come. There's fighting ahead and we've seen enough of that for men who don't carry muskets, only whips; and then we never seen a train under charge of a woman before and we couldn't understand it, and we didn't like it, and we thought we'd break it up, and we've been mean and contrary all day, and said a good many hard things and you've treated us like gentle-men. We hadn't no right to expect that supper from you, a better meal than we've had in two years. And you've been as polite to us as if we'd been the General and his staff, and it makes us ashamed. And we've come to ask your forgiveness. We shan't trouble you no more."

My forgiveness was easily obtained. I reminded them that as men it was their duty to go where the country had need of them. As for my being a woman, they would get accustomed to that. And I assured them that, as long as I had any food, I would share it with them. That, when they were hungry and supperless, I should be; that if harm befell them, I should care for them; if sick, I should nurse them; and that, under all circum-stances, I should treat them like gentlemen.

They listened silently and, when I saw the rough, woolen coat-sleeves drawing across their faces, it was one of the best moments of my life. Bidding me "goodnight," they withdrew, excepting the leader, who went to my ambulance, hung a lighted lantern in the top, arranged the few quilts inside for my bed, assisted me up the steps, buckled the canvas down snugly outside, covered the fire safely for morning, wrapped his blanket around him, and lay down a few feet from me on the ground.

At daylight I became conscious of low voices and stifled sounds, and soon discovered that these men were endeavoring to speak low and feed and harness their teams quietly, not to disturb me. On the other side I heard the crackling of blazing chestnut rails and the rattling of dishes, and George came with a bucket of fresh water, to undo my buckle door latches, and announce that breakfast was nearly ready.

I had cooked my last meal for my drivers. These men remained with me six months through frost and snow and march and camp and battle; and nursed the sick, dressed the wounded, soothed the dying, and buried the dead; and if possible grew kinder and gentler every day.

The next big battle, Fredericksburg, did not take place until December 1862. General Robert E. Lee had posted his Confederate troops on the south bank of Virginia's Rappahannock River. The Union commander, General Ambrose Burnside, delayed revealing his plans. Clara wrote: "Of army movements nothing can be said with certainty; no two persons, not even the generals, agree. . . . I have received calls from two generals today and in the course of conversation I discovered that their views were entirely different. General Burnside stood a long time in front of my door today, but to my astonishment he did not express his opinion—STRANGE!" Eventually Burnside tried a foolhardy frontal assault across the river.

■ One soft, hazy winter's day the army prepared for an attack. . . . I stood and watched the engineers as they moved forward to construct a pontoon bridge. . . . The rebel army occupying the heights of Fredericks-burg previous to the attack was very cautious about revealing the position of its guns. A few boats were fastened and the men marched quickly on with timbers and planks. For a few rods it proved a success. . . . On marches the little band with brace and plank, but never to be laid by them. A rain of musket balls has swept their ranks and the brave fellows lie level with the bridge or float down the stream. . . . Maddened by the fate of their comrades, others seize the work and march onward to their doom. For now, the balls are hurling thick and fast. . . .

At ten o'clock of the battle day when the rebel fire was hottest, the shell rolling down every street, and the bridge under the heavy cannonade, a courier dashed over and . . . placed in my hand . . . a request from the lion-hearted old surgeon on the opposite shore, establishing his hospitals in the very jaws of death. The uncouth penciling said: "Come to me. Your place is here."

General Ambrose Burnside, the Union commander at Fredericksburg, was bald on the top of his head but had impressive sidewhiskers, which he wore with a heavy mustache and a smooth chin. This style of facial hair arrangement has since been known as "sideburns," a play upon the general's name.

The faces of the rough men working at my side, which eight weeks ago had flushed with indignation at the very thought of being controlled by a woman, grew ashy white as they guessed the nature of the summons, and the lips which had cursed and pouted in disgust trembled as they begged me to send them, but save myself. I could only permit them to go with me if they chose, and in 20 minutes we were rocking across the swaying bridge, the water hissing with shot on either side. . . .

An officer stepped to my side to assist me over the debris at the end of the bridge. While our hands were raised in the act of stepping down, a piece of an exploding shell hissed through between us, just below our arms, carrying away a portion of both the skirts of his coat and my dress, rolling along the ground a few rods from us like a harmless pebble into the water. . . .

In the afternoon of Sunday an officer came hurriedly to tell me that in a church across the way lay one of his men shot in the face the day before. His wounds were bleeding slowly and, the blood drying and hardening about his nose and mouth, he was in immediate danger of suffocation. (Friends, this may seem to you repulsive, but I assure you that many a brave and beautiful soldier has died of this alone.) Seizing a basin of water and a sponge, I ran to the church, to find . . . my patient. For any human appearance above his head and shoulders, it might as well have been anything but a man.

I knelt by him and commenced with fear and trembling lest some unlucky movement close the last aperture for breath. After some hours' labor, I began to recognize features . . . and there to my gaze was the sexton of my old home church!

I have remarked that every house was a hospital. . . . Being alone, and the only woman visible among that moving sea of men, I naturally attracted the attention of the old veteran, Provost Marshal General Patrick, who, mistaking me for a resident of the city who had remained in her home until the crashing shot had driven her into the street, dashed through the waiting ranks to my side, and, bending down from his saddle, said in his kindliest tones, "You are alone and in great danger, Madam. Do you want protection?"

Amused at his gallant mistake, I humored it by thanking him, as I turned to the ranks, adding that I believed myself the best-protected woman in the United States. The soldiers near me caught my words, and responding with "That's so! That's so!" set up a cheer. . . . The gallant old General, taking in the situation, bowed low his bared head, saying as he galloped away, "I believe you are right, Madam."

It would be difficult for persons in ordinary life to realize the troubles arising from want of space merely for wounded men to occupy. . . . Among the wounded of the 7th Michigan was one Faulkner, of Ashtabula County, Ohio, a mere lad, shot through the lungs and, to all appearances, dying. When brought in, he could swallow nothing, breathed painfully, and it was with great difficulty that he gave me his name and residence. He could not lie down, but sat leaning against the wall in the corner of the room.

I observed him carefully as I hurried past from one room to another, and finally thought he had ceased to breathe. At this moment another man with a similar wound was taken in on a stretcher by his comrades, who sought in vain for a spot large enough to lay him down, and appealed

This panorama of the Union army's preliminary bombardment of Fredericksburg, before it began its assault on the Confederate army there, also shows work proceeding on the pontoon bridge across the Rappahannock River on which the troops advanced. Miss Barton almost lost her life during the battle crossing this pontoon bridge so that she could nurse the wounded on the far side.

to me. I could only tell them that when that poor boy in the corner was removed, they could set him down in his place.

They went to remove him, but, to the astonishment of all, he objected, opened his eyes, and persisted in retaining his corner, which he did for some two weeks, when, finally, a mere bundle of skin and bones, for he gave small evidence of either flesh or blood, he was wrapped in a blanket and taken away in an ambulance to Washington, with a bottle of milk punch in his blouse, the only nourishment he could take.

On my return to Washington, three months later, a messenger came from Lincoln Hospital to say that the men of Ward 17 wanted to see me. I returned with him, and as I entered the ward 70 men saluted me, standing, such as could, others rising feebly in their beds, and falling back—exhausted with the effort.

Every man had left his blood in Fredericksburg. . . . My hand had dressed every wound—many of them in the first terrible moments of agony.

I had prepared their food in the snow and winds of December and fed them like children. How dear they had grown to me in their sufferings, and the three great cheers that greeted my entrance into that hospital ward were dearer than the applause. I would not exchange their memory for the wildest hurrahs that ever greeted the ear of conqueror or king.

When the first greetings were over and the agitation had subsided somewhat, a young man walked up to me with no apparent wound, with bright complexion, and in good flesh. There was certainly something familiar in his face, but I could not recall him, until, extending his hand with a smile, he said, "I am Riley Faulkner, of the 7th Michigan. I didn't die, and the milk punch lasted all the way to Washington!"

In northern Maryland, as elsewhere at the front, Clara dressed as simply as possible so she could readily move about and waste as little time as possible in dressing. Just after she returned to Washington from her searing experiences in December 1862 at the battle of Fredericksburg, she was startled to find in her home a box of things meant for her—not for the soldiers. She wrote her friend Annie Childs:

■ Worn, weak, and heartsick, I was *home from Fredericksburg;* and when, there, for the first time I looked at myself, shoeless, gloveless, ragged, and blood-stained, a new sense of desolation and pity and sympathy and weariness, all blended, swept over me with irresistible force, and, perfectly overpowered, I sank down upon the strange box, unquestioning its presence or import, and wept as I had never done since the soft, hazy, winter night that saw our attacking guns silently stealing their approach to the river, ready at the dawn to ring out the shout of death to the waiting thousands at their wheels.

I said I wept, and so I did, and gathered strength and calmness and consciousness—and finally the *strange box,* which had afforded me my *first rest,* began to claim my attention . . . and a few pries with a hatchet, to hands as well accustomed as mine, soon made the inside . . . visible. . . . The while I was busy in removing the careful paper wrappings a letter, addressed to me, opened—*"From friends in Oxford and Worcester"*—no signature.

Mechanically I commenced lifting up, one after another, hoods, shoes, boots, gloves, skirts, handkerchiefs, collars, linen—and that beautiful dress! look at it, all made—who!—Ah, there is no mistaking the workmanship—Annie's scissors shaped and her skillful fingers fitted that. Now, I begin to comprehend; while I had been away in the snows and frosts and rains and mud . . . these dear, kind friends, undismayed and not disheartened by the great national calamity which had overtaken them, mourning, perhaps, the loss of their own, had remembered *me,* and . . . had prepared this noble, thoughtful gift for me at my return. . . .

A new chord was struck; my labors, slight and imperfect as they had been, had been appreciated; I was not alone; and then and there again I re-dedicated myself to my little work of humanity, pledging before God all that I *have*, all that I *am*, all that I *can*, and all that I *hope* to be, to the cause of *Justice* and *Mercy* and *Patriotism*, my *Country*, and my *God.* . . .

Annie, if it is not asking too much, now that I have gathered up resolution enough to speak of the subject at all (for I have never been able to before), I would like to know *to whom* besides yourself I am indebted for these beautiful and valuable gifts. It is too tame and too little to say that I am thankful for them. . . . I will say that, God willing, I will *yet wear them where none of the noble donors would be ashamed to have them seen.*

THE SIEGE OF CHARLESTON

These new clothes were, in fact, worn by her on the islands near Charleston, South Carolina, where the Union forces were trying to capture the city that had started the war by firing on Fort Sumter in April 1861. The siege of Charleston began on April 7, 1863, the very day she arrived at nearby Hilton Head, but in her diary a few days later she noted that the first assault "had fizzled. . . . I thought from the first that we had 'too few troops to fight and too many to be killed.' "

During the relative lull, as further assaults were planned, a letter from an editor friend, T. W. Meighan, urged her to press for an early peace. Her thoughtful answer shows her deep grasp of the whole involved politico-military situation caused by the Civil War.

■ Where you in prospective see *peace*, glorious, coveted peace, and rest for our tired armies, and home and happiness and firesides and friends for our war-worn heroes, *I* see only the *beginning of war*. If we should make overtures for "peace upon any terms," then, I fear, would follow a code of terms to which no civilized nation could submit and present even an honorable existence among nations. God forbid that *I* should ask the useless exposure of the life of *one* man, the desolation of one more home. . . .

If my poor life could have purchased theirs, how cheerfully and quickly would the exchange have been made . . . and yet among it all it has never once been in my heart, or on my lips, to sue to our enemies for peace. First, they broke it without cause; last, they will not restore it without shame. True, we *may* never find peace by *fighting*, certainly we never shall by *asking*. "Independence?" They always *had* their independence till they madly threw it away. . . .

I grant that our Government has made mistakes, sore ones, too, in some instances, but ours is a *human government*, and like *all* human operations liable to mistakes. . . . I would that so much of wisdom and foresight and strength and power fall to our rulers as would show them tomorrow the path to victory and peace, but we shall never strengthen their hands or incite their patriotism by deserting and upbraiding them.

To *my* unsophisticated mind, the Government of my country *is* my country, and the *people* of my country, the Government of my country as nearly as a representative system will allow. I . . . look upon our "Government" as the band which the people bind around the bundle of sticks to hold it firm, where every patriot hand must grasp the knot the tighter, and our "Constitution" as a symmetrical framework unsheltered and unprotected, around which the people must rally, and brace and stay themselves among its inner timbers, and lash and bind and nail and rivet themselves to its outer posts, till in its sheltered strength it bids defiance to every elemental jar—till the winds cannot rack, the sunshine warp, or the rains rot, and I would to Heaven that so we rallied and stood today. If our Government is *"too weak"* to act vigorously and energetically, *strengthen it till it can.* Then comes the peace we all wait for.

Meanwhile, there was war. A major assault on Fort Wagner began on July 11, 1863, with the advance charge led by her friend Colonel Robert G. Shaw, with his Negro regiment, backed by heavy artillery including the "swamp angel," a cannon that could send its shells five miles. Some 30 years later, in her Red Cross rescue work after a hurricane in this same group of islands, she would meet some of these Negro heroes again. Colonel Shaw was among the many killed, together with masses of the colored troops who were the particular targets of the Confederate defenders. But Clara effectively nursed numerous wounded survivors.

■ I remember so well these islands, when the guns and gunners, the muskets and musketeers, struggled for place and foothold among the shifting sands. I remember the first swarthy regiments with their unsoldierly tread, and the soldierly bearing and noble brows of the patient philanthropists who volunteered to lead them. I can see again the scarlet flow of blood as it rolled over the black limbs beneath my hands and the great heave of the heart before it grew still. And I remember Wagner and its 600 dead, and the great-souled martyr that lay there with them when the charge was ended. . . .

I saw the bayonets glisten. The "swamp angel" threw her bursting bombs, the fleet thundered its cannonade, and the dark line of blue trailed its way in the dark line of belching walls of Wagner. I saw them on, up, and over the parapets into the jaws of death, and heard the clang of the death-dealing sabers as they grappled with the foe. I saw the ambulances laden down with agony, and the wounded, slowly crawling to me down the tide-washed beach. . . .

The walls are reached, the torpedoes, and the pikes. Up—up—over the parapets, into the fort, hand to hand, foot to foot. Does any man say that this war showed no bayonet wounds? He did not scale the walls of Wagner. Hand to hand and hilt to hilt they wrestle. . . .

What is that? The sides of the fort are black with men—are these re-enforcements? Ah, would to God! Back! Out! Down, over torpedo and pike into moat and wave, sinking, striving, fainting, crawling, dying! . . . The fort was gained, the center reached. Bravely they fought, but all too few. They waited, braving death, for the help that came not. Leader after leader fell. And there side by side with those of fairer hue, lay the tawny hand of Africa, which that night for the first time . . . had been permitted to strike a lawful, organized blow at the fetters which had bound him body and mind and soul.

That broad, dark, heaving chest, and struggling breath, that great patient eye and gaping wound! "Ah, Sam, that's bad for you." "Yes, miss, I knows it. Dey's too many for us dis time—I'm a gwine, but thank God my childers free."

After eight months of siege, Charleston still held out—it was not to surrender until virtually the end of the war, in 1865. The Union assaults died down, and Clara—who had been ill—decided to return to Washington. On December 9 she wrote a friend:

■ Eight months and two days ago we landed. . . . The first sound which fell upon my ear . . . was the thunder of our guns in Charleston Harbor, and still the proud city sits like a queen and dictates terms to our army and navy. Sumter, the watch-dog that lay before her door, fell, maimed and bleeding, it is true; still there is defiance in his growl, and death in his bite. . . . We have captured one fort—Gregg—and one charnel house—Wagner—and we have built one cemetery, Morris Island. The thousand little sand-hills that glitter in the pale moonlight are a thousand head-stones, and the restless ocean waves that roll and break upon the whitened beach sing an eternal requiem to the toil-worn, gallant dead who sleep beside.

HUMOR AND HORROR AT THE FRONT

Back in Washington early in 1864, she began to prepare herself for the bitter fighting that would surely come with the end of winter, and for the political stresses of a presidential election year. She attended a number of Lincoln's receptions, and wrote of the "great, sad-eyed Commander" that his "care-worn face is very dear to me." When a friend asked what man or party she would support in the election, she answered that it would definitely be the Republican candidate.

However, she was willing to back either President Lincoln or the party's candidate of 1856, General John C. Frémont.

■ I *honor* Mr. Lincoln and I have believed, and still do, that his election was ordained, that he was raised up to meet this crisis, but it may also be that *no one* man could be constituted who should be equal to both the beginning and enduring of this vast, this mighty change—the same mind that could guide safely in the outset may be too slow now, for war has had its effects upon us. . . . I can trust either President Lincoln or General Frémont—on some accounts a change would be well. I think it would root out the traitors more effectually.

The title of this caricature in "Harper's Weekly" just after the 1864 election is "Long Abraham a Little Longer." Lincoln beat Democratic candidate George McClellan, 212 electoral votes to 21, but his margin in popular votes was much narrower.

177

At the time of John Brown's raid and execution in 1859, Clara had disapproved of the whole affair. Now, in April of 1864, she attended an abolitionist meeting with Brown's brother Frederick and showed a rather different attitude.

■ I went early with Mr. Brown. . . . At eight the orator of the evening entered the Hall in the same group with President Lincoln, Vice-President Hamlin . . . and others. . . . His remarks touching John Brown were strong, and, sitting as I was, watching the immediate effect upon the brother at my side, and when in a few minutes the band struck up the familiar air dedicated to him the world over, I truly felt that John Brown's Soul *was* marching on, and that the mouldering in the grave was of little account; the brother evidently felt the same. There was a glistening of the eye and a compression of the lip which spoke it all and more; he was evidently proud of the gallows rope that hung Old John Brown, "Old Hero Brown!"

On leaving the Hall, Mr. Parker joined us, and we all took a cream at Simmod's.

Clara had a sense of humor, which not only helped in times of stress—but often helped in her dealings with other people. Near the close of her life, she commented that the talent which had served her best—because it had eased so many tense situations—was a sense of humor. It certainly came to her aid during the terrible slaughter of the Wilderness and Spotsylvania in May 1864.

■ The soil was red clay. The 10,000 wheels and hoofs had ground it to a powder, and a sudden rain had converted the entire basin into . . . a lake. . . . Standing in this plain of mortar-mud were at least 200 six-mule army wagons, crowded full of wounded men waiting to be taken upon the boats for Washington. . . . No entire hub of a wheel was in sight, and you saw nothing of any animal below its knees and the mass of mud all settled into place perfectly smooth and glassy.

As I contemplated the scene, a young, intelligent, delicate gentleman, evidently a clergyman, approached me, and said anxiously, but almost timidly: "Madam, do you think those wagons are filled with wounded men?" I replied that they undoubtedly were. . . .

Miss Barton was a guest at various presidential receptions during the Lincolns' years in the White House. This engraving depicts the party that Mr. and Mrs. Lincoln held there on February 5, 1862.

"What can we do for them?" he asked, still more anxiously. "They are hungry and must be fed," I replied. For a moment his countenance brightened, then fell again as he exclaimed: "What a pity; we have a great deal of clothing and reading matter, but no food in any quantity, excepting crackers."

I told him that I had coffee and that between us I thought we could arrange to give them all hot coffee and crackers. "But where shall we make our coffee?" he inquired, gazing wistfully about the bare wet hillside. I pointed to a little hollow beside a stump. "There is a good place for a fire," I explained . . . and very soon we had some fire and a great deal of smoke . . . and presently a dozen camp-kettles of steaming hot coffee. My helper's pale face grew almost as bright as the flames and the smutty brands looked blacker than ever in his slim white fingers. . . .

We moved down the slope. Twenty steps brought us to the abrupt edge which joined the mud. . . . If you could have seen the expression of consternation and dismay depicted in every feature of his fine face, as he imploringly exclaimed, "How are we to get to them?"

"There is no way but to walk," I answered. . . . In spite of all the solemnity of the occasion, and the terribleness of the scene before me, I found myself striving hard to keep the muscles of my face all straight. As it was, the corners of my mouth would draw into wickedness, as with a backward glance I saw the good man . . . take his first step into military life. But thank God, it was not his last.

This long line of wagons full of wounded, Clara discovered, reached "so far out on the Wilderness road that I never found the end of it." And the arrangements for medical care were nonexistent. In this emergency, she turned with swift decision to one of her most useful friends, Senator Henry Wilson of Massachusetts, who as chairman of the Senate's Military Committee had considerable influence. Her "political" intervention in this crisis saved many lives—and showed the skill at cutting through confusion and red tape that she used so forcefully and well in her later Red Cross career.

A tall, lumbering, genial senator, Henry Wilson of Massachusetts was one of Miss Barton's most effective champions in Congress. He was later Vice-President under Grant.

■ No one has forgotten the heart-sickness which spread over the entire country as the busy wires flashed the dire tidings of the terrible destitution and suffering of the wounded of the Wilderness whom I attended as they lay in Fredericksburg. But you may never have known how many hundred-fold of these ills were augmented by the conduct of improper, heartless, unfaithful [Union] officers in the immediate command of the city and upon whose actions and indecisions depended entirely the care, food, shelter, comfort, and lives of that whole city of wounded men.

One of the highest officers there has since been convicted a traitor. And another, a little dapper captain quartered with the owners of one of the finest mansions in the town, boasted that he had changed his opinion since entering the city the day before; that it was in fact a pretty hard thing for refined people like the people of Fredericksburg to be compelled to open their homes and admit "these dirty, lousy, common soldiers," and that he was not going [to do anything whatsoever] to compel it.

This I heard him say, and waited until I saw him make his words good, till I saw, crowded into one old sunken hotel, lying helpless upon its bare, wet, bloody floors, 500 fainting men hold up their cold, bloodless, dingy hands, as I passed, and beg me in Heaven's name for a cracker to keep them from starving (and I had none); or to give them a cup that they might have something to drink water from, if they could get it (and I had no cup and could get none); till I saw 200 six-mule army wagons in a line, ranged down the street. . . .

Every wagon [was] crowded with wounded men . . . wrenched back and forth by the restless, hungry animals all night . . . and how much longer I know not. The dark spot in the mud under many a wagon told only too plainly where some poor fellow's life had dripped out in those dreadful hours. I remembered one man who would set it right, if he knew it, who possessed the power and who would believe me if I told him. . . . Four stout horses with a light army wagon took me 10 miles at an unbroken gallop, through field and swamp and stumps and mud to Belle Plain and a steam tug at once to Washington. Landing at dusk I sent for Henry Wilson. . . .

He listened to the story of suffering and faithlessness, and hurried from my presence, with lips compressed and face like ashes. At ten he stood in the War Department. They could not credit his report. He must have been deceived by some frightened villain. No official report of unusual suffering had reached them. . . . Still the Department doubted.

It was then that he proved that my confidence in his firmness was not misplaced, as, facing his doubters he replied: "One of two things will have to be done—either you will send some one tonight with the power to investigate and correct the abuses of our wounded men . . . or the Senate will send some one tomorrow."

This threat recalled their scattered senses.

CLOSING STAGES OF THE WAR

The Civil War now had less than a year to run, and Clara spent most of that time as Superintendent of the Department of Nurses for the Army of the James, which was commanded by her warm supporter General Benjamin F. Butler. This position gave fresh scope to her imagination and ingenuity, though her family and friends feared that she was overdoing. But she refused to let anyone slow her down, and wrote her brother David: "I suppose I should feel about as much benefited as my goldfish would if some kind-hearted person should take him out of his vase where he looked so wet and cold, and wrap him up in warm, dry flannel. We can't live out of our natural element, can we? I'll keep quiet when the war is over."

She brought a warm, personal, feminine touch not only to the hospitals she supervised with the Army of the James but also to the emergency work she continued to do on the field in battle crises, such as the explosion of the great

Miss Barton often paid tribute (as on this page) to the courage and character of Negro soldiers and civilians. One incident that epitomized the new Negro status—and delighted Northerners—is pictured here: a Negro sentry, fearing a possible fire hazard, warns General Grant, "You must throw away that cigar, sir!"

mine at Petersburg. If a wounded lad craved a pie with thumb-printed edges, she baked it. If the exhausted surgeons were ready to drop (and in those days when the concept of antisepsis was not widely known, surgeons would often operate more than 24 hours at a time without even pausing to wash their hands), she revived their spirits with homelike touches. During the bloody battles of 1864, she wrote: "Got supper of boiled eggs, crackers, toast and tea for the men. Set the table with a sheet for a tablecloth. Dr. Lamb at the head and how my little supper did seem of relish to them. My little stove is a jewel."

Meanwhile, she did not pamper herself. Her own tent near Petersburg was "bare as a cuckoo's nest—dirt floor, just like the street, a narrow bed of straw, a three-legged stand made of old cracker boxes, and a wash dish." As she also observed: "I have always refused a tent unless the army had tents also, and I have never eaten a mouthful of my own soft bread or fresh meat, until the sick of the army were abundantly supplied with both."

Nevertheless, despite all the strains she underwent, her morale stayed high, as shown in the following excerpts from three letters she wrote to old friends during July and September of 1864:

■ Here in the sunshine and dust and toil and confusion of camp life . . . the atmosphere and everything about black with flies, the dust rolling away in clouds as far as the eye can penetrate, the ashy ground covered with scores of hospital tents shielding nearly all conceivable maladies that soldier "flesh" is heir to, and stretching on beyond the miles of bristling fortifications, entrenchments, and batteries encircling Petersburg—all ready to blaze—just here in the midst of all this your refreshing letter dropped in upon me. . . .

Yesterday in passing through a ward (if wards they might be termed) filled mostly from the U.S. Colored Regiments I stopped beside a sergeant who had appeared weak all day, but made no complaint, and asked how he was feeling then. Looking up in my face, he replied, "Thank you, Miss, a little better, I hope." "Can I do anything for you?" I asked. "A little water, if you please." I turned to get it, and that instant he gasped and was gone. Men frequently reach us at noon and have passed away before night. . . .

I find a large number of colored people, mostly women and children, left in this vicinity, the stronger having been taken by their owners "up country." In all cases, they are destitute, having stood the sack of two opposing armies—what one army left them, the other has taken. On the plantation which forms the site of this hospital is a colored woman, the house servant of the former owner, with thirteen children, eight with her and five of her oldest taken away. The rebel troops had taken her bedding and clothing, and ours had taken her money, $40 in gold, which she had saved, she said, and I do not doubt her statement in the least. I gave her all the food I had that was suitable for her and her children and shall try to find employment for her. . . .

Thus far I have remained at the Corps (which is, in this instance, only an overburdened and well-conducted field) hospital. This point, from its peculiar location, is peculiarly adapted to this double duty service, situated as it is at one terminus of the line of entrenchments. . . .

I scarce write at all; and no one would wonder if they could look in upon my family and know besides that we had *moved* this week . . . a family of 1,500 sick men. . . . Our old cook John and his assistant Peter both came down sick. . . . I stepped into the gap and assumed the responsibility of the kitchen and . . . I held it and kept it straight till I selected a new boss cook and got him regularly installed and then helped him all the time up to the present day. I wish I had some of my bills of fare preserved as they read for the day. The variety is by no means so striking as the quantity. Say for breakfast 700 loaves of bread, 170 gallons of hot coffee, two large wash-boilers full of tea, one barrel of apple sauce, one barrel of sliced boiled pork, or 30 hams, one half barrel of corn-starch blanc-mange, 500 slices of butter toast. . . .

For dinner we have over 200 gallons of soup, or boiled dinner of three barrels of potatoes, two barrels of turnips, two barrels of onions, two barrels of squash, 100 gallons of minute pudding . . . or a large washtub full of codfish nicely picked, and stirred in a batter to make 150 gallons of nice home codfish, and the Yankee soldiers cry when they taste it. . . . Some days I have made with my own hands 90 apple pies. This would make a pie for some 600 poor fellows who had not tasted pie for months, it might be years. . . .

Last Saturday night we learned that we were to . . . go up in front of Petersburg, and their first loads of sick came with the order. . . . Since dark 40 wounded men have been brought in . . . one with the shoulder gone, a number of legs off, one with both arms gone, some blown up with shells and terribly burned. . . . Oh, what a volume it would make if I could only write you what I have seen, known, heard, and done since I first came to this department, June 18th. The most surprising of all of which is (tell Sally) that I should have *turned cook*. Who would have "thunk it"? I am writing on bits of paper for want of whole sheets. . . .

My range here is very extended; this department is large, and I am invited by General Butler to visit every part of it, and all medical and other officers within the department are directed to afford me every facility in their power. . . . Yesterday morn we had terrible firing along the whole line, but it amounted to only an artillery duel. Yet it brought us 14 wounded, three or four mortally.

Of another day's work near the end of the war, she wrote:

■ I have had a barrel of apple sauce made today and given out every spoonful of it with my own hands. I have cooked ten dozen eggs, made cracker toast, corn-starch blanc-mange, milk punch, arrow-root, washed hands and faces, put ice on hot heads, mustard on cold feet, written six "soldiers' letters home," stood beside three death beds—one the only son of a widowed mother, who up to this time knows nothing of her bereavement—and now, at this hour, midnight, I am too sleepy and stupid to write even you a tolerably readable scrap. It has been a long day, and the mercury is at something over 100°, and no breeze.

Clara could, fortunately, keep her sense of humor even under grim circumstances—and even when, at this late stage of the war, she saw people who were thoroughly unrealistic in their reaction to the problems that war posed. Thus, near Petersburg late in 1864, she who was ever so thoroughly practical could write wryly about a thoroughly impractical agent of the Sanitary Commission, who was supposed to be helping soldiers—not hindering them. The agent thought it was better to dress dead men than live ones.

■ I had been making the rounds of the hospital tents and for a moment stepped into the commission quarters when this tall, sun-burned, honest-faced soldier stepped in after me and approaching the agent said he should like to get a pair of stockings.

The agent replied with great kindness that he was very sorry that he could not oblige him, but they were out of stockings, except some very fine ones they had saved for *dead men!*

If you could have seen the look of puzzled astonishment which spread over the veteran's face, as he strove to comprehend the meaning of the reply! He looked at me, at his own turtle-backed feet, innocent of stockings for months, until finally giving it up, he broke out with, "Stockings for dead men!" And turning on his heel he stalked out of the tent, no richer and apparently no wiser than when he entered. Doubtless he went back to the camp and trenches in disgust.

And the young agent who had been from home only a fortnight, and had never learned by observation that men could lie quietly in their graves without stockings and shirts was just as deeply puzzled to comprehend the astonishment of the soldier and stood gazing after him in silent wonder as he walked away.

THE SEARCH FOR MISSING MEN

As the war approached its close, Clara decided to establish an agency to locate missing soldiers. On February 28, 1865, her friend Senator Henry Wilson urged President Lincoln to authorize her to do this. Lincoln did so on March 11. The need for such work was pressing. At least 143,155 graves of Northern soldiers were unidentified; some 44,000 other deaths were recorded with no graves listed; while in countless other instances, nobody seemed to know where soldiers still presumably alive were located. To eliminate these huge omissions, a whole register had to be set up, and Clara had to organize it from scratch. As she later reported to Congress:

■ During the last year of the War, I became aware from letters received from various parts of the country, that a very large number of our soldiers had disappeared from view without leaving behind them any visible trace

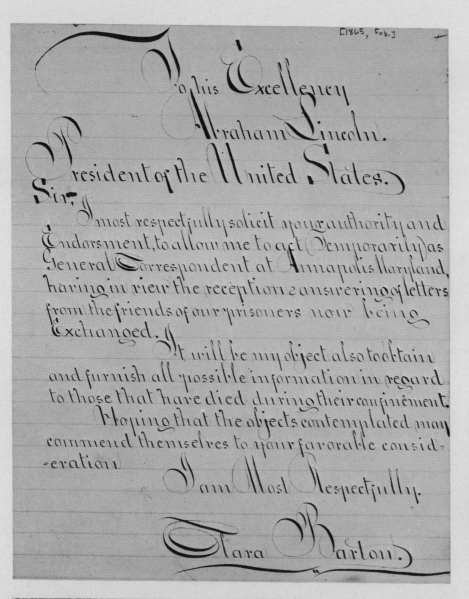

[1865, Feb.]

To his Excellency
    Abraham Lincoln.
President of the United States.
Sir,
    I most respectfully solicit your authority and
Endorsment, to allow me to act Temporarily as
General Correspondent at Annapolis Maryland,
having in view the reception & answering of letters
from the friends of our prisoners now being
Exchanged. It will be my object also to obtain
and furnish all possible information in regard
to those that have died during their confinement.
    Hoping that the objects contemplated may
commend themselves to your favorable consid=
=eration
        I am Most Respectfully.

           Clara Barton.

Some of the different styles of Miss Barton's handwriting appear here. The "copperplate" of her most formal correspondence is shown in the letter she wrote Lincoln early in 1865 asking his authorization for her prisoner-of-war work. The entries in her diary for two successive days a few weeks later, covering Lincoln's assassination and death, show her more informal penmanship.

FRIDAY, APRIL 14, 1865.

Assasination of President
Lincoln
was returng from a call at
Mr Uppermans. when it was
rumored on the sheet,

SATURDAY, APRIL 15, 1865.

President Lincoln died at
7 oclok this morning
the whole city in gloom
no one knows what to do

Dr Sidney came

185

or record. . . . Any information respecting them would have afforded the most grateful relief to their families. . . . I caused printed lists of all missing soldiers who had come to my knowledge, to be posted in conspicuous places, in all the towns and considerable villages in the country, requesting information from all who might be able to furnish any.

Congress was so impressed by the work she did on this project, largely with money out of her own pocket, that it appropriated $15,000 to repay her. Her most striking work in this field was accomplished at the Confederate prison camp of Andersonville, Georgia, after she located a discharged prisoner, Dorence Atwater of Connecticut, who had secretly made a record of deaths and burials at Andersonville. With the authorization of the Secretary of War, she led an expedition that set up a suitable cemetery there. Later she wrote:

■ To speak of Andersonville is but reasonable, knowing that I have looked upon its terrible face. . . . I have looked over its 25 acres of pitiless

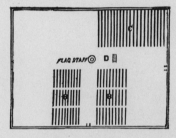

In this picture, sketched by I. C. Schotel for the issue of "Harper's Weekly" dated October 7, 1865, Miss Barton is shown at "A" in right center raising the American flag at the Andersonville National Cemetery. The accompanying chart (above) indicates that "B" represents rows containing from 100 to 150 headboards each, "C" has rows with 300 headboards each, while "D" has the graves of six men who were hung in the prison camp.

stockade, its burrows in the earth, its stinted stream, its turfless hillside, shadeless in summer and shelterless in winter; its well, and tunnels and graves; its seven forts of death; its ball and chains; its stocks and tortures; its kennels for blood-hounds; its sentry boxes and its dead line; my heart went out, and I said, "Surely this was not the gate of hell, but hell itself," and for comfort, I turned away to the nine acres of crowded graves, and I said that here at last was rest, and this to them was the gate of Heaven.

Then I saw the little graves marked . . . raised over them the flag they loved, and died for, and left them to their rest. . . . They starved in Andersonville. There, side by side, we found their graves, and marked the spot for you.

The original burials at Andersonville had simply been by numbered boards. Comparing these numbers with Atwater's list, Clara and her companions were able to re-inter and give reverent burial in deep individual graves to

12,920 men, with "a uniform and comely tablet, bearing name, company, regiment and date of death of the soldier who slept beneath." This and other postwar work kept her occupied almost as long as the great conflict itself. She recalled:

■ Our war closed in the spring of '65, but for four years longer, in an awful aftermath, I worked among the debris, gathering up the wrecks, and sometimes during the lecture-season, telling a few simple war stories to the people over the country in their halls and churches.

Her work on missing soldiers involved some 105,000 letters handwritten by Clara or her few assistants during a four-year period. This correspondence with distraught relatives was often quite harrowing for her—and also quite expensive. Senator Grimes, addressing his fellow senators, reported: "I personally inspected the vouchers. In tracing the missing men Clara Barton expended $2,000 more than the Government gave her for the expenses."

However, her labors in this field did produce some wryly amusing sidelights. For she often located a missing soldier who did not want to be located! Thus the sister of one "J.H.H." of Lockport, New York, begged Clara to find her brother, "who was engaged in the 2nd Maryland Regiment under General Goldsborough, and from whom we have not heard in nearly two years. His mother died last winter, to whom his silent absence was, I assure you, a great grief." Clara duly had his name posted on bulletin boards everywhere, and shortly heard from an indignant "J.H.H." who objected strenuously to having "my name blazoned all over the country. If my friends in New York wish to know where I am, let them wait until I see fit to write them."

In turn, Clara wrote him as follows:

■ Sir: I enclose copies of two letters in my possession. The writer of the first I suppose to be your sister. The lady for whose death the letter was draped in mourning I suppose to have been *your mother*. Can it be possible that you were aware of that fact when you wrote that letter? *Could* you have spoken thus, knowing all?

The cause of your name having been "blazoned all over the country" was your unnatural concealment from your nearest relatives, and the great distress it caused them. "What you have done" to render this necessary *I* certainly *do not* know. It seems to have been the misfortune of your family to think more of you than you did of them, and probably more than you deserve from the manner in which you treat them. They had already waited until a son and brother possessing common humanity would have "seen fit" to write them. *Your mother died waiting*, and the result of your sister's faithful efforts to comply with her dying request *"mortify"* you. I cannot apologize for the part I have taken.

You are mistaken in supposing that I am "anxious for your welfare." I assure you I have no interest in it, but your accomplished sister, for whom I entertain the deepest respect and sympathy, I shall inform of your existence lest you should not "see fit" to do so yourself.

She also felt deeply for the widows and orphans of the war, and she used the fame she had deservedly won, both by her labors and by the risks she had taken, to extend her task of comfort and mercy to those who now needed it as much as the soldiers had needed it in battle. Her success as a public speaker—she gave 300 lectures in 1867 and 1868 alone and used the money from them for her work—was largely owing to the vividness and immediacy with which she could describe her experiences.

Miss Barton used an agent to book her talks but also booked some of them herself, at fees averaging more than $75 per lecture and ranging up to $125. She had an effective range of oratorical devices, many of them gained from speakers she had heard address Congress.

She could rouse the imagination and pluck the heartstrings of her Victorian-era audiences. The power of her eloquence and pathos reminds one even of her famous contemporary, Charles Dickens, as he described the death of Little Nell. This is such a lecture excerpt:

■ Having occasion to pass through a somewhat western city in the winter of '65 and '66, my attention was one day suddenly arrested by the figure of a singularly attired, weird looking little boy, with a basket on his arm standing in front of a bakery. A soldier's cap and pantaloons in which his tiny form seemed nearly lost and the faded light blue cape of a storm-beaten overcoat reaching to his knees, with the once bright buttons still striving to adorn its tattered edge, comprised the uniform of the little shivering hero.

He stood perfectly motionless, evidently unconscious of any presence save the large, warm, nut-brown loaves within the window. As I could not pass such a picture, I stopped, and asked if he were hungry! "Not very," he said, hesitatingly, "not very, but Annie is." "Who is Annie?" I asked. "My little sister." "Have you no father and mother?" "Father was killed at Chattanooga, and ma's sick." His voice trembled a little. "No brothers?" I asked.

"I had three brothers," and his little voice grew smaller and trembled more, "but they all went to the War. Willie was shot in the woods when they were all on fire" (he meant the Wilderness) "and Charlie, he starved to death in Andersonville, and Jamie, he was next to me, and he went for a Drummer Boy, and died in the Hospital. And then there was only Ma and me and Annie. Annie was a baby when they went away, and Ma's grown sick and Annie's often hungry and cold and I can't always get enough for her. I pick up chips and wood, but Ma doesn't like me to ask for food, she says it's a bad habit for little boys to learn," and the tears slid quietly down his child cheeks, wan and care-worn.

I went home with him—far on the outskirts of the city, long beyond the reach of sidewalks, through alternate frost and mud—a cheerless room, and as we entered a thin hectic woman partly rose from her bed to greet me. Her story was only a confirmation of what I had heard. Her boys enlisted first and early, and the father, partly to be near them, and partly through dread of the draft, followed them. One by one they had met their

Washington. Jany 2nd 1866

Tuesday

the water is running. the keys have
been handed over to me, and I am
much more comfortably situated. than un
heretofore.

It must be nearly time for
the Senate to meet again. but the
House will not be in full session
until the 8th or 9th – at which time
I shall expect cousin Robert, and
possibly Mrs. Gage. I must make
all the progress I possibly can with
my lectures before this. as I can
probably never write as well as I
am doing just now all alone.
I began to think I might like the
life of a writer. and it yet remains to be seen if I can assume
it — I began late it is true if atall
. but it may be the true course.
for me after all. If I were only
sure that I could read my lectures)

fate. . . . One by one her hopes [for their survival] had died. . . .

As she talked on quietly and tearfully, Baby Annie stole out of her hiding place, and peered wistfully into the basket. And the little military guardian drew up to my side with simple, childlike confidence, as he said, "This was Jamie's cap and cloak. They sent them home from the hospital when he was dead. But they didn't send Jamie home. Nor Willie, nor Charlie." I said "No!" "Nor Papa. There's only Ma and me and Annie—that's all!"

And these were more than there would be long, poor child, for already the pale messenger waits at the gate, and his weird shadow falleth ever nearer.

A SPEECH FOR WOMAN'S RIGHTS

Clara became extremely effective as a public speaker, though it always remained a strain for her. John B. Gough, then considered one of the country's outstanding orators, said of a lecture by her, "I never heard anything more touching, more thrilling, in my life." The Syracuse Times *said of a speech there, "Few eyes but were dim; few hearts but were saddened."*

Among those most pleased by her platform success were the leaders of the woman's rights movement, notably Susan B. Anthony, who tried to enlist her active support. They pointed out that her audiences contained a high percentage of men, which was not the case with any suffragette speaker, and that she thus had a unique opportunity "to make woman's plea for the right to a voice in government."

Susan B. Anthony (above) and Miss Barton were very friendly for some 40 years, and in the lecture excerpt starting on this page Clara eloquently defended Susan. The diary entry opposite includes some of Miss Barton's thinking as she wrote out the lectures she planned to give and considered the possibility of becoming a full-time writer. The "Mrs. Gage" mentioned is the woman's rights leader Frances D. Gage, cited by Clara on page 192.

Clara never became one of the active suffragettes. She wanted (and generally got) their full support for the causes that most concerned her, and she invariably opened her lectures with the phrase "Gentlemen and Ladies." But she was a lifelong friend of the chief suffrage leaders. And when, in 1867, she was placarded in an Iowa town before she spoke there as a speaker of "patriotic eloquence" but no lecturer "upon women's rights after the style of Susan B. Anthony and her clique; Miss Barton does not belong to that class of woman," she made her basic attitude abundantly clear.

■ My blood boiled as I read. I went upon the platform and faced an audience of which the most exacting speaker might be proud, not even standing room in the aisles. I treated them to their feast of "patriotic eloquence" with a vim. . . . I held firm to my subject till my address and all pertaining to it was ended, and when they shouted and cheered to a "tiger," I resumed in the following text:

"Soldiers, you have called me here to speak to you of the war we lived together. I have done it. Now I have a word to you. I wish to read to you this paragraph which you have used to help fill your hall." I read it very slowly and distinctly.

"That paragraph, my comrades, does worse than to misrepresent me as a woman; it maligns my friend. It abuses the highest and bravest work

Elizabeth Cady Stanton was one of the woman's rights leaders most fervently admired by Miss Barton. In 1848 Mrs. Stanton produced a "Declaration of Sentiments" listing 18 grievances and wrongs women were suffering from men. A warmly humorous woman, Mrs. Stanton kept active in feminist causes while rearing seven children.

ever done in this land for either you or me. You glorify the women who made their way to the front to reach you in your misery, and nursed you back to life. You called us angels.

"Who opened the way for women to go and made it possible? Who but that detested 'clique' who through years of opposition, obloquy, toil and pain had openly claimed that women had rights, should have the privilege to exercise them. The right to her own property; her own children, her own home, her just individual claim before the law, to her freedom of action, to her personal liberty. Upon this, other women claimed the right and took the courage, if only to go to an army camp, and drag wounded men out of a trench, and try to save them for their families and their country.

"And, soldiers, for every woman's hand that ever cooled your fevered brows, staunched your bleeding wounds, gave food to your famishing bodies, or water to your parching lips, and called back life to your perishing bodies, you should bless God for Susan B. Anthony, Elizabeth Cady Stanton, Frances D. Gage and their followers.

"No one has stood so unhelped, unprotected, so maligned as Susan B. Anthony, no one deserves so well; and soldiers, I would have the first monument that is ever erected to any woman in this country reared to her; and that monument *will* be reared, and your daughters, boys, will help proudly, gratefully help to set its granite blocks like glistening silver, for everlasting. Aye, set it where all may see, and I would recall the eloquence of Webster at Bunker Hill, 'Let the earliest light of the morning gild it, and parting day linger and play on its summit.'

"*Boys, three cheers for Susan B. Anthony!* And the very windows shook in their casements."

FIRST GLIMPSE OF THE RED CROSS

In 1868 Clara's health collapsed; the medical term used for her ailment was "nervous prostration." In 1869 she was still far from recovery, and her doctor ordered her to "do nothing for three years"—and to do it in Europe. "You must rest," he said. "You can't rest in your own country. They won't let you." She was nearly forty-eight and (thanks to some earnings, some bequests and her own strict economy) had enough financial means to live on for the rest of her life.

She sailed for Europe and tried to do nothing. But for her, this was almost impossible. Thus, not long after she settled at Geneva, in Switzerland, she was visited by a group of Red Cross officials, headed by Dr. Louis Appia, who wished to know why the United States had never ratified the Geneva Convention for the relief of sick and wounded soldiers, with its symbol of the Red Cross. She later recalled:

■ They introduced themselves as the officers of a society known as the International Convention of Geneva—more familiarly, the Red Cross—

having for its object the amelioration of the sufferings of war. . . . This society had been formed in 1865, at the instance of Dr. Louis Appia. . . .

This treaty, consisting of 10 articles, and making material changes in the articles of war governing the medical and hospital departments of all armies, provided among other things for entire neutrality concerning all hospitals for the care of sick and wounded men; that they should not be subject to capture; that not only the sick and wounded themselves, but the persons in attendance upon them, as surgeons, hospital stewards and nurses should be held neutral, and free from capture; that surgeons, chaplains and nurses, in attendance upon the wounded of a battlefield at the time of its surrender, should be regarded as noncombatants, not subject to capture, and left unmolested to care for the wounded so long as any remained upon the field, and, when no longer needed for this, should be safely escorted to their own lines, and given up; that soldiers too badly wounded to be capable of again bearing arms should not be carried away as prisoners, but offered to their own army; . . . that all supplies designed for the use of the sick or wounded should be held as neutral and entirely exempt from capture by either belligerent army; that it should be the duty of both generals in command to apprise the inhabitants, in the vicinity of a battle about to take place, of the fact that any house which should take in and entertain the wounded of either side would be placed under military protection, and remain so as long as any wounded remained therein, and that they would also be exempt from the quartering of troops and ordinary contributions of war, thus literally converting every house in the vicinity of a battle into a furnished hospital and making nurses of its inmates.

In order to carry into effect these great changes, it would be needful to have some one distinctive sign, a badge by which all these neutral peoples and stores could be designated. There must be but one hospital flag among all nations within the treaty, and this same sign must mark all persons and things belonging to it. The convention studied diligently for this sign [and] said . . . This little Republic of Switzerland . . . has had the courage to invite us here to consider our cruelties and call upon us for some better system of kindness and humanity. . . .

We cannot take her flag . . . but if she permits we will reverse its colors —a white cross upon a red ground—and make a red cross on a white ground the one distinctive sign of humanity in war, the world over. The consent was given and this committee of gentlemen who had called the convention, with Monsieur Gustave Moynier as its president, was re-elected by all the nations as the international medium and head of war relief throughout the civilized world. . . .

There were at this time 31 nations in this great compact, comprising all the civilized and even some of the semi-civilized nations of the globe, all with one great and incomprehensible exception, the United States of America. It had been three times presented to our Government . . . without success, and without any reason which . . . seemed sufficient or intelligent. And it was to ask of me the real nature of the grounds of this

Henri Dunant, who founded the International Red Cross, deservedly became the first winner of the Nobel Peace Prize. The novelist Victor Hugo wrote Dunant, "You are arming humanity and are serving freedom," while the philosopher Ernest Renan told him, "You have created the greatest work of the century."

declination that the interview had been sought. . . .

In their perplexity they had come to me for a solution of the problem. What could I say? What could each or any of you have said. . . . Simply that you did not know anything about it, and you were sure the American people did not know anything about it, or ever had heard of it. That the Government, or rather some officer of the Government . . . had decided upon and declined it individually. . . . I knew it must be so: that it had simply gone by default with no real objection . . . and I hoped it could be better presented at some future time.

THE FRANCO-PRUSSIAN WAR

A few months after this visit of Dr. Appia and his colleagues had first acquainted Clara with the Red Cross, France declared war on Germany in a dispute over the crown of Spain; the German chancellor, Bismarck, had proposed that Prince Leopold, of Germany's ruling Hohenzollern family, be named Spanish king. France's Emperor Napoleon III thought this a threat to encircle him. Still too sick, at first, to do as much as she wished to do in this emergency, Clara nevertheless went to the front, where she did some work and made some keen observations:

■ On the 15th of July, 1870, France declared war against Prussia. Within three days a band of agents from the International Committee of Geneva, headed by Dr. Louis Appia . . . equipped for work and *en route* for the seat of war, stood at the door of my villa inviting me to go with them and take such part as I had taken in our own war. I had not strength to trust for that, and declined with thanks, promising to follow in my own time and way, and I did follow within a week.

No shot had been fired—no man had fallen. Yet this organized, powerful commission was on its way, with its skilled agents. . . . These men had treaty power to go directly on to any field, and work unmolested in full cooperation with the military and commanders-in-chief; their supplies held sacred and their efforts recognized and seconded in every direction by either belligerent army. Not a man could lie uncared for or unfed.

I thought of the Peninsula in McClellan's campaign, of Pittsburg Landing, Cedar Mountain, and second Bull Run, Antietam, Old Fredericksburg, with its . . . dead, and starving wounded, frozen to the ground, and our commission and their supplies in Washington, with no effective organization to get beyond; of the Petersburg mine, with its 4,000 dead and wounded and no flag of truce, the wounded broiling in a July sun, dying and rotting where they fell.

I remembered our [Civil War military] prisons, crowded with starving men whom all the powers and pities of the world could not reach even with a bit of bread. I thought of the widows' weeds still fresh and dark through all the land, North and South, from the pine to the palm; the shadows on the hearths and hearts over all my country. Sore, broken hearts, ruined, desolate homes! Was this a people to decline a humanity in war? Was this a country to reject a treaty for the help of wounded soldiers? Were these the women and men to stand aloof and consider?

I believed, if these people knew that the last cloud of war had forever passed from their horizon, the tender, painful, deathless memories of what had been would bring them in with a force no power could resist. They needed only to know. . . .

As I journeyed on and saw the work of these Red Cross societies in the field, accomplishing in four months under their systematic organization what we failed to accomplish in four years without it—no mistakes, no needless suffering, no starving, no lack of care, no waste, no confusion, but order, plenty, cleanliness and comfort wherever that little flag made its way—a whole continent marshaled under the banner of the Red Cross —as I saw all this, and joined and worked in it, you will not wonder that I said to myself, "If I live to return to my country, I will try to make my people understand the Red Cross and that treaty." But I did more than resolve, I promised other nations I would do it. . . .

France, Germany and Switzerland had been in the international compact for years past, all organized, every town and city with its Red Cross Relief Committee, its well-filled workrooms like our relief societies in our war, but all prepared in times of peace and plenty, awaiting the emergency. . . . My first steps were to the storehouses, and to my amazement I found there a larger supply than I had ever seen at any one time in readiness for the field at our own Sanitary Commission rooms in Washington, even in the fourth year of the war; and the trains were loaded with boxes and barrels pouring in from every city, town and hamlet in Switzerland, even from Austria and northern Italy; and the trained, educated nurses stood awaiting their appointments, each with this badge upon the arm or breast, and every box, package or barrel with a broad bright scarlet cross, which rendered it as safe and sacred from molestation (one might almost say) as the bread and wine before the altar.

The French city of Strasbourg fell to the Germans on September 28, 1870, after a siege led by the Grand Duke of Baden that left the city in smoking ruins. Clara happened at that moment to be visiting the Grand Duchess of Baden, who became one of her closest, lifelong friends, and who supported her generously during her vigorous relief activities in Strasbourg. She found that many of the wounded there were women, "a phase in military observation new, even to me." But wounded women would become ever commoner in following decades, as war became ever more total.

Two of her key assistants were Antoinette Margot and Anna Zimmermann, the latter a clergyman's daughter who was a governess at Baden's royal court. Of the former, Clara wrote:

■ As good fortune would have it, there comes to me at this moment a kind-featured, gentle-toned, intelligent Swiss girl . . . my faithful Antoinette . . . Swiss by birth, French by cultivation, education and habit.

Antoinette Margot, daughter of a silk manufacturer, was one of Miss Barton's best aides in Europe and later helped her for a time in the United States. Clara heartily praised her for being "lovely, gentle and mild."

The two national characteristics met and joined in her. The enthusiasm of the one, the fidelity of the other, were so perfectly blended and balanced in her, that one could never determine which prevailed. No matter, as both were unquenchable, unconquerable. She was raised in the city of Lyons, France, an only daughter, and at that age, an artist of great note, even in the schools of artistic France. Fair-haired, playful, bright and confiding, she spoke English as learned from books, and selected her forms of expression by inference. One day she made the remark that something was "unpretty." Observing a smile on my face, she asked if that were not correct? I replied that we do not say unpretty in English. "No. But you say unwise, unselfish, unkind and ungrateful—why not unpretty?" "I do not know," I answered. I didn't either. . . . This slender little lady . . . went with me every step, over broken ranks, through fire and blood.

It was during her relief work in Strasbourg that Clara first realized the dangers in mere indiscriminate giving—that in the long run it was far better to help even the worst-hit victims to help themselves. Germany's "Iron Chancellor" Bismarck was also at the moment Governor General of Alsace, so when he visited Strasbourg and wanted to know what she was doing, she wrote him a masterful letter that not only shows her diplomatic skill and her political insight but also foreshadows her later techniques.

■ I learn that Your Highness will kindly permit me to communicate with you in reference to the work I am endeavoring to perform. . . . But speaking no German, lacking confidence to attempt a conversation in French, and fearing that English may not be familiar to you, I decide

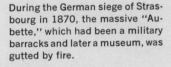
During the German siege of Strasbourg in 1870, the massive "Aubette," which had been a military barracks and later a museum, was gutted by fire.

to write, subject to translation, the little explanation I would make of my work, its origin, progress and design.

I entered Strasbourg the second day after its fall, and, observing both the distress of its inhabitants and their bitterness toward their captors, who must always remain their neighbors, I deemed it wise, while they should receive the charity so much needed, that something of it be presented by German hands. In this view I was most cordially met by that noblest of ladies, the Grand Duchess of Baden. . . . I returned with an assistant to do what we could in the name of Germany.

At first, we could only give indiscriminately, to the hundreds who thronged our doors. But, directly, I perceived that a prolonged continuance of this system would be productive of greater disaster to the *moral* condition of the people than the bombardment had been to their physical. . . . Only a small proportion of these families had been accustomed to receive charity, but one winter of common beggary would reduce the larger part to a state of careless degradation from which they would scarcely again emerge. It seemed morally indispensable that remunerative employment in some form should be given them. . . .

We opened our present "Workrooms for Women" in the month of October . . . to aid not only the inhabitants of Strasbourg, but those in other portions of Alsace. . . . I thought that to be just to all and produce the best moral influence, the employment, and the payment, should be given to Strasbourg, thus making of the inhabitants *workers*, instead of *beggars*, but that the warm garments made by them should be sent to the half-naked peasants of the villages. . . . To the extent of my means I have done this. . . . This population must always be the neighbors, if not a part, of the German people; it will be most desirable that they should

Here Strasbourg undergoes severe German bombardment. The French finally raised the white flag of surrender on the cathedral tower at center rear.

also be friends; they are in distress—their hearts can never be better reached than now; the little seed sown today may have in it the germs of future peace or war.

But pardon my boldness, Honored Count; I am neither a diplomatist nor political counselor; I am only a maker of garments for the poor.

Bismarck replied immediately to this letter of December 9, 1870. He met her the next day; 48 hours after that he visited her workrooms and gave the project his full approval. Doubtless he had already decided that France must yield Alsace-Lorraine to Germany in the peace treaty to be negotiated in 1871, and so may have figured that any friendly gestures meanwhile might well be useful. A few months later, feeling better than she had for years, Clara took time out for a sprightly letter to her longtime dressmaker and friend, Annie Childs:

■ If I were to make an apology as long as my offense, I could write nothing else, but I don't like apologies; you don't either, do you? Then let me hasten to proclaim myself an idle, lazy, procrastinating, miserable do-nothing and good-for-nothing; if that isn't enough, I leave the sentence open for you to finish and I sign it squarely when you have done and call it "quits" .... I have neglected everybody in general, not you in particular ....

I wanted all last winter to tell you about my "dressmaking" and describe to you my "shop." I knew it would interest you if no one else. Now, wasn't that the last thing you would have thought of, that *I* should come to Europe and set up *dressmaking*, and *French* dressmaking at that? I knew the fact would be a little surprise to most of my old friends ... but to you I imagine it a matter of bewildering astonishment. Well, you should have seen the patterns!

"Did I have patterns?" Didn't I? And didn't I cut them myself? And didn't I direct all the making until I had imparted my wonderful art to others? And *you* think my garments were fearfully and wonderfully made! Well, that opinion comes of your being an *old* maid and so particular. I assure you, Miss Annie Childs, that they were nice garments and prettily cut and well made, and I found them in excellent demand; every one wanted them and never a word of *complaint of the price.* ...

I don't think they were gored and flounced and frilled as much as yours ... but they were strong and warm and handsome. ... Don't you wish now that you had come and worked at the head of my "shop"—didn't *I* wish it? More than once I sighed in my inmost soul for you. ... I shall write to Fannie sometime when "I hain't told all the news" to you—please hand her this if she looks patient and strong enough to stand it.

To the head of an English committee that had sent a contribution of $2,500 for her work, Clara described more bluntly what she had been trying to do in Strasbourg, Lyons, and Paris:

Bismarck was one of the most redoubtable world leaders of his century. But Miss Barton won his blessing on her work by her shrewdly perceptive letter to him, plus the fine personal impression she made on him when he inspected her Strasbourg workrooms.

■ My attempts to clothe the people of France have not been the result of a desire to improve the personal appearance, but to aid in ridding them a little, if possible, from the scourge of pestilence and vermin which the war has so terribly spread among them. It is to be hoped that few will die of outright hunger during the next six months, but thousands must fall pitiful victims to disease lurking in the only old rags, in which months ago they escaped from fire and destruction.

Disease is spread from one family to another, until thousands who are well today will rot with smallpox and be devoured by body lice before the end of August. Against the progress of these two scourges there is, I believe, no check but the destruction of all infected garments; hence the imperative necessity for something to take their place. Excuse, sir, the plain, ugly terms which I have employed to express myself; the facts are plain and ugly.

Throughout her life, Clara had a discerning eye for social patterns and behavior. Accordingly, when Paris was only beginning to recover from its wartime and postwar upheavals, she gaily took time off from her relief work in September 1871 to contrast the feminine fashions of several nations:

I am spending some fine days in Paris, just what I most desired. I wanted to see some American people; it had been so long since I had seen them—and indeed there is no lack of them here. . . . Some I am proud of, and some I am ashamed of; some speak remarkably well, and some cannot utter a proper sentence. Generally they are "well dressed," as the world goes, but to my eye "over-rigged," as a sailor would say, but always much better than the English, who are the most fearful dressers in all Christendom.

English women are solid and sensible, learned and self-possessed, and all the world respects them; but the art of selecting and putting clothes onto themselves is something quite beyond their line of vision. Not that they do not wear enough—oh, Heavens, no, not that—there is always enough and to spare, but there is no calculation what portion or member of the body corporate it will be found dangling from, and Joseph's coat [of many colors] bore no comparison.

Still [the English] are splendid women, and handsome, 50 per cent more beautiful than the French. The French declare that the Germans cannot dress in decent manner, but I have seen much good, comfortable-looking dressing in Germany, and I rather liked it. I don't know *what* has induced me to write so much upon the silly matter of dress, unless that some of my "sisterin" abroad annoy me a little with theirs.

By 1872, when the pressure of her war work was again relaxing, Clara's nervous illness was returning in full force. But as her biographer Blanche Colton Williams has noted of the years she spent in Europe, 1869–1873: "Long before this phase, Clara Barton was a neurotic. Hers was a neuroticism apparently affecting neither judgment nor emotion when work must be done,

Miss Barton's observations on this page indicate that she could make quite penetrating comments on the feminine styles of her time. Then as later, France was famous for its millinery; here are two Paris hats of the late nineteenth century.

but a state of nerves that induced unhappiness or bodily illness in seasons of comparative idleness."

Outwardly, she often kept up her spirits so well that even her close associates received an impression not of gloom but of firm thinking firmly expressed. Thus, in January of 1872, while she was visiting the Grand Duchess of Baden, she minced no words:

■ The Grand Duchess . . . sent for me about a week ago to spend an evening and she spoke of little else than the progress of woman and schools for girls in America. She had evidently been reading something, I presume some German criticism upon the too liberal spirit of America, and wished to compare notes, I think.

I told her all as it was, and I said I believed in special training for all kinds of life, but that I thought it possible to train too much till the original spirit was crushed out and ashes left in the place of coals, and there was danger of Germany's doing this with her great respect for discipline; that I thought them too strict, and that they cramped their people by rules and regulations and hurt many good original minds. This was plain speech for a woman in a plain black gown without even a ring on her hands to address to a Princess and Sovereign, but when I am asked I answer, let it be where it will. I guess it didn't offend, for she sent me a very pretty letter next morning.

She spent the winter of 1872–1873 under the leaden skies of London, feeling herself "already in a metallic coffin, only waiting to be closed in a little snugger, and have the screws turned down." Even then she "tried to be cheerful and full of life and fun." Not only Antoinette Margot but also Clara's niece Mamie Barton shared her London lodgings. In a third-person note to Mamie wryly signed "Old Dolorous," she showed some of her technique for attempting to lift herself by her mental bootstraps:

■ Auntie wants to write Mamie a little letter. She is more sorry than she can tell that she has such a stupid illness that forbids her to be company for anyone. Auntie does not feel less social for this and although it is hard and painful, she will not feel despondent a moment but hopeful and cheerful for the present and future. . . . Her head is strong physically. (She will not refer to its mental qualities.) . . .

But when she feels herself imposing a dull dead silence on all persons about her, those whom she loves most dearly and for whose hourly comfort and happiness she would sacrifice anything in reason and see her dear little girls gliding about without speaking a sentence—never sees a laugh or scarce a smile—it makes her feel herself such a restriction, such a detractor from their happiness. . . . Nothing so much as a good funny time a day would so shorten and deaden the pain. . . .

Now if the two dear good little girls could only bring themselves to have the same chatty day that Auntie knows they would have if they were in their own room by themselves, laughing, singing, doing nonsense

. . . Auntie would be more grateful to them than for anything else they could do for her. And she has faith in the good understanding of her dear Mamie, to . . . have a good jolly time in spite of her disagreeable old Auntie who can't just now help a bit to make it but who needs it more than ever, and most of all.

LONELY STRUGGLE FOR RED CROSS

In October 1873, still feeling not at all well, she took ship back to the United States, and returned to the home she had bought in Washington shortly before she left America in 1869. But she was not truly effective again for several years.

On April 17, 1877, she wrote a long and revealing letter to Professor Theodore Pfau. This German scholar, planning to visit America and wishing to meet her, asked her to send a photograph. From this letter, accurate as it was at that moment, it would be hard to credit that her most important 25 years still lay ahead:

■ I have in these exhausted days only a given amount of strength, and if, by any accident or oversight, I overdraw on my accounts, I am at once bankrupt, and can carry on business no further. Having been in former days accustomed to draw from an unlimited and ever-recruiting stock of strength and health, I find it a difficult problem to solve, how to bring myself down to the necessary economies of my present condition. I cannot realize that a few hours, a few rods, a few steps even, a little overwork at my desk, the quiet arranging of a simple room, a little overrun of company, may use up all my little capital. . . .

My illness . . . is what is known as "prostration of the nervous system," and very complete at that, I suppose. I am not aware of any decided organic disease . . . but . . . the price of not only my liberty, but my life is "eternal vigilance". . . .

As a *picture*, my photograph is not at all to be coveted. If natural, it must be uncomely. I was *never* what the world calls even "good-looking," leaving out of the case all such terms as "handsome," and "pretty." My features were strong and square, cheek-bones high, mouth large, complexion dark; my best feature was perhaps a luxuriant growth of glossy dark hair shading to blackness, but that is comparatively thin now, and silver gray, all within the last three years. It changed from its original blackness to its present shade in the first six weeks of this present illness in 1874.

I never cared for dress, and have no accomplishments, so you will find me plain and prosy both in representation and reality if ever you should chance to meet either. I beg you to *believe* this . . . to avoid any disappointment which might possibly occur, not that I think it could change the friendship of a sensible person, but I like people, and especially my friends, to know me as I am, and not hold a false estimate of me.

Louis Appia, the first Red Cross official Miss Barton ever met (see pages 46 and 192), did much to encourage her own subsequent Red Cross activities, both in Europe and North America.

Just a month later, on May 17, 1877, she finally felt well enough to write Dr. Louis Appia that she was ready to help get the Geneva Convention ratified by the United States Government, and to organize the American Red Cross:

■ Four long years have found and held me powerless to strike a blow on the great anvil of humanity. . . . Once more I begin . . . to reach out. . . . I see again the flash of the bayonet, the march of armies trampling down the harvests; the terror-stricken fly for rescue, and the wounded cry for help. Again the Red Cross, like the bow of promise, rises over the scene, again . . . its clear, brave tones reach me even here in my quiet chambers . . . and my heart . . . bids me seize my pen and say to you that what there is of me is still ready for my work. . . . Though I may not do what I once could, I am come to offer what I may. . . .

In spite of all efforts which you have so generously made to spread the knowledge of your society and its great objects in this country, it is almost unknown, and the Red Cross, in America, is a mystery. . . . Not one person in 100 on this side of the Atlantic ever heard of it; not one in 500 has any clear idea of its uses or design. . . .

It must be brought into active use. It must have a national headquarters, sanctioned by the Government, where the flag of the beautiful Red Cross floats day and night, in war and in peace. It must have its different State organizations, and its smaller relief societies all working under its insignia. . . .

If you feel that I can serve your cause, and humanity through it . . . let me know your desires *at once.* If you will write me immediately upon receipt of this, asking . . . that I do all in my power to aid you in the work . . . I will have your letter placed before our President and Government and ask their sanction. . . .

If you have already some person in your mind who will do it . . . only see that he does his duty. . . . But if you have not such a person in mind, and feel that I can serve you acceptably . . . I will do all in my power. . . . I am now at my best by far since 1873.

Dr. Appia promptly replied, warmly approving of her becoming the active leader of the Red Cross in America. On August 19, 1877, Gustave Moynier, president of the International Committee, sent her a letter addressed to the President of the United States asking that America ratify the Geneva Convention and establish an American branch of the Red Cross. Moynier added: "We have already an able and devoted assistant in Miss Clara Barton, to whom we confide the care of handing to you this present request."

Early in 1878 she presented this letter in person to President Rutherford B. Hayes at the White House. She had already begun pressing her cause in every significant quarter in Washington, and had published and circulated a pamphlet, "What the Red Cross Is." In the pamphlet she added what became her own notable addition to the world service of the Red Cross—its use in peacetime calamities. The Red Cross had never done this type of peacetime work anywhere until Clara herself began the practice.

■ To the People of the United States. . . . Having had the honor conferred upon me of appointment by the Central Commission holding the Geneva Convention, to present that treaty to this Government, and to take in charge the formation of a national organization . . . it seems to me but proper that, while I ask the Government to sign it, the people and their representatives should be made acquainted with its origin, designs, methods of work, etc. To this end I have prepared the following statement, and present it to my countrymen and women, hoping they will be led to endorse and sustain a benevolence so grand in its character and already almost universal in its recognition. . . .

The Red Cross is a Confederation of relief societies in different countries, acting under the Geneva Convention. . . . The aim of these societies is to ameliorate the condition of wounded soldiers in the armies in campaign on land or sea. . . . The relief societies use . . . whatever methods seem best suited to prepare in times of peace for . . . service in time of war. . . . In the Franco-Prussian War this was abundantly tested. . . .

And it may be further made a part of the *raison d'être* of these national relief societies to afford ready succor and assistance to sufferers in time of national or widespread calamities, such as plagues, cholera, yellow fever and the like, devastating fires or floods, railway disasters, mining catastrophes, etc. The readiness of organizations like those of the Red Cross to extend help at the instant of need renders the aid of quadruple value and efficiency compared with that gathered hastily and irresponsibly, in the bewilderment and shock which always accompanies such calamities. . . .

Organized in every State, the relief societies of the Red Cross would be ready with money, nurses and supplies, to go on call to the instant relief of all who were overwhelmed by any of those sudden calamities. . . . It is true that the Government is always ready in these times of public need to furnish transportation, and often does much more. . . .

But in such cases one of the greatest difficulties is that there is no organized method of administering the relief which the Government or liberal citizens are willing to bestow . . . or, if there be organization, it is hastily formed in the time of need, and is therefore comparatively inefficient and wasteful. . . .

In all such cases, to gather and dispense the profuse liberality of our people, without waste of time or material, requires the wisdom that comes of experience and permanent organization. Still more does it concern, if not our safety, at least our honor, to signify our approval of those principles of humanity acknowledged by every other civilized nation.

Although American women could not vote in presidential elections until 1920, Clara never hesitated to make campaign speeches for those she favored. In 1880, when James A. Garfield was the Republican candidate, she was asked to address the voters at Dansville, New York, just before the November poll. She wrote her address in inch-high letters so she would not have to wear glasses, and spoke in characteristic terms to "Soldiers, Comrades, Citizens of Dansville, Republican Voters." Among her observations:

Gustave Moynier, an early collaborator of Red Cross founder Henri Dunant, was a logical, smoothly-functioning lawyer who knew how to turn Dunant's noble dream into an idealistic yet practical reality. Moynier kept a firm control over the central leadership of the Red Cross organization for 47 years.

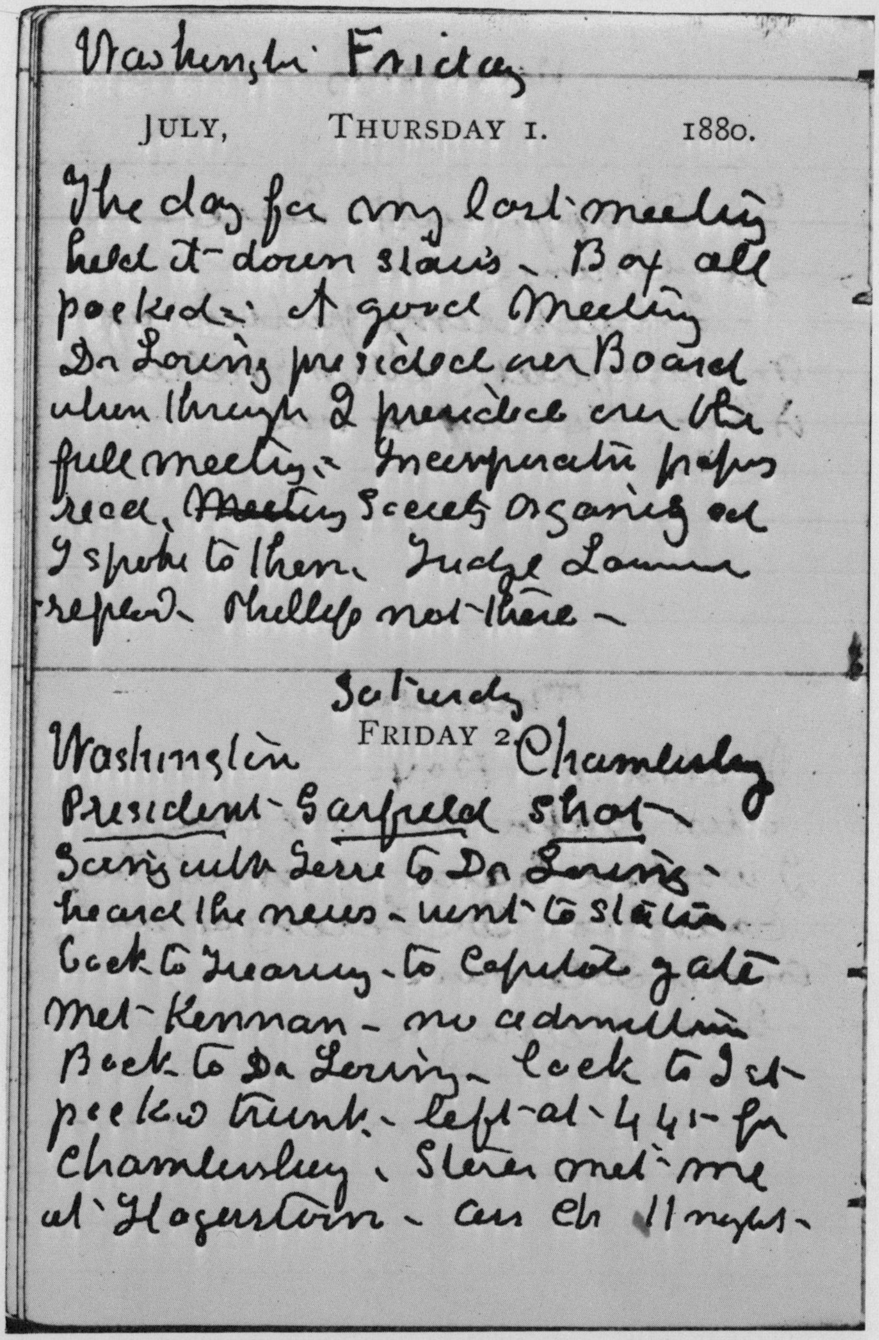

Washington Friday

JULY,   THURSDAY 1.   1880.

The day for my last meeting
held it down stairs. Box all
packed. A good Meeting
Dr Loring presided over Board
when through I presided over the
full meeting. Incorporation papers
read. Meeting Society organized
I spoke to them. Judge Lawrence
represented Phillips not there.

Saturday
FRIDAY 2 Chambersburg
Washington
President Garfield shot
Seriously with Serre to Dr Loring.
heard the news. went to station
back to Treasury. to Capitol gate
Met Kennan. no admission
Back to Dr Loring. back to Oct
peeks trunk. left at 4 41 for
Chambersburg. Steven met me
at Hagerstown. am th 11 nyf.

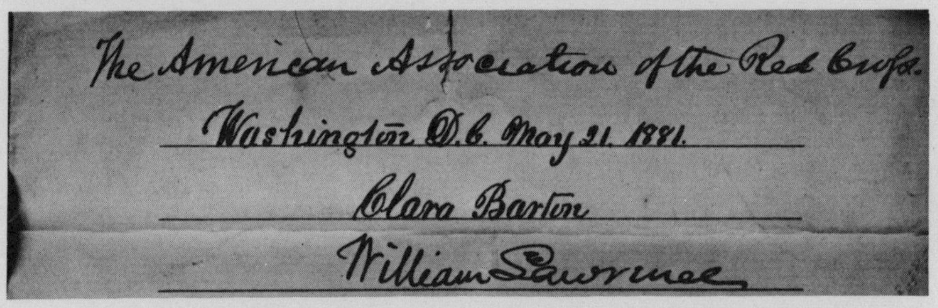

The American Association of the Red Cross.
Washington D.C. May 21. 1881.
Clara Barton
William Lawrence

Part of Miss Barton's economical New England heritage was her hatred of any form of waste. Thus, in 1881 she was using up an unused diary for 1880—carefully writing "Friday" for "Thursday," "Saturday" for "Friday," and so on. Her handwriting is still a little shaky after her long illnesses of the 1870's. The July 1 entry records one of the first meetings of the American Red Cross, with the "Incorporation papers read." Judge William Lawrence, also mentioned in the entry, was chairman of the organization's original executive board, and signed the list of those who attended the May 21 meeting directly after Clara. The July 2 entry notes that President Garfield has been assassinated; however, Clara left Washington that day as she had previously planned.

204

■ No political organization had ever such a burden of responsibility laid upon brain and heart and hand to perform. . . . You need no wiser head or truer heart, no better man than James A. Garfield. I have known him 15 years, and . . . I could unhesitatingly give him a recommendation for personal honesty. . . . You have chosen well: a statesman, a scholar, a patriot, a true-hearted honorable man. . . . See to it that next Tuesday you add to this illustrious list [she named some great past Republicans including Lincoln and Charles Sumner] not a dead but a living leader.

It took Clara long years of persistent pressure at all levels of government to get the Geneva Convention ratified—as it finally was in 1882. America was the world's last great civilized nation to ratify, and as one biographer has observed: "If ever a great enterprise came into being as the result of the persistent, indefatigable effort of one person, that result was achieved by Clara Barton in securing the adhesion of her own country to the international agreement which included the Red Cross."

In 1881, with success at last in sight, she organized a National Society of the Red Cross and was promptly elected its president. A few weeks later, she helped organize America's first local Red Cross society at Dansville, New York, the pleasant and friendly town whose medical facilities had helped her regain her health. Other local chapters were soon organized—none too soon, since after a hot summer there were disastrous losses in forest fires that raged through Michigan. Clara promptly issued a call for help—for the first time in the name of the Red Cross. She later recalled:

■ If we did not hear the crackling of the flames, our skies grew murky and dark and our atmosphere bitter with the drifting smoke . . . of Michigan whose living thousands fled in terror, whose dying hundreds writhed in the embers, and whose dead blackened in the ashes of their hard-earned homes. . . . Our relief rooms were instantly secured and our white banner, with its bright scarlet cross, which has never been furled since that hour, was thrown to the breeze, telling to every looker-on what we were there to do, and pointing to every generous heart an outlet for its sympathy.

Soon after she had established the American Red Cross, however, Clara's career took a temporary, yet fascinating, detour. At the urging of her old friend and Civil War admirer, General Benjamin F. Butler (now governor of Massachusetts), she served for eight months in 1883 as superintendent of that state's prison for women, at Sherborn. Though she later called it "the most foolhardy step I have ever been led to take," she worked very hard at Sherborn in her own highly personal way and was widely praised for the reforms she introduced. Clara summed up this episode in a report she made while at Sherborn and in an address the next year. Excerpts from the two follow:

■ Sherborn Prison . . . has at present 275 to 280 women convicts, and, with those who so kindly care for them, make up a family of something over 300. These convicts [are in jail for] causes . . . as various and widespread as the sins and mishaps which beset erring humanity, but if you asked me what proportion I thought would be left, after all the temptations of liquor and men were removed, I should not require a large sheet on which to write it down. . . .

These women . . . are more weak than wicked, often more sinned against than sinning. This, to my mind, invites a parental, maternal system of government, and to this they are all amenable; even the most obstinate yields to a rule of kindness, firmly and steadily administered. . . .

I well remember the one question which always confronted me from visitors at Sherborn—"Miss Barton, how is it, do you really reform any one here?" My reply was, "That depends upon what *you* consider reform to consist in. If you mean to ask if we take women here, badly born, worse raised, with inherited, habitual, vagrant crime in their natures, with the grogshop and the brothel for their teachers . . . and that by a residence of a few months here we are able to send them out to you . . . proof against all the temptations and vices which you of the free community on the outside may throw in their path . . . then, No, we reform no one, and our prison is a failure. But, if reform may mean that the habits which must incidentally grow up in . . . these women during a term of two years of sober, industrious, and instructed life . . . and a *resolution* at least to try a better life—if all this may be accounted in the direction of reform, then, Yes, a thousand times Yes, we reform all that come within our reach."

The prison in itself is all well, but the danger lies beyond in the temptations, the lures, and the traps of the community into which this poor, weak creature is plunged in her first hour of regained liberty. . . . I recall once an official visit from about 20 members of the State Legislature. . . . They appealed . . . what I would recommend to them to do. . . . I replied . . . "Gentlemen, the Institution from which you come has the making of the laws by which this Institution exists; any time when you *there* will find a way to make it impossible for the people of this State to get intoxicating liquors, upon which to get drunk, I will guarantee that in six months the State of Massachusetts may rent Sherborn for a shoe manufactory." I am not sure that *they* believed what I said, but *I* did and still do. . . .

I regard drunkenness as the great father of crime, and the mother of prisons, almshouses, asylums, and workhouses—the parent of vice and want and the instigator of murder. . . . Then follow in their mournful train the sin-bound cortege of primal and secondary causes of vice and crime and which make necessary the various methods of treatment which have been so ably discovered that . . . I can only . . . perhaps express suggestively some preferences which may have presented themselves to me. . . .

I am unequivocally in favor of an unfixed term of imprisonment when the sentence is given. A fixed time of release is an independence to the prisoner beyond the power of his keepers and stands directly in the way of all reform. . . . [As to] the relations and feeling to be maintained between the inmates of a prison and those in charge of them, I would recommend not only a uniform kindness and firmness of course on the part of every

As her words on this page vigorously testify, Miss Barton was a strong opponent of alcohol. The cartoon above, from "Puck" in 1886, warns that "Prohibition is coming!" The prohibition amendment did not actually come for another generation and then endured for only a relatively few years, but Clara and many of her friends long crusaded against drinking.

attendant, but a uniform politeness as well [on their part].

Like begets like in spite of everything. It increases self-respect. This they have lost, and this they need to have restored so far as may be. Make punishment as rare as possible, but *sure,* and in all instances as light as the case will admit of. I regard undue severity of punishment as far more harmful than no correction at all. Cultivate the love of the convicts by all proper means; it is more potent than punishment.

I believe the record of my last month at Sherborn shows not a single punishment among between 300 and 400 women. They grew to feel that the only hurt of their punishment was the pain it gave me. When I met them for the last night in the chapel, and told them we should not meet again, and invited each to come and bid me goodbye . . . the tears that went over my hands as I held theirs for the last time, were harder for me than all the eight months' work I had done among them. . . .

It was too much to bear. I sought my own room—sank down, cold and shivering with the terrible thought that rushed over me. . . . Was I far enough removed from them? Surely we must be too near alike, if not akin, or they would never have clung to me with that pitiful love.

The quite individualistic and rather freewheeling methods of operation that Clara adopted, from the start, for the American Red Cross—"realizing that to be of any real service as a body of relief for sudden disasters, we must not only be independent of the slow, ordinary methods of soliciting relief, but in its means of application as well"—were summed up by her as follows:

■ *First.* To never solicit relief or ask for contributions.

Second. Not to pay salaries to officers—paying out money only to those whom we must employ for manual labor—and as our officers served without compensation they should not be taxed for dues.

Third. To keep ourselves always in possession of a stated sum of money to commence a field of disaster—this sum to be independent even of the closed doors of a bank which might prevent leaving for a field on a Sunday or holiday.

Fourth. To take this sum of our own, going directly to a field with such help as needed, giving no notice until there, overlooking the field, and learning the extent of the trouble and conditions of the people, making immediate and reliable report to the country through the Associated Press, some of whose officers were our own Red Cross officers as well. These reports would be truthful, unexaggerated, and non-sensational statements that could be relied upon.

Fifth. That if, under these conditions, the people chose to make use of us as distributors of the relief which they desired to contribute to the sufferers, we would do our best to serve them while at the field—make report directly to each and all contributors, so far as in our power, and proceed to carry out any directions and apply the relief at hand, in the wisest manner possible, among a dazed and afflicted community.

To inaugurate this method, I, as president, placed a sum of three thousand dollars, free of bank or interest, upon momentary call, at the service of the association. On more than one occasion it has been taken on Sunday, when every bank in the country was closed and charitable bodies were at their prayers. Even the relief of Johnstown was thus commenced. . . .

It is as good at this moment as it was in 1883, and from the same source. It may not have been a "business-like" method nor one to be approved by stated boards of directors nor squared by bank regulations. But the foes we had to meet were not thus regulated, and had to be met as they came; and so they always must be if any good is to be accomplished.

Until the Government and society can control the elements, and regulate a spring freshet, a whirlwind or a cyclone, they will find that red tape is not strong enough to hold their ravages in check.

RED CROSS RELIEF IN ACTION

The Michigan fires of 1881 were also the first disaster in which Dr. Julian B. Hubbell served as field agent for the Red Cross. He became Clara's right-hand man for the next 23 years in the Red Cross, and remained close to her thereafter until her death in 1912. To her, he was "Buz" or "Bub"—to him, 25 years her junior, she was a second mother he called "Mammie" or "Mamie." Warmhearted and practical, as knowledgeable in agriculture as he was in medicine, never-failing in solicitude and loyalty, he did more than can readily be stated to make her whole Red Cross career triumphant. In the Mississippi and Ohio river floods of 1882 and 1883, he again headed the relief work.

■ Our infant organization sent its field agent, Dr. Hubbell, to the scene of the disaster . . . where the swift-rising floods overtook alike man and beast in their flight of terror . . . sweeping them ruthlessly to the Gulf . . . or leaving them clinging in famishing despair to some trembling roof or swaying tree-top. . . . When Dr. Hubbell retired from the field, having completed the work, he had still unexpended funds in hand. But they were soon needed.

In 1884, in fact, came far worse floods on both the Ohio and the Mississippi. Now Clara herself, with Dr. Hubbell accompanying her, set off on her own first major mission of mercy on behalf of the Red Cross.

■ I chartered my first boat, with captain and crew, at 60 dollars per day, to be at once laden to the water's edge with coal—our own supplies to be stored on the upper deck—and at four o'clock in the afternoon, as the murky sun was hiding its clouded face, the bell of the "Josh V. Throop," in charge of her owner, announced the departure of the first Red Cross relief-boat ever seen on American waters.

I found myself that night with a staunch crew of 30 men and a skilled captain, and a boat under my command. I had never until then held such a command. We wove the river diagonally from side to side—from village to village—where the homeless, shivering people were gathered—called for the most responsible person—a clergyman if one could be found, threw off boxes of clothing, and hove off coal for a two weeks' supply, and steamed away to the opposite side, leaving only gratitude, wonder at who we were, where we came from, and what that strange flag meant? We improved every opportunity to replenish our supply of coal, and reached Cairo in five days.

Waiting only to reload, we returned up the river, resupplied the revived villages of people, too grateful for words, reaching Evansville at the end of three weeks, where more supplies than we had taken awaited us. St. Louis and Chicago had caught the fever of relief, had arranged societies, and had asked permission to join our aid. . . .

We prepared to feed and rescue the perishing stock—as well as people adown the Mississippi. The animals had never been saved in an overflow; and besides the cruelty of letting them starve by thousands, the loss to the people was irreparable, as the following year must inevitably be replete with idleness and poverty till more stock could be obtained to work with.

We found as commissary at St. Louis, General Beckwith, the historic commissary-general of the old Civil War, who had personally superintended the loading of my wagons in Washington, year after year, for the battlefields of Virginia. He came on board the "Mattie Bell" and personally superintended the lading—clothing, corn, oats, salt and hay—besides putting upon the Government boats large quantities of supplies which we could not take on at first, and giving us his blessing, watched us steam out on our joint mission; they putting off rations of meat and meal—we supplementing with clothing for the people and feed for the stock.

We purchased all we could at cities as we passed, picked our course among the broken levees and roaring crevasses, all the way to New Orleans. The hungry were fed, the naked clothed, and the stock saved. The Negro had his mule, and the planter his horses and cattle to carry on his work when the flood should disappear. We had lighter boats, still lighter purses, but lightest of all were the grateful hearts that a kind Providence and a generous people had given to us the privilege of serving.

By May of 1884 the floodwaters along the two rivers had somewhat subsided. But the post-flood conditions, particularly along the Ohio, were so serious as to demand additional relief work at once. Clara continued in action without a pause.

■ From St. Louis we crossed over to Evansville, rechartered the "Josh V. Throop," and put on accumulated supplies. The waters of the Ohio had subsided and the people were returning to the old spots of earth that once had been their home, but there was neither house to live in nor tool to work the land with. We reloaded with pine lumber, ready-made doors, windows, household utensils, stores and groceries, farming utensils, and with a good force of carpenters proceeded up the Ohio once more. The sight of the disconsolate, half-clad farmer waiting on the bank told us where his home had been—and was not.

Three hours' work of our carpenters would put up a one-room house, meanwhile our efficient men and women helpers, among them the best ladies of Evansville, would furnish it with beds, bedding, clothing, provisions for the family, and farming tools ready to go on with the season's work.

Picture, if possible, this scene. A strange ship with a strange flag steaming up the river. It halts, turns from its course, and draws up to the nearest landing. Some persons disembark and speak a few minutes with the family. Then, a half dozen strong mechanics man a small boat laden with all material for constructing a one-room house—floor, roof, doors, windows. The boat returns for furniture.

Within three hours the strange ship sails away, leaving a bewildered family in a new and clean house with bed, bedding, clothing, table, chairs, dishes, candles, a little cooking-stove with a blazing fire, all the common quota of cooking utensils, and meat, meal, and groceries; a plow, rake, axe, hoe, shovel, spade, hammer, and nails. We ask few questions. They ask none. The whistle of the "Throop" is as welcome to their ears as the flag to their eyes.

At one of these wrecked villages the entire little hamlet of people stood on our decks. Only four, they said, were left at home, and these were sick. They had selected their lawyer to speak their thanks. No word will ever do justice to the volume of native eloquence which seemed to roll unbidden from his lips. He finished with these sentences:

"At noon on that day we were in the blackness of despair—the whole village in the power of the demon of waters—hemmed in by sleet and ice, without fire enough to cook its little food. When the bell struck nine that night, there were 75 families on their knees before their blazing grates, thanking God for fire and light, and praying blessings on the phantom ship with the unknown device that had come as silently as the snow, they knew not whence, and gone, they knew not whither."

Returning to Washington after the four months of prolonged flood-relief strain was over, Clara once more came close to physical and emotional collapse. But, for a change, a high government official knew exactly what to tell her:

■ We came to Pittsburgh, discharged our empty boat, bade a heart-breaking goodbye to our veteran volunteers from Evansville, who had shared our toil and pain and who would return on the boat, we taking train once more for Washington. We had been four months on the rivers, among fogs, rain, damp, and malaria—run all manner of risks and dangers, but had lost no life nor property, sunk no boat, and only that I was by this time too weak to walk without help—all were well. . . .

On arriving home I found that I was notified by the International

Committee of Geneva, that the Fourth International Conference would be held in that city in September, and I was requested to inform the United States Government, and ask it to send delegates. With the aid of a borrowed arm, I made my way up the steps of the Department of State (that was before the luxury of elevators) and made my errand known to Secretary Frelinghuysen, who had heard of it and was ready with his reply: "Yes, Miss Barton . . . I appoint you as our delegate."

"No, Mr. Frelinghuysen," I said, "I cannot go. I have just returned from field work. I am tired and ill. Furthermore, I have not had time to make a report of our work." . . .

"I don't want any report; no report is necessary," answered the Secretary. . . . "Regarding your illness—you have had too much fresh water, Miss Barton. I recommend salt—and shall appoint you."

RECOGNITION AT HOME AND ABROAD

Clara caught the eye of everyone at this 1884 Geneva conference. She was the only woman among the 400 delegates from more than 30 nations. Her old friend and fellow delegate from America, Judge Joseph Sheldon of Connecticut, proposed an amendment to the Geneva Convention based squarely on what she had been doing in America. Some national societies were dubious. They considered that "secondary" Red Cross work in emergencies other than those directly related to war might cause confusion. But the resolution, since known as the "American Amendment," passed.

■ That the Red Cross Society engage in time of peace in humanitarian work analogous to the duties devolving upon them in periods of war, such as taking care of the sick and rendering relief in extraordinary calamities where, as in war, prompt and organized relief is required.

While in Europe, Clara renewed old ties, notably in Germany and Switzerland, and arranged for many nations to send exhibits to the Cotton Centennial Exposition at New Orleans, which would also feature a "Red Cross Day." Probably the best of these exhibits, thanks to her royal friends in Germany, was that of handiwork from German women.

The Exposition celebrated "German Day" on March 22, 1885, the eighty-eighth birthday of Emperor Wilhelm I, who had awarded Clara the Iron Cross for her relief work in the Franco-Prussian War. The day inspired Clara—who enjoyed writing verse that was often rather close to doggerel—to write a poem linking the Emperor to the Red Cross. It has been called "the most rousing of all her 'occasional' verse":

Emperor Wilhelm I of Germany had a shrewd common sense, plus the wisdom while he was still only king of Prussia to let Bismarck take the initiative as his chief minister. Wilhelm believed in the "God of battles"— and a successful series of wars eventually made him the ruler of a united Germany.

■ The watch-tower of the people's weal, the guardian of the poor,
   The impersonate of charity, wide opening every door;
And where your Eagles black are borne, or your Lions crouch in gold,
   The crimson Cross of love and peace entwines in every fold.

In 1887 Clara was a delegate to another world meeting of the Red Cross, with representatives from 32 nations. This was held at Karlsruhe in Germany, home of the Grand Duke and Grand Duchess of Baden. The Grand Duchess was the daughter of Emperor Wilhelm I. During Clara's stay in Karlsruhe she met the Emperor again:

■ It was difficult to realize all the ninety years, as he stepped toward us with even, and steady, if no longer elastic, tread. He approached with cordially extended hand, and in his excellent French expressed satisfaction for the meeting. "In the name of humanity, he was glad to meet and welcome those who labored for it." In recalling the earlier days of our acquaintance . . . the Grand Duchess . . . selecting two from a cluster of decorations which I had worn . . . drew the attention of the Emperor to them. The one he knew; it was his own, presented upon his seventy-fifth birthday. The other he had never seen. It was the beautiful decoration of the "German Waffengenossen"—the "Warrior Brothers in arms" of Milwaukee.

It was puzzlingly familiar, and yet it was not familiar. There was again the Iron Cross of Germany, but it was on the American shield. The "American Eagle" surmounting the arms for defense; and the colors of Germany, the red, white and black of the Empire uniting the two. His Majesty gazed upon the expressive emblem . . . and turned inquiringly. . . . The explanation was made that it was from His Majesty's own soldiers, who, after the "German-Franco War," had gone to the United States and become citizens; and this device was designed to express that . . . they bound the old home to the new. . . .

The smile of the grand old Emperor, as he listened, had in it the "Well done" of the benignant father to a dutiful and successful son. "And they make good citizens?" he would ask. "The best that could be desired," I said; "industrious, honest and prosperous, and, sire, they are still yours in heart, still true to the Fatherland and its Emperor."

"I am glad to hear this; they were good soldiers, and thank God, true men everywhere," was the earnest and royal response. . . . At length His Majesty gave a hand to both Dr. Hubbell and myself in a parting adieu, and walked a few steps away, when turning back, and again extending a hand, said, in French, "It is probably the last time," and in English, "Goodbye."

She had barely returned to America from these imperial splendors when she found herself, at sixty-six, working tirelessly again at a disaster. Once more she was back in the Midwest, and later wrote:

■ In February, 1888, occurred the Mt. Vernon, Ill., cyclone, cutting a broad swath through one-half of the beautiful county-seat, tearing down all heavy buildings, picking up the lighter ones and sweeping them along like cardboard. In three minutes the work of destruction was over. Ten minutes later the sun shone out brightly over the ruins of the town, the wails of the maimed and dying, and the lifeless bodies of the dead.

Fires broke out on every hand, and the victims pinned down under the wreckage were subjects for the flames. Appeals for assistance went out, but by unfortunate press representation failed to arouse the public, till after several days, when we were reached, through their representative in Congress, begging that in mercy we go to them. We arrived in the night, found homes destroyed, hospitals full, scant medical care, few nurses, food scarce and no money, a relief committee of excellent men, but little to distribute.

At daylight we looked over the situation and sent this simple message to the Associated Press: "The pitiless snow is falling on the heads of 3,000 people, who are without homes, without food or clothing, and without money. American National Red Cross, Clara Barton, President."

This was all. We assisted their relief committee to arrange for the receipt and distribution of funds, sent for experienced helpers to take charge of supplies, to distribute clothing, and aid the hospital service. We remained two weeks, and left them with more supplies than they knew how to distribute, and the Citizens' Committee, with accumulating cash in its treasury of $90,000, full of hope, life, and a gratitude they could not speak. . . .

We paid our own expenses and no dollar but our own had passed our hands. We were only glad to do this, in the hope that we were building up an institution of self-help of the people, that would one day win its way to their favor and aid.

One of those to whom she appealed for aid for Mount Vernon was the redoubtable Republican orator Robert G. Ingersoll, who had taken his bar examination there. In writing to him, she rephrased a famous proverb and applied it to herself:

■ Several times, I have heard it indirectly spoken, "If Col. Ingersoll could only give one of his masterly lectures for our benefit," and so full of heart and confidence was the expression, that it comes to my thought to pass it on to Col. Ingersoll himself. It is well that he should know how warmly and hopefully he is turned to, by his old friends. They may never tell him this, but long ago I added to the true old adage of "What is everybody's business is nobody's business," another clause which, I think, more than any other principle has served to influence my actions in life. That is, What is nobody's business is *my* business. I act upon it in this matter, and you, my friend, will forgive me, for your heart is so good and kind you *can* do no other way.

Two letters to her niece Mamie, written soon after the one to Ingersoll, show how she juggled Red Cross matters and her own domestic desires. The Philadelphia meeting of 1888 included a reception for her—"in honor of the most sensible, practical, generous, courageous, modest and talented woman one can hope to meet." She does not mention that tribute.

Robert Green Ingersoll, one of the outstanding lawyers and lecturers of his day, was a Civil War cavalry colonel and later coined the rather inappropriate term of "plumed knight" to describe James Blaine. Yet he was perhaps best known as an opponent of organized religion. He observed: "Is there a God? I do not know. Is man immortal? I do not know. One thing I do know and that is that neither hope nor fear, belief nor denial, can change the fact. It is as it is, and it will be as it must be. We wait and hope."

■ I had intended to write you just a line on the train to and from Philadelphia, but one was in the night—the other so full of other things and the trip so short, I did not get to it. . . . We had informal meetings with officers . . . then attended a lecture given in the regular course of the Red Cross Society. Then I gave a lecture. Then home to dress for the reception . . . in Union League Hall, very large, with a band of music. The dignitaries of the city attended in bodies. The physicians—the clergymen—the lawyers—the judges—the military army and navy in uniform. I received and shook hands with all. . . . It was a splendid reception. There was still a meeting at the hotel . . . so we are only in bed by two o'clock next morning, got a hasty breakfast and hastened to the nine o'clock train for home. . . .

Then just think what a washing there was on hand; had never had time to have a full wash done since our return from Mount Vernon . . . and all ironed yesterday, and clothes put away this very minute, and I . . . am just dropped down . . . while Alfred brings compost from the stable alongside ready to make up some flower-beds, etc., and I direct him from the window as I scribble, to lose no time. . . . Tell Gaby we have moved the rosebushes all down to the front of the yard, and they didn't mind it a bit, and went right on putting out buds, and he will appreciate how much better chance we had with a washing of 20 sheets, 30 pillow-slips, and other things in proportion. . . .

We are making out our foreign conference accounts for the Government and I have the report to make out directly and a bill to draw up for Congress this week and a host of correspondence. . . . I found time one night by moonlight to plant lettuce and peppergrass and radishes, and in two days they come up and are green and pretty. Yesterday we set out two dozen tomato plants a foot high. . . . [Yesterday also] I had to meet a Senate committee at the Capitol and address them at 10 o'clock. Then I go with Mrs. General Logan and others to the War Department and manage business there. And now it is eight-thirty the next morning, and at 10 I must be at the War Department with another committee.

THE TERRIBLE JOHNSTOWN FLOOD

One of the great catastrophes of all American history struck on May 31, 1889: the Johnstown Flood in western Pennsylvania. Clara spent the next five months there.

■ If ever a people needed help it was these. . . . It was at the moment of supreme affliction when we arrived at Johnstown. The waters had subsided, and those of the inhabitants who had escaped the fate of their fellows were gazing over the scene of destruction and trying to arouse themselves from the lethargy that had taken hold of them when they were stunned by the realization of all the woe that had been visited upon them. . . .

For five weary months it was our portion to live amid the scenes of destruction, desolation, poverty, want and woe; sometimes in tents, sometimes without; and so much rain and mud, and such a lack of the commonest comforts for a time, until we could build houses to shelter ourselves and those around us. Without a safe and with a dry-goods box for a desk, we conducted financial affairs in money and material to the extent of nearly half a million dollars. . . .

Not a business house or bank left, the safes all in the bottom of the river; our little pocketbook was useless, there was nothing to buy, and it would not bring back the dead. With the shelter of the tents of the Philadelphia Red Cross, that joined us en route with supplies, when we could find a cleared place to spread, or soil to hold them . . . our stenographer commenced to rescue the first dispatches of any description that entered that desolate city. . . . Soon supplies commenced to pour in from everywhere, to be . . . distributed by human hands, for it was three weeks before even a cart could pass the streets. . . .

The little untried and unskilled Red Cross played its minor tune of a single fife among the grand chorus of relief of the whole country, that rose like an anthem, till over $4,000,000 in money, contributed to its main body of relief . . . had modestly taken the place of the $12,000,000 destroyed. But after all it was largely the supplies that saved the people at first; as it always is. . . . From one mammoth tent which served as a warehouse, food and clothing were given out to the waiting people . . . for the love of humanity symbolized in the little flag that floated above them. . . .

This drawing, from "Frank Leslie's Illustrated Newspaper" of June 15, 1889, shows the arrival and shipment of relief supplies—at the Pennsylvania Railroad station in Philadelphia—for the victims of the Johnstown Flood.

June 14. Tuesday

1892.

A little cooler than yesterday, still 90°
There are several points over which to feel
very anxious, The Mississippi valley is in
great need. no move can be publicly made
towards its relief, and no encouragement
for special help. Titusville needs help,
not in food. clothes nor people it says
but money to rebuild,

In either of there cases we could be
of service. on the ground, but Penn.
has said it didn't "want a rival for its
Red cross, and we offer none.

Emma Southmayd with her partner
Mrs Barnard called at 9½ will call
again. Business women in chicago.

I used my little type writer to good pur
pose. got up the current letters. and got
the Dr's letter ready to publish.

Went to the house. decided to paper the
hall. thus save removing old paper. have
some changes in plans. and some outside
mending done up.
Williams was to come with franklin
but did not.
· Delegates not get all home. cannot
get the Bill in.
Saw an enormous flag. with an
emblem floating over the Riggs' house
some fraternity.
·· Did some grocery shopping at Pages
This is Cora's last full day in office.

By 1892, Miss Barton was in her
seventies but in far better health
than she had been a decade or so
previously. Her penmanship was
once again close to "copperplate." Her diary entry for June
14 shows her wide variety of lively
interests: places that need Red
Cross relief; Dr. Hubbell's letter
from Russia on the famine there
to be prepared for publication;
some wallpapering she will do
herself (see page 18); a bill being
prepared for Congress, etc.

Six buildings of 100 feet by 50, later known as "Red Cross Hotels," were quickly put up to shelter the people, furnished, supplied, and kept like hotels, free of all cost to them. . . . The record on our books showed that over 25,000 persons had been directly served by us. They had received our help independently and without begging. No child has learned to beg at the doors of the Red Cross. . . .

I remained five months with these people without once visiting my own home. . . . In that time, it was estimated, we had housed, handled and distributed $211,000 worth of supplies—new and old. . . . The value of money that passed through our hands was $39,000, as stated in the official report of the general committee. . . . It was a joy that in all the uncertainties of that uncertain field not a single complaint ever reached us of the non-acknowledgment of a dollar entrusted to us.

On her return from Johnstown—Dr. Hubbell stayed there another six months —she was tendered a banquet in Washington. The tables were formed in a cross, and a bouquet was presented to her from President and Mrs. Benjamin Harrison. More than ever she was a national figure. But the Red Cross was still a quite small institution—far smaller than it was in most leading nations around the globe. Clara Barton was superb at working alone or with a tight little group of loyal followers. Her colorful actions and her natural flair for publicity had given the American Red Cross a reputation that could scarcely have been achieved in any other way.

But now, as later, she was incapable of·showing the wide organizational skill that alone could have founded hundreds and thousands of local chapters across the land and then welded them into the truly national Red Cross of her dreams. Often she was still using her own personal funds for its operating expenses. In 1891, as her tiny, though widely known, institution celebrated its tenth birthday, she casually took off with the number two person in the Red Cross on a long Western camping trip with her nephew Stephen. She wrote other relatives from Lake Chelan in the state of Washington:

■ We have pitched a tent and made a camp, living out of doors and eating fish and game. We took in the Yellowstone Park on the way . . . and then came on to this point near the Columbia River for the hunting and fishing that Steve hoped to find. That he is not entirely disappointed would appear from the fact of his having the day before yesterday, caught and brought into camp 93 brook trout. He has gone up rowing to the head of the lake today [and looks] for game on this trip. The rest of the party stay in camp—Lizzie because she does not enjoy boating and climbing—Dr. Hubbell and I to work. Our table under the trees is cleared of all appearance of breakfast and spread like a mammoth desk. . . .

The jays, woodpeckers and chewinks twitter over my head, a couple of chipmunks are tugging away at the bread bag, having succeeded in rifling a box of gingersnaps. Now all this seems very trifling and wasteful for grown people. But after all there is more of real time and opportunity in it than in keeping up the formalities of home in hot weather, entertaining friends, and keeping well. . . . I wish you both were here. I think it would be a healthful change, if any change is needed, but it is a great way, isn't it? I don't know how I get into such distances!!

In March 1893 her colleagues Dr. and Mrs. Joseph Gardner, who had helped on Ohio flood relief and would later do yeoman work with her in Cuba during the Spanish-American War, offered the Red Cross 782 acres of land in Indiana, which she at once, and idealistically, accepted:

■ This land, as the property of the American National Red Cross, will be the one piece of neutral ground on the Western Hemisphere, protected by international treaty against the tread of hostile feet. . . . While its business headquarters will remain, as before, at the capital of the Nation, this gift still forms a realization of the hope so long cherished—that the National Red Cross may have a place to accumulate and produce material and stores for sudden emergencies and great calamities. . . .

I will direct that monuments be erected defining the boundaries of this domain, dedicated to eternal peace and humanity, upon which shall be inscribed the insignia of the Treaty of Geneva. . . .

Not only our own people, but the peoples of all civilized nations will have published to their knowledge that the American National Red Cross has a home and a recognized abiding-place through all generations.

For this I have striven for years, mainly misunderstood, often misinterpreted, and it is through your clear intuition and humane thought that the clouds have been swept away and my hopes have been realized.

Clara named this tract in Indiana "Red Cross Park" and gave a reception for 2,000 people in Washington in honor of the Gardners as its donors. But it developed that the Gardners wanted an appreciable sum for the tract, that it was not really suitable for the purposes Clara had in mind, and that the man she put in charge of it (of whom she had written, "He had grown very dear to us, like a brother or a son") was an irresponsible rascal. When she visited it, in May 1893, she found many possibilities in the tract. But she was now nearing seventy-two, and in a private letter she admitted her doubts:

■ I have only been there a part of two days and have seen *these* things, but the acres I have *not* seen tire me to think of, and it confuses me to know that I hold the deed to all this, and am expected to direct it, "during my natural life." It is new and crude as new land is, but its possibilities are immense, and one day—not in my day—they will develop into beauty and usefulness.

Far from developing into "beauty and usefulness," this Indiana property was a steady drain on the Red Cross and Clara—and a decade later turned into a nightmare for her. At the congressional investigation into Red Cross affairs in 1904, John Morlan (the man to whom Clara had entrusted "Red Cross Park") claimed that she had paid the Gardners $12,000 for it instead

218

of the "token dollar" Clara had recorded in the Red Cross accounts. He never produced any documentation, and his testimony at the investigation was in general shown to be full of lies, but the whole episode clearly indicates that Clara was no longer capable of keeping in complete control of a complex situation.

THE SEA ISLANDS DISASTER

But what she could still triumphantly accomplish in the face of disaster was shown later in that same year of 1893, when a hurricane and tidal wave swept the Sea Islands off the coast of South Carolina and Georgia—an area where Clara had done notable work in 1863 during the Civil War.

■ These islands had 35,000 inhabitants, mainly Negroes. . . . Some four or five thousand had been drowned, and . . . 30,000 remained with no earthly possession of home, clothing, or food. . . . Calls went out for help. . . . In a dark, cheerless September mist, I closed my door behind me for ten months, and . . . carried on until the following July. . . .

The submerged lands were drained, 300 miles of ditches made, a million feet of lumber purchased and houses built, fields and gardens planted with the best seed in the United States, and the work all done by the people themselves. . . .

Free transportation for supplies continued till about March. No provisions in kind were sent from any source after the first four weeks of public excitement. After this all foodstuffs were purchased in Charleston and distributed as rations. Men were compelled to work on the building of their

The steamer "City of Savannah" was driven ashore and wrecked during the hurricane in the Sea Islands late in August of 1893, a storm that wrought unprecedented destruction to life and property throughout the region.

own homes in order to receive rations. We found them an industrious, grateful class of people, far above the ordinary grade usually met. They largely owned their little homes, and appreciated instruction in the way of improving them. The tender memory of the childlike confidence and obedience of this ebony-faced population is something that time cannot efface from either us or them.

On the third day after our arrival at Beaufort four middle-aged colored men came to the door of the room we had appropriated as an office, and respectfully asked to see "Miss Clare". . . . The tallest and evidently the leader, said: "Miss Clare, we knows you doesn't remember us. But we never fo'gits you. We has all of us got somethin' to show you." Slipping up a soiled, ragged shirtsleeve, he showed me an ugly scar above the elbow, reaching to the shoulder. "Wagner?" I asked.

"Yes, Miss Clare, and you drissed it for me that night, when I crawled down the beach—'cause my leg was broke too," he replied. "And we was all of us there, and you took care of us all and drissed our wounz. I was with Colonel Shaw, and crawled out of the fote. The oth's nevah got in". . . .

One by one they showed their scars. There was very little clothing to hide them—bullet wound and sabre stroke. The memory, dark and sad, stood out before us all. It was a moment not to be forgotten. . . .

The contributions of food and clothing had been sent to Beaufort. . . . This had naturally drawn all the inhabitants of the scores of desolated islands for 50 miles to Beaufort, until . . . 15 to 20,000 refugees had gathered there, living in its streets and waiting to be fed from day to day. As the food was there they could not be induced to return to the islands. Indeed, there was more often nothing on the islands to return to. The description given . . . was this: If all had been swept out to sea and nothing remained, it was described as, "done gone." But if thrown down and parts of the wreck still remained, it was described as "ractified". . . .

We sat daily in counsel with the local committee . . . and . . . on the first of October, decided to accede to the request of the Governor made at first, and take sole charge of the relief. Our first order was to close every storehouse, both of food and clothing, and inform the people that all dis-

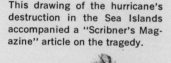

This drawing of the hurricane's destruction in the Sea Islands accompanied a "Scribner's Magazine" article on the tragedy.

tributions would hereafter be made from the islands . . . a system that was to restore to active habits of life a body of utterly demoralized, and ignorant people, equal in numbers to a small new State. . . .

The goods and rations were at once shipped across the bay. . . . It is needless to say that the multitude followed the food. . . . Then followed the necessity for material to rebuild the "done gone," and to repair the "ractified" homes. . . . Each man received his lumber by order and receipt, and was under obligation to build his own house. The work was all performed by themselves. A garden was insisted upon. At first this proposition was resisted as impracticable.

"No use, Mistah—no use—'cause de pig eat it all up." It was suggested that a fence might be made enclosing at least a quarter of an acre about the house to keep "de pig" out, as we should later send, for planting, the best seed to be obtained in the country. . . . The fact that the building of the fence, and its subsequent keeping in strict repair, had some bearing on the weekly issuance of rations, was evidently not without its influence. There were no poor fences and "de pig" did no damage. But there were such gardens, and of such varieties, as those islands had never before seen.

The earliest crop to strive for, beside the gardens, was the Irish potato, which they had never raised. . . . I recall a fine, bright morning in May, when I was told that a woman . . . waited at the door to see me. I went to the door to find a tall, bright-looking woman in a clean dress, with a basket on her head, which, after salutation, she lowered and held out to me. There was something over a peck of Early Rose potatoes in the basket—in size from a pigeon's to a pullet's egg. The grateful woman could wait no longer for the potatoes to grow larger, but had dug these, and had come ten miles over the sea, in the night, to bring them to me as a first offering of food of her own raising. If the tears fell on the little gift as I looked and remembered, no one will wonder or criticize. The potatoes were cooked for breakfast, and "Susie Jane" was invited to partake. . . .

Domestic gardens were a new feature among these islanders, whose whole attention had been always given to the raising of the renowned "Sea Island Cotton," the pride of the market, and a just distinction to themselves and the worthy planter. The result of this innovation was that, when we left in July, it was nearly as difficult for a pedestrian to make his way on the narrow sidewalks of Beaufort because of piled-up vegetables for sale from the islands, as it had been in October to pass through the streets because of hungry, idle men and women. . . .

If any practical woman reading this should try to comprehend what it would be to undertake to clothe and keep clothed 30,000 human beings for a year, and to do this from the charitable gifts of the people, which gifts had all done more or less service before—often pretty thoroughly "ractified"—this woman will not wonder that sewing societies suggested themselves to us. . . .

The women were called together . . . with the result that an old time "sewing circle" was instituted in every community. Its membership, officers, dues, and regulations were properly established—one-half day in each week devoted by each member to the work in its sewing-rooms, with a woman in charge to prepare it. The clothing was given out to them as received by us. Many a basket came proudly back to show us the difference between "den an' now"—good, strong, firmly mended garments. . . . Provision was also made that the little girls from 10 years old should attend and be taught to sew. Many a little dress was selected at headquarters for them to make over or repair. . . .

The money contributed and received for the entire relief of 10 months was $30,500 and a few additional dollars and cents. It aggregated one dollar apiece for the entire maintenance of 30,000 people for 10 months. . . . A report was made and passed into the hands of our legal counsellor, who, on seeing that no change could be truthfully made in it, advised that it be not published, as no one would believe it possible to be done, and we would get only distrust and discredit. . . . But back of the hard facts there is compensation.

A half dozen years later, when our Negro protégés of the Sea Islands heard of the disaster that had fallen upon Galveston, they at once gathered for aid and sent in their contributions. "'Cause dey suffers like we did, and de Red Cross is dar," they said.

Of course I would not permit one dollar of this holy gift to Galveston to go to other than the hands—hard, bony, and black—such as had raised it in their penury. I also wanted to do more. Searching for the most reliable colored people in the city . . . I informed them that I had a little money from their own people of the Sea Islands for them. . . . I told them that I had desired to do more than merely make a gift for distribution. I wished to plant a tree. I could have given them their peach, which they would eat, enjoy, and throw the pit away. But I wished them to plant the pit, and let it raise other fruit for them. . . .

They all sat quiet a few moments. . . . At length their president, the school superintendent, spoke for them. "Miss Barton," he said, "we all appreciate this, and in the name of all I promise you that the pit shall be reverently planted, and I trust the time will come when I can tell you that our tree is not only bearing fruit for ourselves, but for all suffering brethren, as theirs have done for us."

I then handed them the check for $397. . . . The pit has been successfully planted in Galveston, and we are from time to time informed of its bearing.

AID AFTER ARMENIAN MASSACRES

In February of 1896, Clara reached Constantinople to undertake Red Cross relief for the survivors of the massacres that had been widespread in the Armenian areas of the Turkish Empire. This was a different sort of disaster for her—not a natural calamity or an out-and-out war, but "a man-made massacre, with delicate political elements involved." Only the international fame she had gained for good works made it possible for her personally to enter Turkey—or for the work to be done at all. Here is her later account of it:

■ Our correspondence commenced to enlarge with rumors of Armenian massacres, and . . . it was suggested from Constantinople that the Red Cross be asked to open the way. . . . A written request from the Rev. Judson Smith, D.D., of Boston, was nearly identical with one received by us from Mr. Spencer Trask, of New York, who with others was about to form a national Armenian relief committee. . . . Both . . . Mr. Smith and Mr. Trask came in person to urge our compliance with their request that the Red Cross accept the charge and personally undertake the doubtful and dangerous task of distributing the waiting funds. . . .

Human beings were starving, and could not be reached. Thousands of towns and villages had not been heard from since the massacres, and only the Red Cross could have any hope of reaching them. No one else was prepared for field work; it had its force of trained field workers. Turkey was one of the signatory powers to the Red Cross Treaty. Thus it was hoped and believed that she would the more readily accept its presence. . . .

In Constantinople, I called by appointment upon Tewfik Pasha, the Turkish Minister of Foreign Affairs. . . . I proceeded to state our plans for relief [without] which . . . the suffering in Armenia . . . would shock the entire civilized world. . . . If my agents were permitted to go . . . humanity alone would be their guide. . . .

No obstruction was ever placed in our way. Our five expeditions passed through Armenian Turkey from sea to sea, distributing whatever was needed, repairing the destroyed machines, enabling the people to make tools to harvest their grain, thus averting a famine; providing medical help and food as well for thousands of sick; setting free the frightened inhabitants, and returning them to the villages from which they had fled for their lives; restoring all missionary freedom that had been interrupted . . . and through all this, we had never one unpleasant transaction with any person of whatever name or race. . . .

A request was brought to me . . . to turn my expedition through . . . Marash and Zeitoun. . . . Ten thousand people in those two cities were down with four distinct epidemics—typhoid and typhus fevers, dysentery and smallpox. . . . Victims were dying in overwhelming numbers. . . . The medical relief for the cities of Zeitoun and Marash was in charge of Dr. Ira Harris. . . . Dr. Harris's first report to me was that he was obliged to set the soup kettles boiling and feed his patients before medicine could be retained. My reply was a draft for . . . something over $800 with the added dispatch: "Keep the pot boiling; let us know your wants."

The further reports show from this time an astonishingly small number of deaths. The utmost care was taken by all our expeditions to prevent the spread of the contagion and there is no record of its ever having been carried out of the cities where it was found. . . . Lacking this precaution, it might well have spread throughout all Asia Minor, as was greatly feared by the anxious people. . . .

The closing of the medical fields threw our entire force into . . . general relief. . . . The apathy to which the state of utter nothingness, together with their grief and fear, had reduced the inhabitants, was by no means the smallest difficulty to be overcome. . . . Still the land was there, and when seed . . . and farming utensils . . . were brought . . . the faint spirit revived, the weak, hopeless hands unclasped, and the farmer stood on his feet again. . . .

Even while this saving process was going on another condition no less imperative arose. These fields must be replanted or starvation must be simply delayed. Only the strength of their old-time teams of oxen could break up the hard sod and prepare for the fall sowing. Not an animal—ox, cow, horse, goat, or sheep—had been left. All had been driven to the Kurdish Mountains. When Mr. Wood's telegram came, calling for a thousand oxen for the hundreds of villages, I thought of our not rapidly swelling bank account, and . . . the financial secretary was directed to send a draft for $22,000 . . . for the purchase of cattle and the progress of the harvest of 1897. . . .

Unheard-of toil, care, hard riding day and night, with risk of life, were all involved. . . . Among the uncivilized and robber bands of Kurds, the cattle that had been stolen and driven off must be picked up, purchased, and brought back to the waiting farmer's field. There were routes so dangerous that a brigand chief was selected, by those understanding the situation, as the safest escort for our men.

Perhaps the greatest danger encountered was in the region of Farkin, beyond Diarbekir, where the official escort had not been waited for, and the leveled musket of the faithless guide told the difference. At length the task was accomplished. . . . That our work had been acceptable to those who received its results, we knew. They had never failed to *make* us know.

Funds to the total amount of $116,326.01 were cabled us by Mr. Spencer Trask's committee, all of which were placed in the hands of Mr. W. W. Peet, treasurer of the missionary board at Constantinople. All proper receipts were given and taken, and feeling that we had faithfully and successfully accomplished the work we had been asked to perform, we closed the field, and prepared to return to America.

THE SPANISH-AMERICAN WAR

In the battles along the southern coast of Cuba in 1898 that led up to the American capture of Santiago, Clara once again—as in the Civil War but now in her seventy-seventh year—found herself close to the front and tending to the wounded. The Rough Riders, led by Colonel Theodore Roosevelt, had helped to storm San Juan Hill, and when she heard of the growing casualties she hurried to them. General Shafter was the United States army commander in Cuba.

■ News came to us of a serious character. The daring Rough Riders had been hardly dealt by . . . and the wounded needed help. . . . The Red Cross flag was hoisted, Dr. Lesser placed in charge, and scores of our soldiers who had been lying on the filthy floors of an adjacent building, with no food but army rations, were carried over, placed in clean cots, and given proper food [all within a surprisingly short time]. . . .

A few feet away, all the available army tents were put up as additional accommodation. . . . The tents were more than filled with wounded in the battle of San Juan Hill. Three of the five Sisters went into the operating tent, and with the surgeons worked for 30 hours with only a few moments' rest now and then for a cup of coffee and a cracker or piece of bread. . . . On Saturday evening, the second day of the San Juan battle, a slip of paper with these penciled words was brought to the door of the hospital: "Send food, medicines, anything. Seize wagons from the front for transportation. Shafter."

The call for help was at once sent over to [our supply ship] and we worked all night getting out supplies and sending them ashore. . . . I wish I could make apparent how difficult a thing it was to get supplies from our ship to the shore in a surf which, after 10 o'clock in the morning, allowed no small boats to touch even the bit of a pier that was run out, without breaking either the one or the other, and nothing in the form of a lighter save two dilapidated flat-boat pontoons.

These had been broken and cast away by the engineer corps, picked up by ourselves, mended . . . and put in condition to float alongside of our ship, and receive perhaps three or four tons of material. This must then be rowed or floated out to the shore, run onto the sand as far as possible, the men jumping into the water from knee to waist deep, pulling the boat up from the surf, and getting the material on land. And this was what was meant by loading the "seized wagons from the front" and getting food to the wounded.

After 10 o'clock in the day even this was impossible, and we must wait until the calm of three o'clock next morning to commence work again and go through the same struggle to get something to load the wagons for that day. Our supplies had been gotten ashore, and among the last, rocking and tossing in our little boat, went ourselves, landing on the pier, which by that time was breaking in two, escaping a surf which every other moment

This map, showing part of Cuba, indicates a number of the battle areas near Santiago where Miss Barton performed nursing services close to the fighting front. It also indicates several places— such as Daiquiri, Siboney, El Caney, and Santiago itself—where she supervised relief work for Cuban civilians. She also carried out similar relief activities in and around Havana.

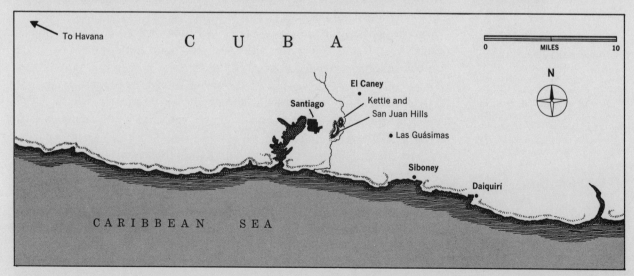

threatened to envelop one from feet to head. . . .

Our "seized" wagons had already gone on, loaded with our best hospital supplies—meal, flour, condensed milk, malted milk, tea, coffee, sugar, dried fruits, canned fruits, canned meats, and such other things as we had been able to get out in the haste of packing. . . . Halting a wagon loaded with bales of hay, we begged a ride of the driver, and our little party, Dr. and Mrs. Gardner, James McDowell, and myself, took our seats on the hay and made our way to the front. . . . Four hours' ride brought us to the First Division Hospital of the Fifth Army Corps—General Shafter's headquarters.

The sight that met us on going into the so-called hospital grounds was something indescribable. The land was perfectly level; no drainage whatever; covered with long, tangled grass; skirted by trees, brush and shrubbery; a few little dog-tents not much larger than could have been made of an ordinary table-cloth thrown over a short rail, and under these lay huddled together the men fresh from the field or from the operating-tables, with no covering over them save such as had clung to them through their troubles, and in the majority of cases no blanket under them.

Those who had come from the tables, having been compelled to leave all the clothing they had, as too wet, muddy, and bloody to be retained, were entirely nude, lying on the stubble grass, the sun fitfully dealing with them, sometimes clouding over and again streaming out in a blaze above them. Fortunately, among our supplies were some bolts of unbleached cotton, and this we cut in sheet lengths, and the men of our party went about and covered the poor fellows, who lay there with no shelter either from the elements or the eyes of the passers-by.

A half dozen bricks laid about a yard apart . . . so low and so near the ground that no fire of any strength or benefit could be made—the bits of wet wood put under crosswise, with the smoke streaming a foot out on either side, two kettles of coffee or soup, and a small frying-pan with some meat in it—appeared to be the cook-house for these men. They told us there were about 800 men under the tents and lying in the grass, and more constantly coming in. . . .

We too gathered stones and bricks and constructed a longer, higher fireplace . . . found the water, and soon our great agate kettles of seven and ten gallons were filled. The rain, that had been drizzling more or less all day, increased. Our supplies were taken from the wagons, a piece of tarpaulin found to protect them, and as the fire began to blaze and the water to heat, Mrs. Gardner and I . . . got material for the first gallons of gruel. . . .

When the bubbling contents of our kettle thickened and grew white with the condensed milk, and we began to give it out . . . to the poor sufferers, shivering and naked in the rain—I felt that perhaps it was not in vain that history had repeated itself. When the nurses came back and told us of the surprise with which it was received, and the tears that rolled down the sun-burned, often bloody face, into the cup as the poor fellow drank his hot gruel, and asked where it came from, who sent it,

General William R. Shafter, who commanded the military siege of Santiago, was so fat that he suffered extremely in the tropical heat of Cuba. But he had been a brave young soldier in the Civil War and effective in Indian fighting. His strong will triumphed over much military mismanagement in 1898.

and said it was the first food he had tasted in three days (for they had gone into the fight hungry), I felt that it was again the same old story and wondered what gain there had been in the last 30 years.

The fires burned, the gruel steamed and boiled—bucket after bucket went out—until those 800 men had each a cup of gruel and knew that he could have another and as many as he wanted. . . .

The operating-tables were full of the wounded. Man after man was taken off, brought on his litter and laid beside other men, and something given him to keep the little life in his body that seemed fast oozing out. All night it went on. . . . Early in the morning . . . they took out 17 who had died in the night, unattended, save by the nurse.

More supplies arrived, and this time came large tarpaulins, more utensils, more food, and more things to make it a little comfortable. . . . There was even something that looked like a table, on which Mrs. Gardner prepared her delicacies.

The Red Cross contingent led by Clara had originally gone to Cuba before the start of the Spanish-American War, in the hope of bringing food and medical aid to the Cuban civilians impoverished and uprooted during the island's long and bloody uprising against its Spanish overlords. After Santiago surrendered, shortly following the battle of San Juan Hill, her Red Cross ship, the "State of Texas," was the first vessel allowed by the victorious American admiral, William T. Sampson, to enter Santiago harbor.

■ These were anxious days. While the world outside was making up war history, we thought of little beyond the terrible needs about us; if Santiago had any people left, they must be in sore distress; and El Caney, with its 30,000 homeless, perishing sufferers, how could they be reached?

On that Sunday morning, never to be forgotten, the Spanish fleet came out of Santiago Harbor, to meet death and capture. That afternoon Lieutenant Capehart, of the flag-ship, came on board with the courteous reply of Admiral Sampson, that if we would come alongside the "New York" he would put a pilot on board. This was done and we moved on through waters we had never traversed. . . . We began to realize that we were alone, of all the ships about the harbor there were none with us. . . .

Leaning on the rail, half lost in reverie over the strange, quiet beauty of the scene, the thought suddenly burst upon me—are we really going into Santiago, and alone? . . . Would it be possible that the commander . . . would hold back his flag-ship and himself, and send forward and first a cargo of food on a plain ship, under direction of a woman? . . . The "State of Texas" was nearing the dock, and quietly dropping her anchor she lay there through the silence of the night in undisputed possessing, facing a bare wind-swept wharf and the deserted city of Santiago.

Daybreak brought quiet to an end . . . 120 stevedores lined up on the wharf . . . told the story of better days to come. . . . Later in the day the flag-ship brought Admiral Sampson and Admiral Schley, who spent several hours with us. . . . When they were about to leave Admiral Sampson was asked what orders or directions he had for us. He replied: "You need no directions from me, but if any one troubles you let me know." . . .

As I was . . . attempting to express my appreciation and thanks to Admiral Sampson for the courtesy of allowing us to precede him into Santiago, Admiral Schley, with that . . . apt turn of expression so characteristic of him, in a half undertone side-remark, cautioned me with "Don't give him too much credit, Miss Barton; he was not quite sure how clear the channel might be. Remember that was a trial trip." . . .

The 30,000 inhabitants of Santiago had been driven to El Caney, a village designed for 500. In two days all were called back and fed, 10,000 the first day, 20,000 the second. Then came our troops, and Santiago was lived and is remembered. . . . Every family or person residing within the city was supplied . . . and all transient persons were fed at the kitchens, the food being provided by the Red Cross.

GALVESTON FLOOD—AND FAREWELL

The last great disaster in which Clara Barton personally led the relief work was that following the Galveston, Texas, hurricane and flood in 1900, when she was nearly eighty.

■ This time there was no . . . warning of approaching danger . . . till the hissing wires shrieked the terrifying word—Galveston. . . . The sea had overleaped its bounds and its victims by thousands were in its grasp. . . . In two days a little coterie of near a dozen left Washington under escort

The destruction suffered at Galveston, shown here in a contemporary drawing by G. W. Peters, was among the worst Miss Barton ever encountered. On the page opposite are her diary entries for September 13 and 14 in 1901, including the death of President McKinley and one of her rather rare misspellings—"medicene."

Glen Echo Friday Sept 13. 1901

I go to the city early. take Silas.
Go to Riggs — draw Mrs. Spencers check $100.
     call at Loan & Trust to see M. Edson
meet Vice Pres: tell him of Alambey no result
     came to Georgetown
Pay coal Bill to D.. Jennicane   39.50
     purchase fruit. groceries, brooms
Home 4 P.m.

President Dead
Glen Echo. Sat. Sept 14 1901

President Mc Kinley died 2.30
News Boy brought Extra
     Pedro went to city —
I get out the Medicines from cellar
     Dr Pratt made his last visit to Harold
who murses his chill.
     I had remained up all night to give the
medicine regularly — it did the work.
     I write Ida twice each day
     Dr Pratt insists That both Harold
& Mrs Rich go north at once to escape
the chills which are becoming epidemic
     Paid $ 4.50

. . . of the New York "World," which had on the first day telegraphed that it would open a subscription for the relief of Galveston, and would be glad to send all supplies and money received to the Red Cross, if its president, Miss Clara Barton, would go and distribute it. . . . The direfulness of the news gathered as we proceeded on our journey. . . .

Here again no description could adequately serve its purpose. The sea, with fury spent, had sullenly retired. The strongest buildings, half standing, roofless and tottering, told what once had been the make-up of a thriving city. But that cordon of wreckage skirting the shore for miles it seemed, often 20 feet in height, and against which the high tide still lapped and rolled! What did it tell? The tale is all too dreadful to recall—the funeral pyre of at least 5,000 human beings . . . told only too fatally what that meant to that portion of the city left alive. . . .

It may be interesting to readers to know what is done first, or just how a relief party commences under circumstances like that. . . . First the ground must be overlooked and conditions learned. This is not easy when it is remembered that broken houses, cars, wagons, church steeples, and grand pianos were liable to be encountered in the middle of the leading streets, themselves buried three feet in the coarse black sand, brought in by the great tidal wave. Nevertheless, a building must be found in which to store and distribute the supplies. . . . A warehouse, fortunately still intact, was generously supplied by Mr. John Sealy. Major James A. McDowell, with the experience of this branch of Red Cross work from Johnstown down, and the record of 26 battles in the old Civil War, was placed in charge. . . .

A poor feeble-looking man, with scant clothing, enters the warehouse

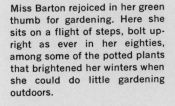

Miss Barton rejoiced in her green thumb for gardening. Here she sits on a flight of steps, bolt upright as ever in her eighties, among some of the potted plants that brightened her winters when she could do little gardening outdoors.

and waits. "Hello there," calls the observant major—with his Grand Army button—overhauling clothes for the visitor. "But, major, I was a Confederate soldier." "Lord bless your poor suffering soul, what difference does that make? Here, this will suit you." . . .

Our men made up their living-room at the warehouse. The few women remained at the hotel. . . . At least 20 counties on the mainland . . . some of which were as badly wrecked and ruined as Galveston itself [also needed help]. . . . I had . . . Red Cross supplies shipped to Houston, and relief for the mainland opened there. These were farming districts, and I directed intelligent inquiry to be made as to what was most needed by the devastated farm lands and their owners. All was swept away—sometimes as far as 40 miles back into the level country; often the soil itself was washed away, the home and all smaller animals destroyed, and no feed for the larger ones to subsist on. The poor farmers walked their desolated fields and wrung their hands.

It proved that this was the strawberry section of Southern Texas, and these were the strawberry growers that supplied the early berries to our Northern market. For miles not a plant was left and no means to replant. This was reported to me on the first day's investigation, and also that if plants could be obtained and set within two weeks a half crop could be grown this year and the industry restored. . . . The messenger was sent back at daybreak to ascertain how many plants would be needed to replant these lands, where they were accustomed to procure them, and what varieties were best adapted to their use. . . .

That night brought again the messenger to say that a million and a half

October 31. Thursday 1901
Worcester Mass. —

This book opens in the midst of one of the finest spells of autumn weather ever known
I have passed the summer in Glen Echo with Mrs. Rich and Harold. Dr. Hubbell returned from his year's absence two weeks ago, and comes here with me.
Steve has broken up in N.Y. and removed his residence to Boston.
The Galveston work is over. The Report is out. Mr. Fred L. Ward has gone home and I have recalled his services here for a few days to help out correspondence.
I am unsettled in regard to the future course to be pursued with the Red Cross. And one object of this visit is to find what form Steve feels like taking.

In this diary entry toward the end of 1901, Miss Barton notes that her "Galveston work is over" and that she is "unsettled in regard to the future course to be pursued with the Red Cross." She was gradually, but reluctantly, beginning to realize that it was time for her to consider resigning as president of the Red Cross.

of plants would reset the lands and that their supply came from the nurseries in North Carolina, Illinois, Arkansas and Louisiana. . . . Within the two weeks this million and a half of strawberry plants were set. It was estimated that fully a third of a crop was realized that year. . . .

I had never left Galveston. Some other thoughtful reader may pitifully ask, what became of these miles of wreckage and the dead on the Galveston seashore? . . . All were burned. The heat grew greater and the stench stronger every day. They tried to remove the debris and get the bodies out for burial. No human being could work in that putrefying mass. Previously had come the glorious thought of getting them into boats and shipping them a mile out to sea. With hopeful hearts this experiment was tried for one day. Alas! the night tide brought them all back to shore. The elements of earth and water had refused—what remained but fire? . . .

The stench of burning flesh permeated every foot of the city. Who could long withstand this? Before the end of three months there was scarcely a well person in Galveston. My helpers grew pale and ill, and even I, who have resisted the effect of so many climates, needed the help of a steadying hand as I walked to the waiting Pullman on the track, courteously tendered free of charge to take us away.

This is a tedious story; but if gone through, one has a little insight into the labor of a Red Cross field of relief. There are 20 in my recollection, and this was by no means the hardest or the most useful. . . .

This is not romance that I am writing, where I can place my characters in the best light, and shape results at will, but history, with my personages still alive, ready to attest the reality of this statement. That grand committee of Galveston relief—than whom no nobler body of men I have ever met—are, I hope, all yet alive to testify to the conditions and statements made.

At the conclusion of the book she published in 1904, "A Story of the Red Cross: Glimpses of Field Work," Clara Barton wrote:

■ I have dedicated this little volume to the people with whom, and for whom, have gone the willing labors of 25 years—initial labors, untried methods, and object lessons. . . . Whatever may betide or the future have in store for the little work so simply commenced, so humbly carried on . . . it bears along with it the memories of pain assuaged, hope revived, endeavor strengthened, and lives saved.

To the noble sympathies of generous hearts these results are due, and yet it is not in its past that the glories or the benefits of the Red Cross lie, but in the possibilities it has created for the future; in the lessons it has taught; in the avenues to humane effort it has opened, and in the union of beneficent action between people and Government, when once comprehended and effected, that shall constitute a bulwark against the mighty woes sure to come sooner or later to all peoples and all nations.

To you—the people of America—this sacred trust is committed, in your hands the charge is laid.

Miss Barton's tombstone at North Oxford, Massachusetts, appropriately includes the Red Cross. She died of double pneumonia at her house in Glen Echo, just outside Washington, at nine o'clock on the morning of April 12, 1912. The next day the New York "Sun" editorialized: "Clara Barton was more than brave. She devoted her life to humanity. She was one of the most useful of women, self-sacrificing to a degree, generous to a fault. Health and fortune she devoted to her great cause. . . . Into the span of what other life have more mercy, tenderness and love entered? Is it not the finest kind of glory that when the American Red Cross is seen or mentioned the name of Clara Barton comes to the mind like a benediction?"

ANNOTATED BIBLIOGRAPHY

Bacon-Foster, Corra. *Clara Barton, Humanitarian.* Columbia Historical Society, 1918.
This book stresses the cause of feminism and has an idealistic overtone throughout. The author is highly favorable to most aspects of Miss Barton's life and career. If anything, the author overplays the "humanitarian" role and underestimates the political sagacity and the strong note of realism that Clara so often displayed.

Barton, Clara. *The Red Cross in Peace and War.* American Historical Press, 1899.
Despite her occasional lapses into rhetoric and sentimentality, Clara Barton was a lively writer and stylist. She tended to be more effective when writing of war than of peace—as this volume demonstrates. She can tell a story rapidly and effectively, and is her own best advocate. While there is little new here, it is a good summary.

Barton, Clara. *A Story of the Red Cross: Glimpses of Field Work.* Appleton, 1904.
A short but informative apologia, this chronological account by Miss Barton—which tells what the American organization she had founded did under her supervision—is balanced and lively. As she says in the preface, such a short volume "must of necessity be but a brief outline, sufficient, however, to convey a clear impression of what the Red Cross really means to every individual in this great country of ours."

Barton, Clara. *The Story of My Childhood.* Baker and Taylor, 1907.
As this important autobiographical item demonstrates, Miss Barton had a vivid memory. She could recall not only the names and events but the feelings and emotions of her early life. Her initial timidity and eventual boldness are reflected in her own story, as is the strain of self-pity that stayed with her through life. Her picture of rural New England is memorable.

Barton, William E. *The Life of Clara Barton* (2 vols.). Houghton Mifflin, 1922.
This is the detailed and official biography, done by one of Clara Barton's favorite cousins. Working closely with her authorized executor, Stephen E. Barton, the author had access to all the material then known. Although it somewhat glosses over the difficulties of her late years, the biography is, in the main, thorough, reliable—and readable.

Boardman, Mabel T. *Under the Red Cross Flag at Home and Abroad.* Lippincott, 1915.
Essentially antagonistic and even unfair to Clara Barton, Mabel Boardman's book should nevertheless be read to show how an opposition viewpoint developed, why it did, and what it asserted. In emphasizing Clara's inability to deal with new and vastly expanded problems, Miss Boardman underestimates her achievement in the Spanish-American War and the opening years of the twentieth century.

Boylston, Helen Dore. *Clara Barton, Founder of the American Red Cross.* Random House, 1955.
This book, designed for young readers, attempts a "balanced" portrait and gets away from the uncritical acceptance of certain Barton episodes that had come to be legendary. The emphasis is on the organization she headed rather than the internal battles she waged. The last chapters are the most informative.

Catton, Bruce. *A Stillness at Appomattox.* Doubleday, 1953.
Few books of this century have caught the mood and feelings of Civil War America as successfully as those of Bruce Catton. Combining careful research with a brilliant and dramatic style, they have won wide acclaim from specialists and general readers alike. This volume, in particular, will help to make the whole conflict—which was so vital for Miss Barton—real to all who live in the Atomic Age.

Commager, Henry Steele (ed). *The Blue and the Gray: The Story of the Civil War as Told by Participants* (2 vols.). Bobbs Merrill, 1950.
The editor attempts, rather successfully, to present "a well-rounded history of the Civil War in the words of those who fought it." More than 450 narratives are included, giving an immediacy to the war years that is often lacking. A number of them deal with areas where Clara Barton was especially active.

Downey, Fairfax. *Disaster Fighters.* Putnam, 1938.
This is a set of rousingly narrated accounts of noteworthy disasters and how the American Red Cross helped at each. It includes—among stories of other calamities where Clara Barton labored—Johnstown, the Sea Islands, and Galveston.

Dulles, Foster Rhea. *The American Red Cross, A History.* Harper, 1950.
Fully and thoroughly researched, this book gives a broad view of the whole Red Cross movement and thus enables the reader to put Clara Barton in perspective. The author is sympathetic to her role as founder, without being as adulatory as some of the earlier chroniclers. The volume is also important for showing the amazing expansion of the Red Cross movement in the twentieth century.

Dunant, Henri. *A Memory of Solferino.* The American National Red Cross, 1939.
Since his reactions to and efforts at Solferino formed the basis on which the whole International Red Cross movement was built, this translated reprint of Henri Dunant's brief, eloquent book is of primary importance. Those who have a romantic view of dashing, nineteenth-century battles will do well to find out, from this volume, how bad were the medical facilities during and after combat before the Red Cross came into being.

Epler, Percy H. *The Life of Clara Barton.* Macmillan, 1941.
Although this book, originally published in 1915, was written without benefit of much material that later students unearthed, it is in some ways the best single volume on Clara Barton. It does not dodge delicate issues or gloss over her errors. Yet it catches her essential largeness of spirit. Epler explains the reason for this authenticity in his foreword: "Her unpublished war diaries and letters upon which I have spent long research, together with her conversations, and observations by eye-witnesses, are my chief original sources."

Freidel, Frank. *Splendid Little War*. Little, Brown, 1958.
A fine one-volume history of the Spanish-American War, with words and illustrations by such war correspondents as Richard Harding Davis, Frederic Remington, and Howard Chandler Christy; graphic and well balanced.

Holbrook, Stewart H. *Dreamers of the American Dream*. Doubleday, 1957.
One should never forget that Clara Barton was not only a nurse, administrator, and politician, but an idealist in the mainstream of American thought. This volume, which deals (through vignettes) with populists, utopians, friends of the oppressed, feminists, and various reformers, helps to establish that mainstream, and thus helps to define the scale of Miss Barton's achievement.

Hurd, Charles. *The Compact History of the American Red Cross*. Hawthorn, 1959.
This volume, which on significant matters is often more detailed than its title suggests, manages to do both full and candid justice to two strikingly different heroines of the American Red Cross: Clara Barton and Mabel Boardman. In some ways Miss Boardman (1860-1946) was as remarkable as Miss Barton—and she was a key Red Cross figure for a much longer time. Miss Boardman so resembled Britain's Queen Mary in dress and dignity that the Duke of Windsor, on first glimpsing her, exclaimed, "Good Lord, there's Mother!" As Hurd notes, one of Miss Boardman's prime qualities was "a running flow of common sense."

Kite, Elizabeth S. *Antoinette Margot and Clara Barton*. American Catholic Historical Society of Philadelphia Records, 1944.
Few people were more important in Clara Barton's life than Antoinette Margot, and no one was more devoted to her. By highlighting their relationship and exploring it in greater depth than any of the standard biographies do, Elizabeth Kite gives new insight into the subject. The volume heavily emphasizes religious themes and events.

Lutz, Alma. *Susan B. Anthony: Rebel, Crusader, Humanitarian*. Beacon, 1959.
Like Alma Lutz's earlier studies of Elizabeth Cady Stanton and Emma Willard, this book helps illuminate the role of women in nineteenth-century America, and thus to illuminate the stage on which Clara Barton appeared. Susan B. Anthony, a good friend of Clara's, faced many of the same problems that confronted Clara during her life.

Memorial to Clara Barton. Government Printing Office, 1917.
Taking the form of an official memorial address, this publication musters all the affirmative clichés and claims. Coming at a time when the country was once again involved in wartime hysteria, it makes much of Miss Barton's role with the Union army and overstresses patriotic zeal.

Randall, James G. *The Civil War and Reconstruction*. Heath, 1937.
This well-known work does not primarily attempt to produce a narrative but rather attempts "to reproduce the feelings and problems of a civilization in a time of distortion, stress, and passion." Randall's book will help any reader to understand the era in which Clara Barton came into national prominence.

Ross, Ishbel. *Angel of the Battlefield*. Harper, 1956.
Emphatically, this is one of the best written and most perceptive of all the biographies of Miss Barton. Ishbel Ross undertook her task at a time when fresh material on Clara made new insights possible, and when various controversies over her had calmed down enough to permit objective judgments. The result is an enjoyable, penetrating book.

Sandburg, Carl. *Abraham Lincoln: The War Years* (4 vols.). Harcourt Brace, 1939.
Lincoln was plainly one of Clara's great heroes. The more one knows about him (especially after 1860), the closer one gets to central areas of her concern. Hence these well-wrought and poetically presented volumes by Sandburg will bring the war years into clearer focus for any reader.

Walcott, Charles F. *21st Regiment Massachusetts Volunteers, 1861-1865*. Houghton Mifflin, 1882.
In many ways, Miss Barton was always a sectionalist, despite her generosity toward "the enemy" at home and toward the afflicted in "other lands" who called upon her. She thought and acted like a daughter of Massachusetts, so Walcott's story of the regiment closest to her home and heart provides a useful though indirect view of her.

Williams, Blanche Colton. *Clara Barton, Daughter of Destiny*. Lippincott, 1941.
Sympathetic without being sentimental, this is one of the finest accounts of Miss Barton's life. That Clara herself suffered much doubt and anguish before discovering her "destiny" is made clear. The book is best in analyzing her motives and inner feelings, weakest on battle scenes.

Young, Agatha. *Women and the Crisis: Women of the North in the Civil War*. McDowell, Obolensky, 1959.
The best study available of the role that Northern women played as nurses, spies, and Sanitary Commission workers. It casts a good deal of light on Clara Barton's life and achievement.

Young, Charles Sumner. *Clara Barton, A Centenary Tribute*. Richard G. Badger, 1922.
Full of resounding phrases and clichés, this "Tribute" contributes little that is new. But it does help show how Miss Barton's reputation had solidified by 1922, and how she had continued to rise in stature even during a postwar period when "debunking" came into prominence.

INDEX